To Maureen
Best Wishes

[signature]

DICKSY'S
FIFTY
YEARS IN
FOOTBALL

DICKSY'S FIFTY YEARS IN FOOTBALL

THE AUTOBIOGRAPHY OF ALAN DICKS

WITH PAUL EVANS

ember

Published by Ember Press in 2023

www.emberprojects.co.uk

© Alan Dicks 2023

A CIP catalogue record for this title is available from the British Library.

ISBN 978-1-7392844-5-9

Editing by CRS Editorial
Cover design by Rawshock Design
Typesetting by Sheer Design and Typesetting

Printed and bound in Poland by B.Z. Graf

Dedicated to Maura, my first and fourth wife.

CONTENTS

ACKNOWLEDGEMENTS

So many people have been important in my life.

Maura, and my children Alan, Mandy, Michelle, Melanie and Patrick.

Jimmy Hill for priceless management experience.

Ron Greenwood for introducing me to coaching.

Harry Dolman for hiring me and giving me time.

Robert Hobbs for his support buying players.

All the players and staff that I worked with, especially Tony Collins.

And in my professional and personal life, Roger Malone, sports presenter, commentator at Bristol City and my golf partner for more than four decades, many a laugh we have had walking the course at Henbury Golf Club.

And to Paul Evans for telling my story.

Alan Dicks

AUTHOR'S NOTE

It was a great privilege to write the story of Alan's life and career. A big thanks to Melanie, Michelle, Nick Boyles, Marc Kirby and Phillip Evans for their support during the journey.

Paul Evans

INTRODUCTION

KICKING A BALL DOWN MEMORY LANE

I'm eighty-nine and live in the same house in Bristol that Gerry Gow, Tom Ritchie and Gerry Sweeney used to visit in the 1970s.

Reliving those days has been a joy and a challenge, memory being a trickier opponent than a trip to Old Trafford.

I still go to Ashton Gate for matches, with my grandson Ben and see Club President Marina Dolman, continuing Harry's great work. During the writing period, so many of my fellow professionals have now sadly left the field forever.

I hope this book helps keep their memories alive, as well as mine.

Alan
August 2023

TESTIMONIALS

In swinging musical terms Alan Dicks was the man who 'Let the good times roll' for Bristol City fans. I listened in on all of his thirteen years in charge at Ashton Gate.

Without a place at the top table for sixty-five long years, the West Country was savouring their team mixing with the likes of Liverpool and Manchester United. Alan needed nine seasons to build a team opposing managers would admire to me as 'very, very fit'. Then he polished it by persuading some big guns to come west – Norman Hunter, Joe Royle, Terry Cooper, Peter Cormack – top internationals all. City fans loved it!

Roger Malone, *Daily Telegraph* and ITV-West

Alan was one of the most forward-thinking managers of his era. He forged a team from young talent good enough for promotion to the top flight. What heady, unforgettable days for Bristol City. He ensured those youngsters were given access to further education, employing my dad to facilitate that. He was the first to introduce video analysis of matches. I was lucky enough to film those games with my dad and edit the tapes for tactical review.

He was hugely influential in BBC Radio Bristol's decision to give me my first job in the industry. For that I will always be indebted to him. But most of all I will always be grateful for one piece of advice. "It is a game to love. Whatever happens, don't lose your love of the game".

Jonathan Pearce, Broadcaster and lifelong Bristol City fan

I knew about Bristol City from as early as I can remember; my father Ron and my Uncle Ted set the mood for Saturday evening on returning from matches. The 1966 World Cup final, as a six-year-old, sparked my interest in football and the trip to John Atyeo's testimonial against Leeds Utd later that year was my first experience of Ashton Gate. However, all that was just the warm-up; it was Alan Dicks and his various teams over twelve years that captured me for ever, defining my growing up and ultimately my career.

Of course, the promotion winning team to the top-flight in 1976 was the high point, but the memories of the entire period are just as vivid. Alan was the man who delivered all of them: FA Cup win away at high flying Leeds Utd on a Tuesday afternoon in 1974; surviving in the First Division at the end of the 1977/78 season at Coventry (celebrating with their manager Gordon Milne afterwards as they stayed up too); beating Man Utd 3-1 at Old Trafford in October 1978. Alan's teams were just like him; thoughtful, committed and passionate, but fun at the right time. Over the past twenty-five years I have come to know him pretty well; it has been a privilege to spend time with him at matches.

It is an honour to write a testimonial for this book. Years have not dimmed his enthusiasm for life, family, football and his (and my) beloved Bristol City.

Richard Scudamore,
Former Chief Executive, Premier League and EFL

1

WAR AND FOOTBALL

I was forced to leave home at just six years old.

Don't blame my parents.

Blame Adolf Hitler.

Before then, football had begun for me, in my street, aged four. Out with the big boys, including my elder bother Ronnie, until mum called me in when it was too dark to see the black, heavy, leather ball. De Laune Street in Kennington with its neat rows of small Victorian terrace houses, had hardly any traffic. With only three cars in the whole street, it made for a pretty good makeshift pitch. But then the bombings started. The Luftwaffe blitzing London meant the game was over. When I returned from evacuation, the devastation the Germans had caused left us with rubble for goalposts. Our football was to be played on a landscape of shattered buildings and skeleton structures. Houses, where my neighbours had once lived, were left with no front and rooms clearly visible. They'd even obliterated the church around the corner. It was 1942 but I was so pleased to be home, even if it was a bombsite.

Fortunately, our house wasn't hit. My mum, dad and Ronnie were all safe and well, relieved to see me and my big sister Joyce back on the manor; the family reunited. The Kennington spirit had meant everyone had just carried on and made the best of it. It was war and like the rest of the country, we just got on with it. And anyway, the ruined church's aisle made a perfect football passing practice corridor and cricket wicket. As an eight-year-old, De Laune Street was less a bombsite, more a massive climbing and playing opportunity.

Kennington is known for its two famous landmarks – the Oval Cricket Ground and the Imperial War Museum. A young Charlie Chaplin played at the Regal Kennington Theatre and down the Lambeth Walk in the early years of the century. My grandfather had a tobacconist shop and would often be part of crowds who gave Chaplin pennies when he nimbly danced on top of beer barrels outside the pub opposite. This was before Chaplin moved to Hollywood and became the biggest star in the world. It was a cultured area with theatres and music halls in Brixton, Kennington, Elephant and Castle and Vauxhall, all with chorus girls, comedians and jugglers.

During the decades before I was born in 1934, there was a gradual decline. The gentry began an exodus to the suburbs, their big houses divided into flats to provide cheap lodgings for lower-paid workers. The lucky ones – families like us – had a whole house, though very modest, with an outside toilet. Just twenty years previously the social historian Maud Reeves wrote that the area was full of '...respectable but very poor people, who live over a morass of such intolerable poverty that they unite instinctively to save those known to them from falling into it'. That was my parent's childhood. Thrifty, hard-working, honest and part of a community that looked after its own.

In uniform; Joyce in girl's life brigade,
me in scouts, De Laune Street.

My evacuation destination was Axminster in Devon, apparently a beautiful part of the country. It might as well have been Mars to a boy from the city. Upon leaving Waterloo station, here I was, staring out of the train window at the grey concrete as it gradually turned into green fields, with my regulation evacuation equipment including gas mask, toothbrush, towel, overcoat and soap. (I was being sent to a place that didn't have soap?)

When we reached the house on the edge of town, with fields stretching into the distance and total silence, it felt like just outside the middle of nowhere. The couple who were my 'evacuation parents' – the Watkins – had a surprise for us. They would accept my big sister Joyce into their home, but not me. Mum protested, shouted and refused to leave, until they agreed to take both of us. 'You can't separate the children from each other as well as from their parents!' Easy mum, I thought, sensing a quick return to De Laune Street. But as always, her fighting spirit held sway and finally convinced them I should stay. Holding back the tears, I held her hand so tight and cried so much as she said goodbye. I almost managed to stop her leaving. Almost.

It turned out that the Watkins had different plans for Joyce than for me. She was constantly busy helping with household chores; cleaning, washing and ironing. Free domestic help, basically. Perhaps that was why they were so keen on her. I, on the other hand, was pretty much left me to my own devices. There was no school, so while Joyce was hanging out the washing, I roamed the countryside, freely; a small boy marvelling at nature – cows, sheep, endless green fields – wondering where all the concrete and cars were. There were highland cattle in the field at the back of the house. I would wander to the edge of town, to the cattle market, once given a stick by the local farmer, 'hey cockney lad, drive them into the pens for us'. I was now a six-year-old farm hand.

The experience of being separated from my parents as a young child, sent to live miles away with strangers, was typical. Millions of children were evacuated in the early war years. If you lived in range of the Luftwaffe, you'd best get out of the way. What could have been a very tough separation from family and mates for a small child, turned out to be an education. I learned a lot about myself. I developed a strong sense of independence and self-reliance. It's not that my new family didn't care. I was well fed and had plenty of everything (including soap) but they were busy with their lives and thought it was fine for a small child to wander the Devon countryside alone. Those two years taught me how to look after myself.

Meanwhile, mum and dad carried on with their lives without two of their three children. Dad worked as an electrician for the General Electric Company so had early access to all the latest technology. In 1949 we had a TV and, a few years later, a microwave. Much to the amazement of our neighbours, we were at the cutting edge of mid-century domestic tech innovation. Dad's family had no history of anything technical, rather a long tradition of boxing. My father looked tough and intimidating, being of a solid build and bald. But he wasn't tough. His father was. Grandad ran a take-on-all-comers boxing booth where he and his two brothers would fight anyone who fancied their chances, with the winner getting a cash prize. As hard men, they very rarely gave any money away.

Dad liked a flutter. From the age of nine, I was regularly sent out to put bets on for him. 'Dicksy sent me', I'd say to this shady looking bloke who stood on the corner of Kennington Lane with a cloth cap pulled over his eyes, taking the money, usually five shillings, to do a round the clock bet on the horses that afternoon. I never really understood how it worked, but it intrigued me, especially as dad was always doing it, even when he kept losing.

Mum was a force of nature. Up at 4.30 a.m. every day to clean an office in the West End, she rushed back home to take us to school, then off to a workshop where she spent the day sewing beautiful, multicoloured, intricate carpets. Works of art in themselves, many ended up in West End theatres like Drury Lane. Her needlework also created beautiful dresses and shirts. Domestically, she was the power behind the throne. Coming from the Lambeth Walk, her family were very business minded and ran a successful shop. She inherited a good business brain, was smart with money, and made the most of what little there was.

One beautiful spring day, I wandered back into my Axminster house after a morning of chasing rabbits, to find her stood there. 'You're coming home'. And so she took Joyce and me back to London. The Watkins were not best pleased. They enjoyed the fee they got from the government to look after us and the help Joyce gave, but mum had spent long enough away from her kids. Also, the Luftwaffe had been put in their place. For now, London was less dangerous.

It was good to be back in SE17. Well, what was left of it. I was back to playing football – the ritual of going to school, coming home and playing in the street. The next day? Repeat. School, home, football in the street, often just with a tennis ball. The only change came in the summer when it was cricket *and* football.

My brother Ronnie, who is ten years older than me, had been conscripted. He took the train up to Middlesbrough to join the artillery and was eventually posted to the Far East, and then North Africa. While stationed in the north-east, he was asked for a trial at Middlesbrough Football Club. The club quickly spotted how talented and versatile he was and signed him. Eventually he played in every position for the team, including as goalkeeper. His favourite role was charging down the wing, leaving flailing defenders in his wake. My brother the professional footballer. He was my hero, though never much a part of my childhood. An absent talisman; living proof of what was possible.

I admired and looked up to him, in every sense. He was a brilliant sportsman – football, cricket, athletics, swimming, you name it. And a great brother. There is one memory from the war years I treasure. Ron took me to see the latest Tarzan movie – *Tarzan's Desert Mystery* – at the Regal in Kennington. It was the biggest film franchise of the 1930s and 1940s, starring Johnny Weissmuller. How excited I was! An eight year old on his first visit to the cinema, sitting in the darkness with expectation higher than the trees Tarzan swings from in the thrilling opening scene.

But just as Johnny landed effortlessly on another branch, a deafening screech rang out. It wasn't the chattering of his monkey mates, it was a screaming air raid siren. We were under attack. With calm, everyone in the cinema stood up and began to file out of the building. It was a sign of how frequent these incidents were, that there was so little panic. All I could think about, rooted to my seat, was Tarzan. Ron had to drag me out, to troop into the gloom of Kennington Road. We were a couple of miles from De Laune Street and we knew mum would be worried sick. Everywhere we looked there was well-ordered panic. Everyone making for any kind of cover – a public air raid shelter, the underground station or the Anderson shelter in their own backyard. Given the distance, we started to run as parked cars and trolley buses emptied. South London was scrambling for safety.

Stressed policemen ordered the few stragglers to take cover. The sirens were still wailing their command as the Dicks' boys, with a ten-year and a five-inch gap, careered down Kennington Road. All I could see was Ron's heels, disappearing. Suddenly, he stopped, saw I was struggling. He ran back and looked down at me as I clutched my side, stricken with a stitch; breathless.

'Sorry... Ron. I'll... run... faster. Honest.' He knew this was rubbish. If we carried on at my pace, the war would be over by the time we got home. His response was instant. Lifting me up, he swung me on his shoulders and set off again, this time carrying four stone of dead weight. And he didn't just run, he sprinted. Driven by a combination of fear and a vision of the panic on our mum's face, through the now deserted streets of Kennington, we turned into Dale Road, then Burton Road, and eventually, De Laune Street. How he managed to outrun the incoming bombs, carrying his lump of a brother was incredible. This speed was later to be seen on a Saturday afternoon, up and down the left touchline of football grounds around the country.

I never did find out what *Tarzan's Desert Mystery* was. But I did learn how fast, strong and brave my brother was. A real-life hero.

Our street was not just a football pitch. It was for cricket, roller skating, and hockey, with occasional Woodbine cigarette breaks for some of us 11-year-olds, in a discreet bomb shelter. We had a winning table tennis team that played after I sang with the choir, and the congregation had left the church. Plus basketball at the local YMCA, leading our Kennington team to an All-London tournament at the famous Tottenham Court Road YMCA, which we won. There was, however, an odd rule at that branch that if you wanted to swim in the pool, you had to be naked; weird but true. I also swam for the school (in trunks) and competed in athletics tournaments. Basically, if it was a sport, I'd play it.

Dad, Joyce, Ron, me and mum, the back of De Laune Street, 1946.

Of course injuries happen and one time, while enjoying a post-match Woodbine, I sat down on shards of broken glass in a bomb shelter. Arriving home in tears, Mum ordered me to lie down on the kitchen table as she pulled them out, piece by painful piece. Bottoms up! Very funny, mum.

In the summer of 1944, the war reached a critical point at the battle of Normandy, resulting in the liberation of western Europe. But the Germans weren't going quietly. They unleashed a deadly new weapon as a final attempt to break us – V2 rockets. The first supersonic long-range, guided ballistic missiles were silent, flying faster than the speed of sound. So, there was no air-raid warning and no sprint home to the shelter. All that was heard was the devastating explosion when it was too late. One afternoon, dad and I heard the very faint sound of something falling through the sky over our bit of south London. 'Some poor bugger's going to get it,' he mourned. It landed on Woolworths in nearby New Cross, killing 168 people, including a schoolmate.

My parents took immediate, evasive action. They sent me to stay with my aunt in Glasgow, out of range and safe from the V2s. Now I was on another train, this time from Kings Cross, heading north. When I reached Susan's house and began to settle in, I quickly discovered that in some ways it was more dangerous here, than in south London. Not many pupils at Strathclyde Juniors were welcoming to the English lad, the only one among 500 Scots. I was the lone foreign import in the under 11's team where I had a busy season in midfield. Off the pitch, things were even livelier, as the less enlightened of my school mates decided to pick on the solo Sassenach. Simple choice: I could back down or fight. I was my grandfather's grandson. Eventually there was one fight too many, though it was me who was disciplined by the headmaster, receiving the leather strap after running smack into a teacher when fleeing from my schoolmates. That punishment hurt, in every way. More lessons in looking after myself.

Football was my salvation. A successful season for the school team finally earned me a begrudging respect and truce. I even went to watch Celtic play at Parkhead. But after a year it was still a relief to get back to the threat of the Germans rather than the Scots. I joined a senior school off the Old Kent Road, near the famous Thomas A Becket Gym, which later became the training centre for some of the most famous boxers of the twentieth century in Henry Cooper, Muhammad Ali, Joe Frazier and Sugar Ray Leonard. I wish I'd known about it before I went to Glasgow. School was over four miles from home, beyond the Elephant and Castle, but most days I would walk and save the bus and tram fare to spend on sweets and bread, which we'd stuff with chips. Good fitness training, though maybe not with all the Kit Kats, Crunchies and packets of Rolos. With a heavy schedule of chocolate to get through, I avoided turning into Billy Bunter by playing three matches every weekend, for three different teams. There was my school team in Kennington and two local youth sides, with two matches on a Saturday and one on Sunday morning. Our school team was useful. We won the London Schools Championship, the Dewar Shield and two other trophies in that 1949/50 season. I patrolled the midfield, protecting the defence, breaking up attacks and feeding the strikers. As the side did well, so I got noticed, eventually called up for a trial for the London Schools' Team.

From the age of twelve, I travelled all over London on my own, going to trials, playing for different teams. I was independent, driven, bursting to match Ron. Maybe that drive off the pitch compensated for the bit of pace I lacked on it. Some players are not the most naturally gifted but they make up by giving more than the required 100%. That was me.

Being selected for the London Schools' Team was an honour. Mum and dad were so proud, as was Ron, who had just returned from helping beat the Japanese in Burma, to play for Middlesbrough in the First Division. A strong attacking team, they finished the season ninth, with Portsmouth winning the title and Manchester City relegated. He was offered a contract by First Division rivals Brentford. But Middlesbrough, like all clubs, owned their players and decided they wouldn't release him, so he had to stay in the north-east, which was tough for mum.

The first London School's team match was a test. New team-mates, new system, new coach, so it was about adapting quickly and clicking with the other players. We trained very hard for the game, which was against, of all teams, Glasgow. So, it was back on a train to Scotland and a chance to prove a point to some of my auld enemies. As is best, revenge was served cold, on a freezing Glasgow afternoon. No fists needed this time, winning comfortably 3-0.

The school team with the Dewar trophy, 1949. I'm front row, second from the right.

Maybe that extra motivation helped my performance because I kept my place in midfield and became a regular in the side. It got me thinking that if I was good enough to represent London Schools', then maybe football could be more than just the thing I did at the weekend. By the age of fifteen, I was completely obsessed with following in Ron's footsteps. A career in football was working for him. He was now settled at Middlesborough, a first-on-the-team-sheet wing half, on the verge of an England call-up.

Like many footballers, academically, I was not a natural. But numbers were my strength and I found maths straightforward; you might say I was in the first team. But for English, geography and history, not even on the bench. In those days at Kennington Secondary, commercial subjects were also taught, alongside the three Rs (reading, writing and arithmetic). So, I took typing, basic accountancy and office skills. Practical abilities which would come in very useful later.

My dad liked football but didn't support anyone, so we would go and watch various teams play. Sometimes, we'd get the tram to Charlton Athletic – the closest First Division side – and join 45,000 at The Valley Stadium. We also braved the Old Den, saw Millwall in the Second Division, in a ground infamous even back then for fans keen to offer forthright advice to opposition players and officials.

In 1945, just months after the end of the war, we saw Chelsea play Dynamo Moscow at Stamford Bridge. There were officially 75,000 crammed in to see the famous Russian side but the actual attendance was closer to 100,000 as people starved of live football for so long went to extreme lengths to see it, including climbing on top of the stands and any nearby roof that gave a view. We were stood in the Shed End, half way back, as an almighty roar went up. I think that meant the teams had come out. Being eleven, all I could see were the backs of the men in front. My dad looked down as I stared at a curtain of trench coats, trying to imagine what the players looked like. He suddenly picked me up, held me above his head, then tapped the shoulder of the bloke in front and passed me over and above him. Soon I was heading closer to the pitch, being passed over a sea of cloth caps, man by man, lifted by supporter after supporter, all helping me continue my journey closer and closer to the pitch. Quickly I had been carried to the front and was sat down a couple of feet from the touchline. The best seat in the house.

And it was some show. The Russian's brand of football was years ahead of the conventional English style, being a revolutionary short passing game that our domestic players had never faced. Chelsea were outclassed but what they lacked in style they made up for in commitment, and so deserved the 3-3 draw. This was eight years before the Hungarians – the best team in the world led by the brilliant Ferenc Puskas – taught England a famous footballing lesson in front of 100,000 at Wembley, winning 6-3. It led to the England team reassessing their training and tactics, and English clubs adopting these international practices.

As inventors of the game, we assumed a natural leadership of world football. But this complacency was shattered by the super-fit Hungarians introducing a revolutionary approach. Alf Ramsey was part of that losing team, I remember him telling me years later of the shock of playing against a team that heralded the arrival of 'total football' to the world game. The sheer physicality and control they had on the pitch had a seismic impact on the English game and dragged us into the modern footballing world.

With Kennington Secondary winning the London Schools' Championship and having been picked for the London Schools' team, it meant I was on the radar of local clubs. An approach came from Dulwich Hamlet – famous for their pink and black shirts – who signed me at sixteen on amateur terms. (You couldn't turn pro until seventeen.) I played a couple of times for their reserves but was soon spotted by Millwall and joined them, much to Dulwich's annoyance. They felt let down and decided I couldn't play for them again, which was tough, as I had many good friends at the club.

Millwall, 1950.

Millwall played me in the reserves and also loaned me out to Rainham Town. Again, there was no pay as I was an amateur, but I had my first taste of the good life with £2 per match expenses. Paid (sort of) to play football! I couldn't wait to tell Ron. My second match was on a wet Saturday afternoon in February, in west Essex. On a pitch like a quagmire, I helped us win again.

As we squelched off at full time, I was approached by a man under an umbrella called Len Gordon, previously of West Ham and England. As I blinked through the monsoon, Len explained that he was from Chelsea Football Club, and that he thought I showed some promise. So much so that he wanted to meet my mum and dad and discuss me joining the Blues.

Blimey. Sign for one of the biggest teams in the country? Jump three divisions? Turn professional??

On the tram home, it just seemed too good to be true. I had made good progress in the past year. But First Division Chelsea? That would be fantasy football.

A few days later, Len is at our kitchen table in De Laune Street, along with a Chelsea scout, Jimmy Thompson, opposite me and my dad. On Len's command the scout pulls out a thick wedge of fivers from his bag and drops them on the table with a thud. My jaw joins them. I've never seen so much money. Neither has my dad.

'Alan, that's £200. 'It's all yours. If you come and sign for Chelsea.'

There's stunned silence.

I'm thinking, *how many Crunchies is that?*

My dad is thinking, *how many TV sets?*

No thought needed. I sign. I'm instantly catapulted from being a Third Division reserve team player to being part of a First Division squad. The pay was £8 per week, more than dad was earning.

But we never saw a penny of that wedge.

Billy Birrell, the Chelsea manager, told my dad the club would get in trouble if they actually paid it. Instead, they shelled out for my parents to go on a week's holiday to Bournemouth. With £200, it should have been a month in the Maldives. It was an early introduction to the role of money making the football world go round.

In the year between leaving school and signing as a professional at Chelsea, to keep me in beer and boots, I joined a firm of chartered accountants as a junior clerk, working there in the week, playing for Millwall or Rainham at the weekend. I'd inherited my mum's ability with numbers, and so did well. One day, the boss called me into his office, sat me down and, beaming, gave me the good news. A full-time position at the firm, with great career prospects was the offer. He pushed a contract across the desk for to me to sign.

So, it came down to a straight choice – accountancy or football? I was nearly seventeen and lucky enough to have two very different career options.

A famous old saying claimed there were just three ways out of south London – football, boxing or crime. For me, you could add chartered accountancy. The disbelieving boss warned me no-one had ever turned down a junior position before. Maybe I wasn't thinking of my future properly. Most footballers' careers were over by thirty. By then, I could be on the board of the firm. Or just bored.

Growing up, I knew some dodgy local characters. My parents influence and a sense of right and wrong meant though I was often tempted, I managed to resist. My best mate, Brian Trodd, lived in the house opposite. We used to chat across the street from our bedroom windows. Ron, Alfie and Ronnie were other mates who were part of a very close community that also helped, along with the Scouts. I had some great adventures on Scout camps and learned some lessons. On a trip to the Isle of Wight there was a serious incident involving stolen knives. When we returned, Father Mike, the Scout leader, told my parents I had bought a stolen knife – but had eventually returned it. Dad gave me such a telling off about how stupid I was.

Some local mates ended up at Her Majesty's Pleasure. I was saved by my parents leading by example, instilling a work ethic. If footballers had tattoos back then, mine would have read – *Work hard on and off the pitch*. Was it really that simple? Somehow, I'd managed to join one of the top clubs, with no real setbacks and no injuries. It was almost like it was meant to be.

2

THE BLUES

Ask any football-mad lad what the perfect seventeenth birthday present is and signing for a top club might be the answer.

My professional daily life began with a journey by underground and tram from Kennington to Stamford Bridge for training, with matches at the weekend. Chelsea were a rich club, owned by the wealthy Mears family, but despite having money were an underachieving First Division side. Billy Birrell managed a team that struggled, narrowly avoiding relegation three seasons in a row in the early 1950s. That said, they did reach consecutive FA Cup semi-finals, losing both times to Arsenal. So I arrived at a challenging time for the club, though they weren't short of options, as I joined a huge squad of over fifty professionals.

Every Tuesday morning, a First Team versus Reserves match was played at Stamford Bridge. It gave us a chance to impress Mr. Birrell. Us, the reserve team, playing in the Eastern Counties League, were hungry to make the big leap up to the first team. It was a busy schedule. Sometimes the league games stacked up. One week, early in that first season, we played on Friday, Saturday and Monday.

At the end of the 1951/52 season, Birrell was fired, with the young, ambitious Ted Drake taking over. His aim was simple: turn this erratic side into a consistent, winning machine. So, he began revamping, from revolutionising the training and fitness programmes to dumping the Pensioners nickname and becoming the Blues. 'Within three years we will win the league', he boldly predicted, about a team who had just finished nineteenth.

He also abandoned the club's long-standing transfer policy of buying big names, who often didn't work out, focusing instead on discovering young talent from the lower leagues and the amateur game. He introduced a tough training regime focused on ball work, something rarely practised at the time.

A season later and the team finished nineteenth again. Not quite the consistency he was looking for.

Drake had a great playing career. Still one of Arsenal's highest-ever goal scorers, he was an affable, handsome man whose ever-present smile masked a will of iron. The reserves now trained with the first team at Stamford Bridge, where his ideas and intensity were inspirational to an impressionable eighteen-year-old. The ground was a vast, wooden bowl with a running track on the perimeter, with endless sloping terraces that could hold 80,000. It had hosted England matches and over-capacity classics, like the one I watched from the touchline against Moscow Dynamo.

When the grass was wet, to avoid damage, we had to run on the dog track, which circled the pitch. We ran again and again. And then again. It was brutal. It was a level of fitness I'd never been close to before. No-one had pushed me this hard, to the absolute limit, and I considered myself very fit. Welcome to the professional life.

If we were on the grass, sometimes the greyhounds would be training on the dog track at the same time, so you'd find yourself competing against streaks of smooth fur, endlessly overtaking, disappearing around the next bend. Following the dogs, it was into the stand behind the goal to play 'head tennis', heading the thick, dense, leather ball. As with the running, this exercise went on. And on. After a while it felt like you were banging your head against a brick wall. Both pointless and painful. It's unsurprising that it's become such an issue, with many players from that era, who had spent their whole careers, in effect, heading a brick wall.

The hard training sessions and some decent reserve performances paid off. In early December 1952, Drake grabbed me after training and said I'd made the first team. My debut was against Manchester City, in front of 25,000 at Maine Road, but sadly not mum and dad. It had taken fourteen months to make the step up. Unsurprisingly the nerves and adrenaline were flowing, the blood pumped like a vessel was going to burst. I'd never been so fired up. I'm finally playing with the big boys. Though in midfield for the reserves, Drake put me as centre back in a 4-3-3 formation, alongside John Harris, a tough, uncompromising Scot, who played over 300 times for the club.

For this match, Manchester City tried something new; a deep lying centre forward – Don Revie. It was a tactical innovation and, fittingly, he caused us endless problems. The traditional No.9 had vanished, replaced by a roaming striker who didn't play by the rules. We did hit the back of the net after ten minutes, but unfortunately it was ours, John Harris with an own goal. At half time, we were two down. In the dressing room, Drake had lost his smile. The motivational speech didn't help as we were run ragged in the second half, losing 4-0. Post-match, there was a mixture of pride and disappointment. Yes, I was now a first team player, but what a way to start.

It was a quiet coach journey home. I hadn't played badly, Drake made a point of reassuring me about my performance. So, I was optimistic, looking forward to, hopefully, a run in the first team. Manchester United at home next.

But then the War Office called. For me, the season was over.

I was conscripted and sent up to RAF Padgate in Warrington, for basic training. The RAF Corps operated signals equipment and maintained communications, often under enemy fire. My role was to learn the rudiments of being a signals operator, mastering the teleprinter and ticker tape. I was being trained to go up in Lancaster bombers, to help defeat whoever we might be at war with next, which was most likely our WWll allies, Russia. I was still a professional footballer but was now expected to do most of my playing on Pitch D, next to Runway Two, at RAF Padgate. The timing. As quickly as the first team chance was given, it was taken away.

I reported for duty on the first day – a freezing November morning – to the flight sergeant, looking sharp in my uniform, boots so polished you could comb your hair in them. I'd had plenty of practice on my Gola football boots. He promptly ordered me to report back again the next morning.

'How long have you been in the RAF, Dicks?'

'Er, one day, sir.'

'One day. Now you think you can just bugger off back to London to play football?'

'I didn't think I could, sir.'

RAF Padgate, middle row, third from right.

He fixed me with a stare.

'Well, Chelsea Football Club have contacted us, requesting your presence on their field tomorrow at 15.00 hours. You are aware that you're in the RAF now son, not the bloody First Division!'

Fair point, that's my career on hold. But he hadn't finished and had a surprise up his sharply creased uniform sleeve.

'I will give you permission to play for Chelsea, Dicks. But on one strict condition. That you also play for the RAF team. There's a match against the army in three weeks.'

'Yes, sir!'

Result. My career was back on track, though in the reserves. Also, I was being paid by the RAF and still by Chelsea, meaning my combined salaries were more than any of the first team players. At eighteen. But, more importantly, I was going to be allowed to carry on doing what I loved, in-between getting through eight weeks of 'square bashing'.

In early 1953, we played Spurs Reserves at Stamford Bridge. With a few minutes to go, defending an attack to preserve our one-goal lead, keeper Bill Robinson went for the ball and got the man. Not an unusual situation, except that this time the man was me. He drilled his knee into the small of my back with huge force. Friendly fire. The pain was excruciating. It shot up my spine and brought me crashing to my knees. I blacked out, sprawled on the penalty spot, dead to the world. Next thing I know, I'm lying on a gurney in Chelsea and Westminster Hospital, waiting for treatment – for over three hours. So, I catch pneumonia, pass out and don't come round for two days. When I finally come to, a nurse advises that I very nearly died – and that the doctor is considering removing my kidney. This brought me to my senses; I pleaded with them, resulting in a stay of execution for my damaged, but not quite dead kidney.

Now it was weeks in hospital. Ted Drake visited and was reassuring about my recovery, return to training and getting back on the pitch. It was a great gesture from the manager. His concern was partly born from his own playing career having been cut short by a spinal injury. Mine had only just begun, though for the moment it was over. The prognosis was that I'd make a full recovery though the thoughts in that hospital bed were dark. At worst, it was the vision of me in a suit, sat behind a desk at the chartered accountants.

Once discharged from hospital, still damaged, I was posted to RAF Compton Bassett, Wiltshire, where it turns out they had an upcoming fixture. On arrival, I'm greeted by another flight sergeant, but my reputation preceded me.

'You play for Chelsea?

Chelsea, 1955.

'Yes, sir.'

'We have a big match next week. You are ordered to play for us Aircraftman 2nd Class Dicks.'

'But, Sergeant I'm....'

'It's vital the RAF win. I can order you to play, Dicks. You know what happens if you disobey an order?'

But I didn't play again for eight months. For anyone.

Almost a year after my first team debut at Manchester City, Drake selected me for the home match with Burnley, though I had to first get permission from the flight sergeant. I was fully recovered, but my pre-match nerves were as much about how my body would hold up, as my mind. Ted Drake was inspirational, pumping up the team, a manager you wanted to win for, who you would fight to the end for. I'm in midfield, my preferred position. Finally, we get out on the pitch in front of over 40,000. My heart's racing, let's hope my body can keep up. Captain Roy Bentley, a Bristol lad and Chelsea legend of over 350 games, kicked off. Seconds later the ball lands at my feet. I instinctively look to John McNichol on the right wing and stroke the ball out to him. But it runs too far, spins out for a throw in. He shoots me a look like I'd just spilled a pint all over his new suit and roars in thick Glaswegian.

'Play it to my fuckin' *feet*!'

Sound advice. I soon settled down, put in a decent performance in a match we won, and kept my place for the away game at Bolton Wanderers. Desperate to learn, another senior player to share his secrets of the game was Ian MacFarlane, a dogged full back. His advice to a naive, young pro just starting out in the game was simple.

'If you are up against a skillful player who has lots of tricks, make sure you sort him out early on'.

'Mark him tightly? Give him no time on the ball?'

'No. Punch him in the back.'

'Eh?'

'Punch him in the back. Hard. Job done'.

Welcome to the beautiful game.

There was great excitement in De Laune Street the next morning as we gathered round to read the Chelsea match report in The Sunday Express.

Left half, Bobby Dicks, playing in his first home game, got the ball to safety.

That made mum laugh.

Dicks made a mistake to allow the first Burnley goal but never let it bother him and continued to play with supreme confidence.

Better.

The ball ran loose to Dicks, who just outside the Burnley area, drilled a low shot towards the goal, it rebounded but was picked up by Bentley who put it away.

Great. My very first match report in the national press.

Well, *Bobby* Dicks.

The RAF now posted me to London, to work for the Air Ministry at Bush House in Kingsway, just over Waterloo Bridge from Kennington. No more RAF matches, barking flight sergeants, uniform or commuting from the north down to Chelsea. I was back living at home, in my old bedroom and eating mum's cooking. And going dancing. I'd always been keen, so took classes with my best mates Brian Trodd and Alfie Vernon, learning the jive, tango and rumba, then hitting the dance floor of The Lyceum in the Strand and the glittering ballrooms of Streatham and Purley.

Every weekend I played for the reserves. Ted Drake had given me those two first team run outs over the past year but felt I was more suited to the level below. Still learning, though I'd tasted the First Division, I wanted to play every week but had to be patient, he said. Chelsea finished eighth that season, so the Drake revolution was beginning to spark, part of which involved broadening the squad's experience. So, the club organised trips abroad, playing top European opposition. It taught us different tactical and physical approaches to the game while helping to bond the squad. The first match was against CSKA Sofia in Bulgaria, where me and John Sillett, defensive partners on the pitch, became good friends off it. He was from a football family. His dad had played for Southampton and his elder brother Peter was also a regular for Chelsea. John was a smart full back, with a natural instinct for the game and great positional and tactical sense.

In Sofia, the evening before the match, we headed out on the town. The club had warned us that the police will not hesitate to arrest if they think there is any 'interaction' between foreigners and local girls. The joys of communism. This policy was tested in a bar, when a man came over and asked whether we'd 'like his wife'.

Sorry?

'You like her? She beautiful.'

He gestured to a very attractive woman on the other side of the bar. Tempting, but we had our orders and made our excuses and left. Back at the hotel we mentioned this to the friendly doorman. He said we were right to decline as it was a set-up to get us arrested. *Depraved, immoral western footballers coming over here and taking our beautiful Bulgarian married ladies.*

The Chelsea squad leaving for Bulgaria, 1957.

In the pre-season of 1954/55, two years into the Drake era, there was an optimism around Stamford Bridge. The team was taking shape, confidence was building, and it felt like we were on the right path to challenge for the title. Players Drake had brought in from the lower divisions, like John McNichol and Frank Blunstone, proved his strategy was spot on. Cost effective and hungry for success, they added the raw element that had been missing in the expensive, sometimes less motivated, established names bought previously.

Wolverhampton Wanderers were the team to beat. They had comfortably just won the league title, captained by the great Billy Wright, and were to be a major force throughout the 1950s, winning it another couple of times. Wolves invited top foreign teams to play at their ground, Molineux. Cultured Hungarians, Spaniards and Germans graced the pitch, spreading new ideas on tactics and strategies that Wolves absorbed and put into practice, contributing to their success.

Until Christmas, results were mixed but in the new year consistency was found – the catalyst being a five goal blitz at Bolton. I was playing for the reserves, impatiently waiting for my next chance. It finally came in the spring, at Tottenham, where we won 4-2, completing the double that season. Great for the club, but sadly not for me. Going in for a 50-50 challenge, I was booted hard in my right thigh – very hard – and should have come off. But with no substitutes, my only thought was to finish the match and impress the boss, so I played on. It was agony. Post-match the physio shook his head and diagnosed a haematoma, with severe bruising and swelling. A huge lump at the top of my right leg, it looked like I'd been stung by 1,000 wasps. He couldn't believe I'd played forty-five minutes with such a serious injury. It was not unusual. Players would play through pain to make the most of their game time, taking their chance when it came, no matter what. I paid a price, playing no part in the five remaining fixtures of the season.

For Drake's revolution to succeed and to deliver on his bold promise when appointed, this season needed to be the one. The team, shaped by the ideas he had implemented in three seasons, now reached the point when everything came together. Fitness, discipline, tactics, confidence, optimism, all coinciding to create the perfect storm. We triumphed, finishing four points clear of the next three teams, scoring an average of two goals a game. Regular crowds of over 50,000 added the vital '12th man'. The decider was a narrow home win over title favourites, Wolves, in front of an ecstatic 75,000. The finishing touch was a thrashing of Sheffield Wednesday to win the title. Champions, for the very first time in the fiftieth anniversary of the club's foundation. It would be another fifty years before it happened again.

The celebrations were wild, peaking on the open bus tour through the streets of West London, ending up at the mayor's office for yet more champagne. As well as the brilliant Roy Bentley in that historic team, there was future England manager Ron Greenwood and lightning winger, Eric Parsons. Being champions meant we qualified for the inaugural European Cup and were drawn against Swedish club Djurgården in the first round. Our excitement was short-lived as the Football League somehow decided that the tournament was a distraction to domestic football and ordered the club to withdraw.

Every year I return to Stamford Bridge for a reunion lunch with the players from that history-making squad, with sadly fewer of us present each time.

I got back to full fitness ready for the 1955 summer European tour, playing an Ajax team that had only just turned professional, then on to face the famous Racing Club de Paris. Memorable times, also for my first visit to a brothel. As a twenty-year-old professional athlete, I had a Paris match, then went straight back for a re-match. 'You 'ave plenty of stamina, monsieur,' noted the madame.

In Lille, Sir Richard Attenborough turned up at our hotel, where I literally ran into him in the lobby. A huge Chelsea fan, he had been invited to watch the game that night.

'Hi Alan, how are you.'

'Er...hi.'

Embarrassingly, though a movie star, I had no idea who he was. Of course, he was a perfect gentleman, looking forward to seeing me play that evening. Only after he'd left did I realise just how many great films I'd seen him in.

Unsurprisingly, the optimism around the club for the 1955/56 season was sky high, reinforced by winning the pre-season Charity Shield against Newcastle United. Yet the opening months quickly brought the club back down to earth, with too many poor results. I spent until Christmas in the reserves, waiting again for Drake to promote me. Meanwhile, the first team couldn't get out of the bottom half of the table. But as the new year arrived, so did my chance. Drake picked me for the FA Cup match at Third Division North, Hartlepool United, which we only just won, narrowly escaping a giant killing. I played in half the remaining games of that season, so it was personally satisfying, though as a team, the magic had gone. We all wondered why. Same players, same manager, same tactics, different performances. Motivation perhaps? Having achieved the goal, players took their feet off the pedal, were coasting. Losing at home to a poor Preston North End was a low.

In March, I got my one and only Chelsea first team goal, driving it home from the edge of the box to equalise late on at Luton Town. We got a £4 bonus for a win and £2 for a draw so I made a few quid for my teammates. But the season was a huge anti-climax. We finished sixteenth, proving that when you have finally battled all your way to the top, it's even harder to stay there.

I was rapidly developing an interest in the world outside of playing, as being a footballer had its obvious limitations. Like my mum used to remind me, chartered accountants can go on until sixty-five. Surprisingly, at twenty-two, I was planning my future. I knew Ron Greenwood held football skills classes with groups of school kids. When he mentioned he was looking for a demonstrator, I volunteered. He'd take me along and ask me to 'Chip the ball over the wall, Alan.' And I would. 'Play it to the feet of that striker.' And I would, though he was forty yards away. My key strengths were my passing ability, comfortable with either foot, and I could read the game well. As for my weakness? I still lacked pace. It's what stopped me from being a first team regular. My brain was faster than my legs. Match-wise, I knew what was going to happen, and where, I just sometimes couldn't get there fast enough.

Alongside the Greenwood classes, Ron recommended I sign up for the first-level FA coaching badge. Already having suffered a couple of nasty injuries, I was aware of the fragility of the body and a career in football. I couldn't imagine being thirty and still playing. Many players who started out at the same time as me, were finished before they'd even started. Injury, loss of form or confidence, or just bad luck. The odds were stacked against a top schoolboy becoming a top pro. So having a plan B, learning the non-playing side of the game, made sense.

Ron's advice turned out to be the best I ever had.

For the close season, I had another plan. I bought a little old van and drove round selling stuff I had bought from wholesalers, to gift shops. Ornamental ship's anchors, yacht steering wheels, Italian marble lights and electrical novelties that doubled as home lighting. Cruising along the south coast from Weymouth to Land's End, up the edge of Cornwall, in two summer seasons I earned enough to buy a brand new Austin van.

That summer, I was driving over Tower Bridge to Kennington, returning from a trip to East Anglia. It had been a good week and I had £100 burning a hole in my pocket. With deserted streets at 1 a.m. and being keen to get home, I drove slightly over the 30mph limit. Suddenly, a policeman appeared out of nowhere and flagged me down. I pulled up, rolled down the window, and smiled as innocently as I could. There were already six points on my licence. Any more and a ban would mean the end of the business. The copper leaned in, looking stern.

'Good evening, officer. Can I be of assistance?'

He looked quizzical, struggling to work something out.

This is going to be bad.

'Alan Dicks? It *is* you!

Ah…

'I'm a Chelsea fan! Saw you against Tottenham.'

He let me off with a warning not to speed again – or let Spurs win next season.

The 1956-57 season. We win just three of the first fifteen games, continuing the erratic form of the last campaign. I'm in and out of the first team as Drake looks for the line up to recapture the form of 1954-55. We lose 4-0 to Spurs in the cup. *Hope I don't run into that copper again.* But I get to play in a great 3-0 win at Everton, a reminder of what the team is capable of.

The next night, me, Alfie and Brian are at the Lyceum Ballroom in the Strand. I'm looking sharp in a four-button suit, hair Brylcreemed in a quiff, with a splash or three of after shave. The young footballer on the pull. As we threw our well-practised moves across the dance floor, I spotted a vision through the crowd. A real beauty with short blonde hair, perfect skin and a sort of glow around her, dancing with two friends.

Like before, when running out onto the pitch in front of 50,000, I took a deep breath and braced myself. I had all the moves – foxtrot, jive, tango – and if I could dribble a ball out of a crowded defence, I could glide around dancers on a busy dancefloor. So, I'm thinking, I'm going over there, give her the full Fred Astaire. She smiled as I offered my hand. *Wow, gorgeous!* I lead her across the floor with my finest tango, gliding under the glitter ball, nimbly avoiding all the other quiffs and beehives. I was at the top of my game. Suddenly, she stopped dead. The smile had vanished, she was now stern. 'Can you please dance properly?' she snapped.

It was like being sliced down by Gerry Harris (feared Wolves defender) and briefly floored me. *Regroup, focus.* So, I concentrated on just staying with her, finding the rhythm, remembering all the advice my supple Argentine dance teacher Juanito had given me, 'Alan. We dance as *one!*'.

We move, settle into a rhythm, find pockets of space on the dancefloor, and find our feet. I'm in control, winning at last.

Come Dancing, here we come!

Then her shoe came off.

A pundit would have said she was dancing too quickly. I said it was my fault with two left feet. Though I could kick the ball perfectly with either. Just ask Ron Greenwood. *Who?*

As midnight and the final whistle approached, I offered Maura a lift to her home in Brockwell, just south of Kennington. She couldn't believe it, thought I was a right Johnny-Big-Boots. A professional footballer *and* with his own car? Away with you! She was training to be a nurse, just eighteen, having arrived from Ballina, County Mayo four months earlier. Mentioning I was a Chelsea player was a potent chat up line, though I'm not sure she believed me. It did all sound like a load of baloney; too good to be true. She was a beautiful, smart, Irish girl and nobody's fool. As I'd been at Chelsea for five years, I got a £500 loyalty bonus and bought a Ford Model C Ten. There were now four cars in De Laune Street. She was still laughing when she sat in the passenger seat when now it seemed, incredibly, that maybe it was all true. On future dates, we'd go dancing at the ballrooms of Streatham, Purley and Tooting. Four months later, she moved into De Laune Street. Separate bedrooms, of course.

From January 1957, I was a regular in a steadily improving team. On a Saturday, supporters would chat to me on the Number 9 bus on the way to Stamford Bridge, asking if we were going to win today, win the league, win *anything*. After a taste of silverware, they wanted more. We enjoyed putting five past Everton, Birmingham City and Newcastle United and scoring four at Luton. Manchester United ran away with the league. We were unlucky to finish thirteenth, goal difference placing Birmingham City above us. At a level similar to before the Drake revolution, our issue – despite having a defence that conceded very few away – was leaking goals at home. Drake had managed to modernise the club in many ways, but lasting success was elusive.

3

THE DARK BLUES

White Hart Lane was an intimidating ground. Over 50,000 fired up for the opening game of the 1957-58 season. Danny Blanchflower, the Northern Irish international, captained the Spurs team, played over 400 times at right half. He was someone I really admired, partly as he played in the same position. He ran the game – early evidence of his eventual Footballer of the Year award. It also saw the debut of a mercurial youth team striker, seventeen-year-old Jimmy Greaves, who got the first of 124 goals in three seasons for us. My last visit to Spurs ended in A&E. This, in a painless draw.

Next up, two league games against Manchester City in one week, in which we conceded eight goals. We were struggling, apart from the prodigy, Greaves. I played in five of the opening eight games and it felt like Drake saw me as the first choice for right wing half. But in early September, a home draw with West Bromwich Albion turned out to be my last. I spent the rest of the season in the reserves. Just when I thought my position in the first team was secure, it was gone. A challenging season with mixed results, ending up mid-table, the only consistency being top scorer Greaves.

Tottenham v Chelsea, White Hart Lane, August 1957.

Pre-season 1958-59, Maura and I wed.

She was the oldest of ten children, raised in a two-up, two-down. Despite their financial challenges, her father managed to send her to private school, funded by his winnings from poker games. In a beautiful white dress, expertly sewn by my mum, we married in Southwark Cathedral, Kennington, with the reception in the White Horse pub around the corner from De Laune Street. It was a big turnout, with Maura's mum, dad and many of her nine brothers and sisters over from Ireland, and quite a party. Then off to Devon for the honeymoon, starting at Axminister, revisiting childhood evacuation spots, then on to the Jurassic Coast. Back in the Smoke we stayed in De Laune Street (same bedroom) before moving into a flat on Kennington Road, found through an estate agent from my local Sunday cricket team at the Oval.

By October, Ted Drake had decided he needed fresh blood, so there had to be sacrifices. Not a great surprise to find out I was on the list. The club had done a deal with Southend United, with immediate effect.

The standard employment terms meant players had a yearly contract, reviewed annually by the club. It was *the club* who would decide whether to keep the player or let him go. But if the player wanted to move, and the club refused, you just had to stay. Your career was out of your hands, something I was now understanding.

We had failed to build on that title-winning season. The team spent the rest of the decade hanging around mid-table, with Drake finally sacked in 1961, replaced by player-coach Tommy Docherty. Drake had transformed the club in his nine years but the peak of 1955 remained the peak. For me, it had been a great education, especially as it was during that historic period. I experienced so much, felt privileged to have played alongside so many great players, learning from Greenwood, McNichol and Bentley, along with all the elements you cannot learn, like luck and injuries. All in all, it was an education that grounded me in being a professional footballer – a great apprenticeship.

After seven years, it was sad to be leaving west London, but I felt optimistic heading to Southend with my Chelsea teammate Les Stubbs. He had previously been there for three seasons, scoring every other game, so unsurprisingly they wanted him back. I was part of the deal that cost the Shrimpers, of Third Division South, £10,000. My final season had started brightly but rapidly faded so the time was right to go.

Les had played alongside me many times. We were mates. He was five years older and had a big brotherly nature. We'd joined

Chelsea around the same time, but he saw much more first team action. Stepping down two divisions was a literal drop in my career. Drake had explained my game time in the first team would be limited, so in the end a transfer to Southend-on-Sea – to be a bigger fish in a smaller pond, a regular first team player – made sense.

Today, if a player who wins the Premier League, transfers to a club in League One, say from Manchester City to Rochdale, it would be very odd, even career suicide. But it was a much more frequent situation then, and as the practical boy from south London soon to have a family to support, I was focused primarily on ensuring I made a living. In post-war times, football was considered much more of a job. An exciting and potentially high-profile job, but just a job none the less. I was proficient at the job – but intent on making it a career, so continued to take FA coaching badges.

Living in Kennington, I drove the forty miles to Southend in the Ford most days and often gave a couple of other players a lift. Located in south east Essex, on the north side of the Thames estuary, Southend was famously home to the longest leisure pier in the world and one of the world's first amusement parks, The Kursaal. It used to be a popular seaside holiday destination favoured by royalty. But as cheap foreign holidays took off in the early 1960s, so the appeal of Southend – often windy, with occasional outbreaks of sunshine – faded. The King's Head pub on the promenade was soon to be the only reminder of its royal past.

Southend United had joined the new national Third Division in 1958 and finished eighth, which was decent for a club with little money. After helping seal the First Division title at White

Hart Lane, I was now playing at The Shay, the home ground of Halifax Town. I earned £18 per week, the maximum allowed being £20 per week, until the maximum wage was scrapped in 1961. Eddie Perry, the manager who signed me, was fired three months later. With no replacement lined up, the club played the second half of the season with the chairman, Major Alf Hay, in charge. Imagine that today. Despite having Dudley Price, a lethal striker who hit twenty-eight goals in forty-one games, we only finished mid-table.

The chairman's management reign ended when he finally decided a real manager was needed. In came Frank Broome, who had been a fine winger for Aston Villa and England. With two successful years managing Exeter City, he arrived at South-end on a wave of optimism. It spread around the club and the confidence he instilled in pre-season promised much for the new campaign. Fresh ideas to galvanise a stale team. All very positive. Though the club had only given him a weekly contract – hardly a vote of confidence. And they restricted him to just three new players during the close season. But we were a more focused group under him and as with every other coach and manager I worked under, I listened, intently. I was a sponge that absorbed all the training routines, fitness codes and practice drills; stored, hopefully to be used later.

It was all over by Christmas. He lasted just six months. Fired by the chairman, who then replaced him with – the *chairman*. Unsurprisingly, any progress was limited, losing six of our last ten games, including a drubbing at Bournemouth and Boscombe Athletic, avoiding relegation to the Fourth Division by just one point. Many players wanted to leave but of course they couldn't. It was up to the club.

Hope arrived this time in the shape of ex-West Ham manager Ted Fenton. He'd spent ten years guiding the Hammers, and establishing The Academy, a revolutionary youth development programme that would go on to produce a string of top players. Ted's Upton Park replacement was my old friend and teammate, Ron Greenwood.

Another new arrival in 1959 was my son, Alan. With a family now to support, the off-season was spent either growing my wholesale business or preparing for the next level FA coaching badge. The Southend manager-go-round, four in as many years, was an early lesson in the vagaries of football management. You can have all the mental strength, conviction and self-belief but come Saturday afternoon when things aren't going to plan, you'll have thousands sharing their view on precisely where you are going wrong. Not a challenge if I'd chosen chartered accountancy. 'You're getting sacked in the morning' was never heard around the offices of financial management. But then, how often does a manager voluntarily leave? You're pushed before you can jump, unless you're the likes of Bill Shankly, Alex Ferguson or Arsene Wenger. It's the luxury afforded to the few. For everyone else, they hang on.

At every club, I listened intently to the manager's briefings and coaching advice. Of course, it's very different when you are out on the pitch. His influence goes – you and your teammates are now in charge. There's not much a manager can change from the touchline apart from substitutes, though there weren't any until 1965. We made our own small changes on the pitch within a game. If you had a problem, you had to react there and then. It was much more physical. You could scythe an opponent down from behind and barely get a wagging finger from the ref. Jimmy

Stirling, my teammate at Southend United, was a hard man. Playing Southampton in the FA Cup, their striker Terry Paine was the danger man. Five minutes in, Jimmy shouts to me.

'Alan, send him down the outside'.

'Why?'

'I want to take him out for a while.'

Jimmy tackled him so hard that Paine suddenly lived up to his name and became a marginal figure for the remainder of the match – a ton of bricks had landed on him. Leading recklessly with his shoulder, and Jimmy didn't even get a yellow. Players like Jimmy and Alf Ramsey, Spurs' right back, had seen action in the war and were not afraid to literally stick the boot in. If you'd survived Dunkirk or El Alamein, Saturday afternoon football was a stroll in the park. No one died on the pitch, but there were some hard knocks and broken bones, most of which went unpunished. The weapon of choice was the shoulder barge. If you raised your hands and pushed a player, it was instant dismissal. But the shoulder was allowed, meaning the more full-blooded defenders like Jimmy could lay down a heavy marker early on in a game by steam rolling an opponent off the ball in a way that would have been considered illegal on a rugby field.

'We take no prisoners' was a wartime phrase that, post-war, entered the language of football. It didn't mean you were going to take their striker out with a bayonet, but it summed up the attitude, the 'never say die' spirit that those who'd seen action in the war were transferring to the pitch. Physical play could significantly help a team win a match. Even during squad training in the local park at Southend, players would put it to the test. Referees offered less protection, so for the vulnerable players it meant you had to look after yourself.

Southend United matchday programme.

But that didn't extend to off-the-pitch health. Some smoked at half time. Others were big drinkers and would often be found running around the pitch at Roots Hall on a Saturday morning before the afternoon's game, sweating off Friday night's pints. Careers ended by injury were far more common.

The post-football job options of pub landlord, sports shop manager and postman waited on the side lines. Many struggled to make it to thirty.

At Southend, there was another fitness strategy. Sex. Yes, we were young fit, sportsmen and those who weren't married would energetically play the field. But at this club there was something a bit more organised. I heard that two of the players shared a house near the ground that had so many girls hanging around that it was like a brothel, except no-one paid. They were presumably big fans of the club and willing to do anything to help morale – after all we were a struggling Third Division side. The bachelors of the team certainly filled their boots in the afternoon. How they did a tough training session and then carried on jogging horizontally was admirable. I'd be safely on the 3.14 p.m. to Liverpool Street Station, returning to Maura. I'd be back home in Kennington by 5.30 p.m. to see Alan, and by Christmas 1961, also Mandy and Michelle, before bedtime.

In the pre-season of 1962, Southend asked me to stay on. We'd finished sixteenth, which was an improvement, but still with no money to strengthen the squad, so when my contract was put in front of me to sign, I hesitated. I hadn't lost my appetite for the game, just hungry for something else. Now twenty-eight, the clock was ticking, I needed to broaden my experience, look for ways to extend my career. The answer was coaching. I'd done a lot for the London County Council and at several private schools, and now had my full FA coaching badge. The FA Training Centre at Lilleshall in Shropshire ran courses, so periodically I went up there to complete my set of badges.

Now fully qualified, I was ready to step up.

4

THE SKY BLUES

Jimmy Hill asked me to come for an interview.

At his wedding.

In the smart reception, near Piccadilly Circus, to the soundtrack of Sam Cooke's 'Twisting the Night Away', Jimmy outlined his grand plans to take sleepy, Third Division Coventry City, into the top flight for the very first time. Of course, it was the happiest day of his life, but there was no reason to stop working. Other than his new bride, Heather, his love was football. The Third Division was very familiar to me after three seasons with Southend. As manager for ten months, he was looking for an assistant, and a coaching agent had recommended me, and he was intrigued. We chatted – well, he talked – outlining his ambitions for the club; a club that hadn't tasted the big time for so long, and how he had plans to end that drought. With such infectious energy and enthusiasm, it was hard not to be excited.

Back in Kennington, Maura asked me what the wedding was like.

'Jimmy was very chatty, with loads of energy and ideas.'

'No, not him. The bride, how was she?'

'She's called Heather.'

'Right. Heather.'

Turned out that Heather Hill and Maura would end up becoming best friends for life.

A few days later, Jimmy called, asked a few more questions and said he'd be back in touch. An hour later, he rang, and offered me a one-year contract as assistant manager/ coach and to play for the reserves. He explained that the best place to coach a team from is not the side of the pitch, but on it – something most clubs hadn't considered. But then, Jimmy was endlessly innovating. After a decade playing as an inside right for Fulham, he retired to become chairman of the Professional Footballers' Association, campaigning for an end to the Football League's maximum wage, where players were limited to earning £20 per week. Jimmy led the movement to end this antiquated law. To force change, he convinced players they should go on strike. Like today, workers – miners, factory staff, bus drivers – protested about pay and/or conditions by downing tools and refusing to work. Or in this case, play. All the Saturday fixtures at the end of January 1961 were scheduled to be cancelled, due to the players' refusal to play. With a worker's ultimatum, the clubs finally gave in. Player power at its most potent.

The most famous beneficiary of this revolution was Johnny Haynes, the Fulham striker, who got an instant wage rise to £100 per week – a 500% increase. Club chairman, Tommy Trinder, said he was happy to pay the rise because Haynes was an entertainer and brought the crowds in, an agreement not all club owners were so comfortable with. Who could possibly predict that fifty years later it would end up at £400,000 a week? Sparked by Jimmy, the fuse was lit that exploded the time-honoured pay structure. The balance of power shifted away from the clubs and was handed to the players, and, eventually, to their agents.

Jimmy wanted me to start straight away. As soon as we could move the family to Kenilworth, into one of Coventry's club houses, the better. We packed up the house in Kennington. The move was exciting and challenging, but sad for my mum. She saw Michelle, Mandy and Alan most days, so it was a wrench. Not easy for Maura either; new city, new home, new friends, but she was a resourceful and sociable person, so these challenges were not mountains to her.

Coventry was among the first of Britain's cities to be redeveloped in the post-war years after bombing destroyed much of the centre, including the ancient cathedral. It rose literally from the ashes, transformed by a vast rebuilding programme. Coventry was a classic example of 1960s concrete architecture: cold, functional and uninspiring. Not dissimilar to the way the team played, shown most recently when finishing fourteenth in the Third Division.

Car factories like Jaguar employed thousands, helping the city become a boom town with such good employment prospects it attracted workers from all over the world. Building on this spirit, Jimmy wanted to make the community feel part of the club. So, he insisted we always used 'we' when referring to the club – a way to bridge the gap between the club and the fans. Also, he made the match-day programme full of club initiatives for the fans. *Inclusivity.* Way ahead of the game, he overhauled Coventry's image with what became known as the Sky Blue Revolution, changing the home kit from navy and white back to the original sky blue colours from fifty years before, plus the introduction of a nickname and a club song. Many elements accepted in modern day sport, like pre-match entertainment and half-time events, were kick-started by Jimmy, who wanted families and the community to be at the heart of the club and the match-day experience.

Of course, the best way to get people through the turnstiles was by getting results. For that we had to refresh the squad, cheaply. First in was my old friend John Sillett – surplus to requirements at Tommy Docherty's Chelsea – a right back who would be part of the defence with George Curtis. Now in his eighth season at the club, George was less flesh and blood, more carved from granite. The hardest player I've ever known. Soon after I joined, he broke his leg at Nottingham Forest. As he lay spread on the ground, we jumped out of the dugout and shouted to the stretcher team. But before they could reach him, George had got up, and stamped his leg down so hard it had pushed the bone back into place. Another time he went up for an aerial challenge and headed the opponent, not the ball, and cracked the poor player's skull. George barely winced. And there was brain with the brawn. After fourteen years at the club, he ended up on the board, having bought shares regularly since he joined, which made him a lot of money. He eventually became joint manager alongside John Sillett in the mid-1980s, winning the FA Cup.

Our cost-effective new signings paid off. That first season, 1962-63, we came fourth, just missing out on promotion. It was progress from the mid-table finishes the club had specialised in for the previous decade.

As a team we were still inconsistent, winning three, then losing three. We were one of the highest-scoring teams, so we needed to tighten up at the back and show more discipline. The reserves, though, won the Combination League, securing the title at home in front of 12,000, with me playing midfield, coaching and managing.

Our final Combination League game was at Fulham and as I stepped off the coach at Craven Cottage, I had a real surprise waiting for me. Mum. She didn't tell me she was coming and explained there was no way of letting me know. After the match, we went back to De Laune Street, where dad was waiting. I hadn't been home for ages, so it was a very special evening. They were both on good form. I told them all about Coventry, how the kids and Maura were all doing well and about my ambition to eventually move into management. Mum jokingly suggested that it wasn't too late for chartered accountancy. Of course, they were so pleased it was working out even if it was so far away. A very special evening.

Next morning, I'm woken by dad, screaming.

'She's gone! She's gone!'

I'm thinking, *where's she gone?* She'd recently retired, so she's not gone to work. Maybe she'd gone to get some shopping in, early?

She had died in her sleep. A brain seizure.

At sixty-two. Much too young, especially for someone so full of life just a few hours before.

My inspiration, gone.

How does such a force of nature fade so quickly?

There had been no warning, just a sudden end.

The shock lasted. And lasted.

Part of my role was recruitment. I'd constantly be watching local youth and junior games, searching for talent. In pre-season we signed a sixteen-year-old called Bobby Gould, who would stay for five years, becoming a twenty-goal-a-season striker. By early October, we were top. And the people came. Attendances were up to 30,000, unheard of for a Third Division club. We then put eight past Shrewsbury Town.

There were also some good players coming through the reserves like Ernie Machin, Willie Carr and Ronnie Rees, who would all go on to be first-team regulars. So good, that we were getting 10,000 fans for *reserve* matches. Day-to-day, I was running coaching for both teams – Jimmy occasionally popped in – and I revelled in the responsibility. Having been at Chelsea, I was quite a well-known player; First Division experience was respected in the lower leagues. Playing in midfield, in the Combination League, at thirty-four, meant proper hands-on coaching – the perfect way to bring on the younger players and still be Jimmy's No.2 with the first team.

Pat Saward (coach), me and Jimmy, 1964.

Jimmy, always the innovator, had studied the rhythms of the body and implemented an unusual training routine for the players. It wouldn't raise an eyebrow today where clubs employ full-time throw-in coaches, but in 1963 it was radical. The standard training approach was peak fitness training sessions in the mornings, with the afternoons for relaxation. Yet, he argued, we played our matches on a Saturday afternoon, meaning the body graph was out of sync. We were going against the natural flow of energy. So, he changed the fitness training to weekday afternoons, 2–4 p.m.

It worked. The season started well, then got better. By late-November, we were nine points clear.

Soon, Jimmy left me to run all of the playing side, leaving him free to focus on other aspects of the club and his next innovation – like his anti-vandalism brainwave. British Rail suffered widespread trouble when supporters travelled to away games. Train carriages were trashed, rival fans fought, and staff were assaulted. So, Jimmy did a deal with British Rail to create the Sky Blue Express, specifically to ferry Coventry fans to away matches in their own space.

He also had his Internationals Club. This was a team comprised of great professionals in their twilight playing years, such as Tom Finney, Danny Blanchflower and Stanley Matthews, who would play exhibition matches. I would be the reserve. Often someone was injured, so then it was a team of legends…and Alan Dicks. Quite an experience.

By early 1964 we were on track for promotion, whatever it took. On a bleak Saturday morning in January at Highfield Road, the snow lay thick on the pitch. Kick off was at 3 p.m. against promotion rivals Brentford. But we were a quick passing team that needed to play on grass. So, we got the groundsman to dig up a patch of snow, spread some water, put the snow back and mark the spot. When the referee inspected the pitch at midday, we led him to that spot and suggested we dig below the snow to see how the ground was. He then revealed that there was ice below.

'Oh no,' we all cried.

'Match abandoned', he said.

There was proper crime in football that season with a match-fixing scandal. Swindon Town striker, Jimmy Gauld, encouraged players in several teams to influence the outcome of matches and take bets on the result. The legal result was ten players being sent to prison and banned from the game for life, with thirty-three players prosecuted in total. One convicted player was actually awarded Man of the Match, despite being found guilty of throwing the game. Not sure how that worked. We were untouched by the scandal, but it shook the game and undermined the supporter's belief in a sport that had turned out to be so easily corrupted.

This second season was another learning curve. I absorbed every bit of club strategy, planning, player management, training and psychology that Jimmy Hill shared. George Curtis summed him up.

'I've never known him lose an argument. When you think you have him cornered, he'll baffle you with science.'

That was Jimmy – smart, highly competitive and always thinking outside the box, on and off the pitch.

In the FA Cup we were the giant-killers, beating First Division Sunderland and Portsmouth to face Matt Busby's Manchester United in the quarter-final with Bobby Charlton, Nobby Stiles and Dennis Law, who scored twenty-nine that season. What chance did the Sky Blues have against the Red Devils? Jimmy had instilled a fearless attitude in our players that ignored the scale of the opposition and focused simply on how good *we* were. So, 44,000 squeezed into Highfield Road to see us take the lead on a pitch made of both mud and snow, when John Sillett began a move ended by Terry Bly, blasting it past Harry Gregg. Maybe the biggest of giants could be killed? It all looked possible until Bobby Charlton grabbed two late on, ending dreams of a Sky Blue Express trip to Wembley.

For the next two months we stuttered, allowing the one-horse title challenge to then become a race between us and Crystal Palace. As happened at Chelsea, there are periods when for no obvious reason, a successful team suddenly self-destructs. Confidence wanes, the luck – and victories – disappear. We rode this nine-game winless period out by signing goal machine George Kirby from Southampton in March, who promptly ended the drought by putting four past Oldham Athletic.

Jimmy had specific rules about dealing in the transfer market. He believed a player's motivation gradually dropped after being in the game a few years, meaning they would be good for a season or two, but not much after. Buying an expensive player was an extravagance only done as a necessity to fill a temporary hole in the team. There had to be a very compelling reason to buy any player over the age of twenty-five. Unorthodox criteria, but it worked.

The season came down to the very last home game in front of over 42,000, close to a Third Division record. Crystal Palace were two points ahead, so it was a must-win match against a stubborn Colchester United. A nervy contest was eventually decided by our single late goal. Palace lost at home to Oldham, so we were champions on goal difference. Promotion in my first full season.

Jimmy's reward for the team, and wives, was a trip to Spain to play a couple of matches and get some sun. Great team bonding.

When we got back, we were off again, as part of one of Jimmy's more unusual ideas – a tour of Europe, promoting the launch of a new British car by playing matches against various local teams. Eighteen days, three countries and 2,500 miles. A Coventry car company, Rover, wanted to launch its new P6 2000 motor – a car so fast that the West Midlands Police ordered a hundred. Research by Rover had found there was a link between productivity in the factory and success at the club. If Coventry were winning, workers were happier and productivity increased. These recent cars were produced in record time.

We drove ten sky-blue P6s through Holland, Germany and Switzerland, promoting the car and the club, proud new members of the Second Division. As an export drive, it was endorsed by no less than Harold Wilson, the Prime Minister, so at each of the cities we stopped in, there was a civic reception, welcoming the footballers who had pulled up in the latest example of cutting-edge British car engineering.

One night in Zurich, me, Jimmy and an English football journalist went to a reception and ended up at a nightclub. We were approached by two ladies and a conversation begins. It's going well but there's three of us and two of them. Someone is going to be disappointed. Jimmy took me to one side.

'Alan, see if that girl can come with me – and get rid of that bloody journalist.'

So, I took the journalist to one side and politely requested that he let the manager of the recently crowned champions of the Third Division have some quality time with this Swiss lady. He thought for a second.

'Sorry, Alan. No can do.'

And with that he was off, ushering his lady out of the bar, followed by me, leaving Jimmy stood on his lonesome. A rare moment when Jimmy lost out.

The new season revealed old habits. We won the opening five, and then lost the next four, although Jimmy did relax his approach to expensive transfers when the club paid a world record £35,000 for Bill Glazier, Crystal Palace's goalkeeper in October 1964. Despite a challenging start, letting five in against Bury, he went on to play nearly 350 times. We finished tenth in this, our first season in the Second Division. A solid start but not Jimmy's plan. Next season, it had to be promotion.

The 1965-66 season started well, winning ten of the first sixteen. During that run, Jimmy organised the very first football beam-back broadcast, when our midweek win at Cardiff City was watched by over 10,000 on a big screen at Highfield Road. The fans got to see the game, and the club had a new revenue stream. Next, he introduced a bonus system, which added to the player's wages for the following season – a delayed payment that worked to incentivise performance and commitment to the club. It was a referred bonus, so not *quite* illegal.

The *Coventry Evening Telegraph* wanted an interview about my role as Jimmy Hill's right-hand man, which was to be my first one-to-one with a reporter. Jimmy's advice about handling the press and TV was my first bit of media training. He boiled it down to a simple mantra. 'Make sure that you read it in your mind before you say it. Visualise what it would look like in print.'

It saved me from many own goals, carried throughout my career when, eventually, facing the media would become an almost daily event. With his increasing schedule, Jimmy asked me to take first team training and manage team selection more and more. He was a pundit for the BBC, regularly away, leaving me in charge. As the club didn't have their own training ground, we used local parks or private sports grounds, often with a curious crowd watching.

We drew Cardiff City in the FA Cup. The team coach left Coventry on Friday for the Saturday game. Jimmy was commentating on a match at Norwich City on the Friday night. He then he drove five hours in his Jaguar on the Saturday to get to Ninian Park at 2.59 p.m. I was becoming manager by default. The balance between his media commitments and club was shifting, though this didn't stop him innovating. He disliked the league points system, how it didn't encourage teams to go for the win. The remedy, he argued, was to award three points for a win, not two. This would motivate teams to attack, with the added point a reward for winning. Jimmy presented his idea to the Football League, who thanked him and promptly filed it away as an unrealistic idea. It was 1965. In 1981, they opened that file and thought differently, implementing it into all four English leagues. A decade later, FIFA did the same.

It was a stroke of genius. An antidote to the dour 0-0 draw, and to those teams who played *not* to lose. It was a big part of the game that had little do with entertainment and bringing in fans.

What would Jimmy do next? One morning, I turned up at the ground and headed towards the physio room to check on Ernie Hunt's hamstring recovery, when one of the ground staff warned me not to go in. So, of course, I marched straight in and found our highly trained physio busy doing treatment on an injury. Except it wasn't Ernie's hamstring, or even anything human. It was a horse. Jimmy's horse, which had a leg problem. He had joined the local fox hunt and had brought him in for treatment. More innovation.

5

MAKING HISTORY

All Jimmy's ideas and ambitions for the club could not have happened without a supportive and forward-thinking chairman. Derrick Robbins was an entrepreneur who backed Jimmy throughout the Sky Blue Revolution that transformed the club in the mid-1960s. It taught me how vital an understanding – and wealthy – chairman was to a manager.

We missed out on promotion by a single point. Despite having a great run-in, winning four of our last six, Southampton were promoted. There's no prizes for third.

Then it was the 1966 World Cup, where I saw England beat Mexico in a group match and Jimmy – as a BBC pundit – got me a ticket for the final at Wembley, which was an unforgettable experience. We'd learned the lessons of the 1950s and were now as fit and tactically smart as the Germans. The coaching had been revolutionised by Walter Winterbottom, who managed England until 1962, continued by Alf Ramsey, and assisted by my old friend Ron Greenwood, who had helped produce three players of that victorious team at West Ham; Bobby Moore, Martin Peters and Geoff Hurst.

It was quite an afternoon. Grown men openly crying with joy, as finally we were crowned the best in the world in a sport that, as originators, we always assumed we were anyway.

During pre-season training, Jimmy called me into his office. He looked stressed, which was a rare sight.

'Where the hell is John Sillett?'

'He's around somewhere, Jim. Why?'

'Apparently, he slept with some girl.'

'Right.'

'And her dad is not pleased. On his way here now with a shotgun.'

Ah.

'I have been talking with Plymouth Argyle and they want to buy him. Now might be a good time to find where he is.'

I shot down to the dressing room, found John and gave him his options.

Chairman Derrick Robbins and trophies.

'It looks like a move to the south coast would be good for your health, John?'

He nodded. So, no shotgun wedding, more a shotgun signing.

Could this be the one? The 1966-67 season. By the end of November, we were adrift in eighth place, well off the pace being set by Wolves. But as the month changed, so did our form. We won at Cardiff City and at Wolves, then put five past Ipswich Town. It was the start of an unbeaten run of twenty-five games in five months. A club record that still stands.

That run included a 5-1 win at home to Portsmouth. Post-match, as usual, it was up to the director's hospitality suite for a celebratory drink. I wandered over to Jimmy who was talking to a smart and dignified man in his seventies. Jimmy, ever the warmest of hosts, introduces me with a flourish.

'Alan! I'd like you to meet Lord Montgomery of El Alamein.'

Blimey, it was the field marshal and war hero.

'Hello Alan. Congratulations on a very convincing victory'.

I was about to say the same to him.

'A real pleasure to meet you, sir.'

'You had a smart game plan. We, on the other hand, never looked at the races, unfortunately.'

Jimmy and I had beaten Portsmouth. 'Monty' and Winston Churchill had beaten Hitler. I found out later he was from Kennington. If I'd known, we could have talked about the old place. Maybe he'd watched Charlie Chaplin dance on beer barrels? He was a very unassuming hero.

The season decider was against Wolves, the winners to be crowned champions. Sometimes the fixtures conspire to produce a classic. It was dubbed the Midlands 'Match of the

Century' and a record 51,000 squeezed into Highfield Road, onto the roof of the stand, and up the floodlight pylons. There were so many supporters, that kids were allowed to sit just behind the touchline.

Wolves took the lead just before half-time. We came out with all guns blazing in the second half and grabbed two quick goals – the second of which caused the fans to invade the pitch, even though they knew it *wasn't* all over. The referee threatened to abandon the game if there was a repeat. Our match-day announcer used all his powers of persuasion to convince them that their high spirits could cost us the match, maybe even promotion.

When Ronnie Rees got the third with minutes to go, the deafening crowd obediently stayed on the terraces until the ninetieth minute. Then they went mad, on to the pitch, players swamped. Unbelievable scenes. Coventry City were in the First Division for the first time. And that sixteen-year-old apprentice from four years ago, Bobby Gould, was now the league's top scorer with twenty-four.

At 5 a.m., in a local hotel, after raucous celebrations, Jimmy and I raised a glass, to us. In four seasons the manager and assistant – both first timers – had ended eighty-four years of waiting. We had guided the club from the depths of the Third Division to the heights, finally joining the top teams.

An open-top victory parade bus tour of the city was a joyful moment for the supporters, who must have thought they would never live to see this day. We proudly showed the trophy from the Lord Mayor's balcony to a vast crowd. As the Movietone newsreel blared the next day, '*THE BOOM TOWN NOW HAS A CLUB TO MATCH.*'

The final fixture of this historic season was a testimonial for George Curtis for twelve years' service, over 400 games. The only person that could ever stop George from playing, was George. Coventry faced Liverpool, in front of 30,000 fans, still drunk on excitement, to get a taste of what they were going to see next season; Ian St John, Emlyn Hughes, Roger Hunt and Ray Clemence.

Chairman Derrick Robbins owned two Rolls-Royces. He had an idea for some pre-match entertainment. 'I'll bring my convertible Rolls and drive slowly around the edge of the ground with George in the back, so he can take the crowd's applause.'

'Good idea!' said Jimmy.

Derrick didn't know Jimmy had joined the local fox hunt. Half an hour before kick-off, Jimmy, wearing the full hunting outfit of black boots, white britches and a black coat, sat astride his huge brown horse. As Derrick waited in his blue Rolls to start the lap of honour, Jimmy got in first, trotting around the pitch before the car had driven off. The crowd loved it.

Shocked Bill Shankly sat incredulous on the touchline.

George Curtis sat in the Rolls, laughing. Strange to think he's no longer with us. Iron Man was not just a nickname, more a player profile.

Once the champagne was drunk, the bubble burst. The club disappointed Jimmy by offering him a five-year contract when he was expecting ten. Two other managers had been given ten-year deals recently and both had not worked out. Robbins thought it was too risky offering Jimmy what he wanted, despite the historic achievement.

So, Jimmy resigned.

He confessed to me that being manager was not improving his lifespan due to the stress and strain that went with a job that relied principally on other people's performances. You never win as a football manager, he said, even when you're winning. The pressure took its toll, despite the amazing success of our five years, so he left to become head of sport at London Weekend Television. After which he went to the BBC with the challenge of modernising Match of the Day, on the way to becoming the most recognisable TV football personality of his time. He never managed a team again. But he changed the game forever.

6

CITY TO CITY

The Rover P6 screeched to a halt, leaving a black tyre mark across the Ashton Gate director's car park. I leaped out and into a football club in chaos.

Manager Fred Ford had been fired just a few weeks into the season as they struggled near the foot of the Second Division. There had been high expectations for The Robins in the previous season, when he had brought in England international Chris Crowe from First Division Nottingham Forest for a club record signing, and prolific striker Hugh McIlmoyle from Wolves. A poor start was saved by a surprisingly good second half of the season, managing a solid mid-table finish. So, optimism was high for the 1967-68 campaign. As always, all the supporters and everyone at the club had dreamed about was promotion. Impatient? Hardly. It had been fifty-six years. A city the size of Bristol – seventh biggest in the UK – deserves its main football club up there with Manchester, Leeds and Liverpool.

It started well with a 1-0 home victory over Swindon Town in the first pre-season friendly, watched by 8,000. Proper support, which coincided with the opening of the first supporters club shop. But it was going to find itself struggling for customers when the season began with four consecutive defeats. The final straw was the home loss to Blackpool; nine games, seven defeats. Ford looked for a vote of confidence from the board, but only found his marching orders. But some of the players felt such loyalty, they went to chairman Harry Dolman's house in Chew Magna, just outside Bristol, demanding that Ford be given his job back. Many strange things happen in football, but reinstating a sacked manager? Ford had been in charge for seven years and had brought them up from the Third Division in 1964-65. He wasn't someone I knew personally, though Coventry had played Bristol a few times, so we'd been in opposing dug outs. He was a popular figure at Ashton Gate.

Despite the crowd of angry players in his living room, Harry Dolman didn't budge and the search for a new manager began while the club physio, Les Bardsley, was made caretaker manager, again. I found out later that Harry's first choice was the manager of Torquay United, Frank O'Farrell. But in another twist, O'Farrell passed on the offer because of the way Ford had been treated by the club. If he hadn't been such good friends with Ford, he would have taken the job, and I wouldn't have found myself outside the Bristol City boardroom, waiting to be interviewed, complete with sweaty palms, but focused. As assistant at Coventry, we'd had a successful five years. But I had not been the manager. No one knew me outside of Coventry. Were they going to be interested in someone who'd only ever been the No. 2?

This was my debut formal interview, aged thirty-three. At Coventry, Jimmy hired me after a chat at his wedding reception. This time, I found myself driving 100 miles from Kenilworth in one of Coventry's sky-blue Rovers to face a row of suited men sat behind a boardroom table. I didn't manage the journey well, underestimated the traffic, so the last mile was completed at a speed not approved by the police. Racing into the Ashton Gate car park, narrowly missing a bollard, I screeched to a halt, got out, straightened my tie, pulled on the jacket of my dark wool suit and found the reception desk.

'Alan Dicks…to see Harry Dolman', I said, a bit breathless.

'They'll be with you in a minute, Mr. Dicks', said the secretary. 'Take a seat.'

It turned out to be a long minute. But it gave me time to compose myself and go through again the answers to potential questions. The position had not been advertised yet. Jimmy had rung round a few clubs when he knew he was leaving Coventry, and this was the only lead. Of course, it's all about the contacts in any business and football is no exception. It's not what you know, but who. And Jimmy was someone who knew everyone in the game. I couldn't have had a better person to spread the word.

'If you'd like to go in, Mr. Dicks?' she finally said.

The heart's racing a little but I'm ready, striding into the large wood-paneled room to find six men behind the boardroom table. Chairman Harry Dolman gestured for me to sit down on the lone chair opposite and led the cross examination, with occasional questions from his fellow directors. I had an answer for everything, hoping it was what they wanted to hear. When the interrogation ended after forty-five minutes, no one gave anything away. Had it gone well? It felt like getting a draw at Old Trafford; hard work but positive. And hopefully my story felt convincing. Coventry had been promoted twice in my five years. Not a bad CV. But they must have been seeing others with more experience and when Harry uttered those words 'We'll be in touch', I genuinely had no idea whether I'd won or lost.

Back in Coventry, Maura had questions. Are we all having to pack up and move to Bristol? Are the kids leaving their friends? Am I leaving mine? If it happened, it would again be a wrench. They were in good schools, she had made many friends, including her best mate, Heather Hill, Jimmy's wife. 'Impossible to call,' I said. The football wife, always at the mercy of the next move.

I found it hard to concentrate, imagining what a life-changing opportunity it would be, but we had a match at Sheffield Wednesday to prepare for. My job was at this City, not the other one. Noel Cantwell was Jimmy's replacement. He'd had a tough introduction to First Division management, winning only two out of the first eleven games. Jimmy had recommended me to the board, but they had rejected me due to lack of experience.

We were not adapting well to the top-flight, a small fish in a big pond, with low confidence. Without Jimmy it was a very different club. I was 99% focused on the Sheffield Wednesday game, with my mind occasionally wandering to the potential transformational verdict.

Next day, the call came. Fifty-five years later I can still feel the excitment.

Bristol City offered me a three-year contract on £4,000 a year, plus a bonus of £1,000 if I kept them in the Second Division. Yes! Maura was delighted for me and began making plans to move five children – Alan, Mandy and Michelle, now joined by Melanie and Patrick – and a house full of stuff down the M5 to a new life.

It was my chance to be the boss. I'd done my apprenticeship under one of the best teachers and realised how fortunate I was to get this opportunity. My last match was a 4-0 drubbing at Sheffield Wednesday. Coventry would finish twentieth, escaping relegation by just one place.

I was now going down a division, but it was really a promotion.

On Friday 13 October, I left Coventry City and started my new position on the Monday. We moved from the club's four-bedroomed house to a similar club-owned property in Stoke Bishop in Bristol. My very first job as a manager was selecting the team for the visit of Cardiff City the very next day. No surprise there, except I hadn't been around the ground, stepped on the pitch or even met the players. So, I opted for experience, dropped young Chris Garland and we managed a 1-1 draw on that Saturday in front of 15,000, all hoping that this was the start of a new era.

First thing Monday morning, I was at Ashton Gate addressing the players and backroom staff. Now I'm the boss. Jimmy had been a great mentor but it was all down to me. Was I ready? And what are the players thinking? Probably, who the hell is he? Ex-Coventry City *assistant* manager? Many were still frustrated that the club hadn't given Fred Ford more time. Was I going to be any better? I was the same age as a couple of the players so I was going to have to really earn respect.

The first challenge was to stop this poor run. I'd done my homework, quizzing journalists, players, coaches, anyone I knew that could give an insight into the team, player strengths, weaknesses, anything. I needed to get a struggling side to build their confidence in me, and in themselves. In practical terms,

I'd handled all the training at Coventry so knew what I wanted – ball skills, ball work, physical and mental training regimes. A number of personnel changes were needed. By the end of the first week, I could see the areas where we had to improve. Losing at Portsmouth next, confirmed them.

First task? Find a centre forward. With only eleven goals in fifteen games, we were not so much goal shy, as goal scared. Just before I arrived, chairman Harry Dolman had sold striker Hugh McIlmoyle – who'd only been at the club a few months – to Carlisle United. Would I have helped him find his touch? My first deal was actually for a stylish right-half, Ken Wimshurst, signed from Southampton for £12,000, with six years' experience in the Second Division. I also liked the look of John Galley, a goal-every-other-game striker who Tommy Docherty had at Rotherham United. Jimmy Hill and I once had Galley on our target list, so I knew all about him. He came from a football family. His elder brothers, Gordon and Maurice, were both professionals and the biggest influences on his career. Following in a big brother's footsteps was something I understood.

The transfer process with Docherty – an inflammable Scot who eventually managed thirteen clubs and then the Scotland national team – was my introduction to the transfer dance, a backwards and forwards routine that many managers demanded of each other. Miss a step out or get one wrong and you risk upsetting the whole exercise. I'd learned the tango and jive, now it was the transfer shuffle. This went on over the course of many days.

'£15,000,' I offered.

'£17,000', he countered,

'£20,000.'

'£23,000.'

'Tom, I'm not giving you any more bloody money.'

'Alan, £25,000 and you got yerself a deal.'

Agreed. But when I called Tommy the next day about the final arrangements, there was something that somehow he'd forgotten to mention.

'He's got tendonitis. His foot's in plaster.'

Achilles tendonitis is an injury of the Achilles tendon, the band of tissue that connects the calf muscles at the back of the lower leg to your heel bone. A common injury, but it can be tricky to shake off. Checking with our club doctor, he confirmed this was the correct way to treat the injury. I agreed to go through with the deal. At the next board meeting, Harry was impatient.

'Well Dicks, have we got him?'

He always called me 'Dicks' and it would be several years before I earned the right to be 'Alan'.

'Yes. Done deal.'

'OK, that's great. Finally, a goalscorer.'

'Yes. But his foot is in plaster.'

'What?

'But once he's fit, he'll be scoring. Great news, isn't it?"

Total silence.

As I leave the boardroom, I heard one of them splutter.

'I don't believe it! He's bought a bloody cripple.'

I had complete faith in Galley. I had to. So much would depend on him and like every manager, it's my decision and I'll be judged on my transfers. There were no directors of football here. A few months ago, it would have been Jimmy's decision, with me advising, but now it's just me. Though I didn't remember him ever buying a player in a foot plaster cast.

On the pitch, we lost the next two, won the two after, and lost the next. Goals were still an issue. By mid-December the plaster was off. Galley trained hard and we decided Huddersfield Town away should be his debut. It was a big test for both of us. Get it wrong, go too early and he could be back in plaster before you can say 'goal drought'. Result? We won 3-0. And he got a hat trick.

If you designed a prototype centre forward it would be Galley. Over six foot, strong, fearless, quick, a defender's nightmare. Fans soon had a song for him, which is always a good sign. 'I'd walk a million miles for one of your goals, John Galley.' The mood around the club changed after just that one result as now it seemed we could score goals; salvation, with being just above the drop zone.

Chairman Dolman held weekly Tuesday morning board meetings. I would be called in after they had finished, to give updates on the team, injuries, potential signings – anything to do with player matters. He ran the club like a business, and I was just another employee. Occasionally, he would invite me to lunch at his engineering factory in midweek, to talk through team issues. A mutual respect gradually grew. Harry hired me, so of course he was determined for it to work.

I was building relationships with the players, some faster than others. There were those who had been there several seasons like Danny Bartley, Mike Gibson and Jantzen Derrick, the nucleus of the Fred Ford team. Only Gibson stayed. Inevitably, I was going to have a different approach and the first time this showed was in the training programme. I was obsessed with fitness. My motto? 'Can't run, can't play.' So, I implemented routines that specifically focused on stamina and speed. One was simply running up and down a very steep hill on the Lady Margaret estate. Up and down, up and down; twenty times. Building up power on the way up, sprints on the way down. It was intense. So intense, that players vomited. Then we would work with the ball; close control, three against one, head tennis, followed by routines to simultaneously focus on fitness and ball control. Mind and movement exercises; observe how to deliver a ball into the space that works for the target and read the game. Finally, there were specific individual, tailored work outs for players where needed. Most of these ideas were new to the squad.

What was it about Ashton Gate? By December, we had won just two home games all season, despite a noisy regular crowd of around 15,000. In November we had great away wins at Plymouth and Preston, then lost at home to Norwich and Charlton. Harry gave me a public reassurance. Though I'd only been manager for two months, with the intensity of the job, it felt longer, every decision mine. It was still early days, but he was tested further on Boxing Day when we lost 4-1 at Birmingham City. Defence was the priority, and despite that last result, it was improving. Jack Connor was a strong leader alongside Alec Briggs, in front of consistent keeper Mike Gibson. With a midfield of Ken Wimshurst and Chris Crowe, up front were Chris Garland and John Galley. All worked hard. There was a team spirit starting to develop, but it had been a tough introduction as we hovered perpetually above danger.

The last game of the year was the rematch with Birmingham, which we won 3-1, meaning a good New Year's Eve. Both Garland and Galley were on target. Resolutions? Keep working hard and results will come, as I told the press, imagining it in

Me and Harry Dolman, Mr. Bristol City, 1967.

print before speaking. In the *Bristol Evening Post* it looked like the classic cliché. But, of course, they are clichés because they are true.

We began 1968 by drawing. January had four in a row plus a home defeat to Millwall, but this did become rarer, so supporters could look forward to games. After a decent score draw at second-placed Blackpool – Galley on target yet again – there was a week's gap, so we stayed at a local seaside hotel to train and bond. We returned for the FA Cup, at home to Third Division Bristol Rovers. In an electric atmosphere, with 40,000 squeezed into Ashton Gate, for ninety minutes, neighbours and friends were enemies, an intensity I hadn't experienced since Chelsea versus Spurs. But they got a stale contest – a goalless draw that did neither team, nor fans, any good. In the equally tense replay at Eastville Stadium, Galley and Crowe's goals topped off a terrific team performance to shut up our neighbours and to set up a tie at Middleborough.

My brother Ronnie came to the match. He had retired a decade earlier after 350 games, a Teesside legend. With no interest in coaching or management, he owned a furniture store, then worked in a sports shop. That day, he saw a lively contest end in stalemate, with us winning the replay, earning a fifth-round tie at Leeds United. My first chance as manager to take on one of the best. Already a feared force, top of the First Division, the week before they had beaten Arsenal at Wembley to win the League Cup. Don Revie's iconic team – Johnny Giles, Jack Charlton, Billy Bremner, Norman Hunter – were maturing into one of the top club sides in the world. Fair to say we were underdogs, though two recent league wins had stopped the rot and lifted us out of our winter slump, though not the relegation zone. Then Galley got injured.

Elland Road was the cauldron for a bad-tempered match. Despite our committed performance, showing no signs of intimidation, they were two up before half time. It was very physical, sometimes nasty, with Giles – a practiced exponent of the cynical challenge – leaving his foot in just long enough after a tackle to take a man down (and sometimes out). It was Leeds' balance of brawn and brain that made them so dangerous. In the second half we pushed forward hard, with Crowe coming close, but couldn't get the breakthrough.

The match highlight was saved for the closing minutes – a bust-up in their box. Chris Garland brought Billy Bremner down and their keeper, Gary Sprake, took exception. A row kicked off between Sprake and Garland, who allegedly spat at him. Sprake responded by trying out his boxing technique, delivering a knockout blow to lay Garland flat out in the mud, and Sprake in an early bath. A fitting end to a bruising experience.

We were out of the cup and some might say that it's OK, that it means you can concentrate on the league, and staying up. Not me. The Leeds game, every game, is about winning. If you win a cup tie it lifts the team for the next league game. Winning becomes a habit. In my whole career I never, ever, put out a weakened team for a cup match. Though we lost on the pitch at Leeds, we won on the money, with over £15,000, so at least Harry was pleased.

As the No. 2 at Coventry, I was protected from having the ulti-mate responsibility, though with five successful seasons, never saw Jimmy under this kind of pressure. We had now lost eight of the last thirteen games. Confidence was shattered. Before Tuesday's board meeting, a gloomy Harry had an uncharacter-istic private word. I reassured him that games were tight, that we were losing to the odd goal, and that when Galley was fit again, results would improve. He had to trust me.

Harry Dolman was originally from the West Country, starting his working life in a local engineering firm at twenty-one as a junior draughtsman. A well-built man, with a formal, business-like manner, after ten years he was managing director. Many of the company's products were Harry's inventions. The most significant being the ticket machine for the London Underground. At its peak, the business employed 1,600 people. He was not just an inspired engineer but a wealthy businessman, warmly welcomed as club chairman in 1949. He combined shrewd running of the football club with engineering innovation, designing the first set of floodlights installed at Ashton Gate in

1953. Officially, his title was chairman; unofficially, he was Mr. Bristol City. He also had a good knowledge and understanding of the game, keenly aware of the team's needs.

'So, Dicks, what's the latest on buying that defender?' was a regular query.

Building a strong team begins from the back. Get the defence right, don't concede, and you have a chance. We conceded 30% fewer goals in the second half of my first season. At the heart of this was captain Jack Connor. With the club for seven years, he would go on to play over 400 times. Jack was a steady central defender who was my age. Wing half Gordon Parr had played for a decade, and then there was fiery fullback Alec Briggs, who when he had a dip in form and I dropped him for a couple of games, threatened to report me to the Professional Footballers Association. We had Gerry Sharpe, outstanding on the left wing, blessed with incredible pace and a trademark scoring technique of cutting inside to shoot. There was also promising youth talent, which included Trevor Tainton and Geoff Merrick, both local lads.

My tactical approach was influenced by the recent World Cup, where the 4-4-2 formation came to the fore. It was the Brazilian and Hungarian teams who implemented this revolutionary set-up, first seen in Brazil in the late 1950s. The beauty is in its simplicity. The defence keep a solid straight line across the edge of the penalty area, moving up with play, perfect for releasing the offside trap. Central midfielders win possession, protect the back four and provide support to the front two. Winger's supply crosses to the strikers from wide positions to get the goals.

Another benefit was that by pulling the two outside forwards back into deep positions, it meant you could outnumber the opposition in midfield. So, it would be four versus two in midfield, making it easier to keep possession. It created a more solid defensive unit, as an outside forward would now be faced against two defensive players, rather than one. It also afforded greater flexibility, with the midfield players able to move forward or back.

It was a reaction to the static post-war WM and WW formations that had predominated for decades. The English game was slowly embracing this new tactic. It was how I wanted us to play. There were some players who could flourish in that formation; others who it would take time to adapt. Today, it's seen as a rather oversimplistic game plan that prevents more cultured play, but in the 1960s, it was revolutionary.

My coaching staff were inherited and though I started bringing my own people in, it would take a while to het it how I wanted. The physio, and sometime caretaker manager, Les Bardsley and I took a while to bond. Before our game at Norwich City, I asked him what his best team would be for the match, as always, interested in his opinion. He had a sharp response. 'They pay you to pick the team, not me.' Fair enough.

Like every new manager, I quickly learned that you can't do everything immediately. It takes time, you make mistakes, you learn from them. Patience is required, from everyone. A tough ask of some. If I'd had those results in my first season in today's game, by February, the chairman would have been speed-dialing Sam Allardyce.

Our battle reached a critical point at the end of March at home to Rotherham United – relegation rivals, and Tommy Docherty's team. Even Galley couldn't find the net as they scraped it 1-0. Losing such a crucial match prompted a crowd response of from some of the 14,000 of 'You don't know what you're doing!' I was learning on the job, getting to know the players, the club and the city. And the supporters.

It wasn't only during the match. My weekly board meeting became less of a conversation and more of an interrogation.

'What happened against Rotherham, Dicks?'.

'Has Galley run out of goals?'

'Why aren't you playing Tainton more?'

'What if we don't get a result against Bolton?'

Eight games to go and home to fellow strugglers Bolton Wanderers, in front of only 11,000, who were fearing the worst. We managed a draw when two points were needed to escape the bottom three. Keeping the confidence up when the press were putting us down was a challenge. Our victory against Plymouth means *they* go bottom.

Four matches left and a crunch game at The Valley with a team also in trouble. I had great childhood memories of visiting Charlton with my dad, though they were not so good as an adult, losing every time with Coventry City. A must win for both teams, they were in excellent recent form, despite their lowly position. It was also a bit of a grudge match as our supporters remembered them coming back from 2-0 down to win in the FA Cup at Ashton Gate a few years earlier. The City contingent were a small part of the crowd but were the loudest in that vast ground. Chris Crowe scored early, and they equalised with twenty-five minutes to go, but one point is not enough. With fifteen minutes left, a close-range winner from Galley sealed it. Where would we have been without him? The Third Division probably.

Seven of the last eight games were against teams also in trouble. It was like the fixtures had been worked out for maximum tension. Preston were on level points, so to put four past them was perfect. The win helped relieve the tension a little and meant a more relaxed, confident side, proven by winning the next two, including a crucial 4-2 victory at Aston Villa, where I gave keeper Barry Watling and Bristol Boys' skipper Geoff Merrick, their debuts.

The crowd were slowly warming. Maybe I did know what I was doing? The chants faded as results improved. You'd go mad if you listened to the advice of 15,000 people every week. I learned to shut it out. Same as when I was playing. Stay focused.

We won four of the final six games, finding our form at the crucial time and finishing nineteenth. Only three points separated the eight teams above relegated Rotherham and Plymouth.

A rollercoaster introduction to management, I'd done what Harry demanded, and had earned the bonus. He naturally wanted much more next season; there was a constant push/pull between us. Success on the pitch was not enough, he needed the club to grow in terms of the stadium, facilities and supporter base. The only guaranteed way to fund improvements at Ashton Gate was to sell players, as the club had no other assets to leverage. Not ideal for my team-building plans.

Every week I faced the board, all very successful local business people, who were constantly looking at where extra revenue could come from. One, Robert Hobbs, who made his money out of quarries, understood the game and became an ally. Each board member invested £10,000 (£160,000 today) into the club when joining and had that hard-nosed business outlook that drove them to push for growth. We all wanted that, but at what price?

My accountancy training came in useful for understanding the financial numbers, but the most important numbers were always goals. Galley got twenty-six, with support from Ken Wimshurst who was a great playmaker. Strike partner Chris Garland, got nine in thirty-two games. A local lad, I'd reintroduced him as he'd fallen out of favour with Fred Ford. Gerry Sharpe got seven goals from the left wing. Ron Greenwood was interested in him for England. He'd come to watch Garland but was impressed by Sharpe. Originally a striker, he was a revelation on the wing.

7

BUILDING A TEAM ON AND OFF THE PITCH

I needed people I could trust as part of my team. Today, top managers have so many in the dugout with them, it looks like a government job creation scheme. My needs were more modest.

Enter, Tony Collins. We first met when I played for Jimmy Hill's Internationals Club at Rochdale's Spotland Stadium. He was manager of Rochdale, a very impressive character with a long and varied CV. We got on and agreed to stay in touch.

A couple of years later, I was going to watch Preston play on a Tuesday night as we faced them on the Saturday, in the vital end-of-season four-pointer. Maura said she'd like to come. 'OK, but you realise it's over 200 miles?' 'Sure, I'll enjoy the drive.' *To Preston, from Bristol?* Over four hours later, after traffic and roadworks, we arrived. She never came again. I bumped into Tony after the match. We spoke about the game and his situation having left Rochdale. I'd driven all this way and yet I knew Tony, who still lived in Rochdale, with great football connections all over the north and Scotland, and who was a great talent spotter and reader of the game. He could have done it. So, I asked him to join as chief scout.

He needed a club that matched his ambition. I told him he could still live at home with his wife and three children and use his nationwide connections to scout for players. There was no need for him to be based in Bristol as good players can be found anywhere. In fact, the further away from the big cities, often the more likely you were to unearth some gold, with less competition. I also needed someone with managerial experience who could not only find the talent but buy them at the right price. A scout *and* a negotiator, something he'd done at Rochdale. Tony would be our football spy. As history has taught us, the great military leaders throughout the ages have won wars by information. Knowledge is power and spies were vital and that was very much my philosophy. To have someone with that rare skill at the club was going to be game-changing. Unsurprisingly, the board had lined up questions that Tuesday.

'A chief scout, who lives 200 miles from Bristol, Dicks?'

Tony Collins was a pioneer, a football trailblazer. He was one of the first black professionals and the first black manager in English football. Growing up in Notting Hill, only a few miles from me, he eventually played for eight clubs. On the pitch, he sped up the left wing, setting up and scoring goals for, amongst others, Crystal Palace, Watford and Norwich City, ending up at Rochdale, where he was swiftly promoted to boss. They were in the Fourth Division, their rundown Spotland Stadium built for 10,000 fans but with barely half that at matches. With basic facilities, limited transfer funds and poor attendances, it was a tough introduction to management. But, incredibly, in only his second season, he took them to the League Cup Final, being the giant-killers of Southampton and Blackburn Rovers on the way. They faced his old team Norwich City in the two-legged final. Though they lost, to have got that far was a real achievement.

He was a strong character; a product of the life he was handed. The one constant was dealing with discrimination – in the dressing room, on the pitch, in his social life. Tony was one of the very first black players when he turned pro with Sheffield Wednesday in 1947. You could count the number of non-white players in the Football League on one hand. Compare his situation with today, where around 34% of players in the English Football League are black. Though it is not at the same level for managers sadly, just over 4%.

Tony was a great tactician and brilliant spotter of talent, which is why the owner of Rochdale – local businessman Fred Ratcliffe, the King of the Springs (his company made bed springs) – promoted him to manager. Most of the time, money was so tight that Tony had to resort to desperate tactics like sending a cheque from the club to the gas company to pay for the electricity, and vice versa. This trick earned him another ten days for each payment as the companies returned the cheques, requesting the correct payment for their bill. It bought him time. Another reason I liked him – he was good with money.

You must be a strong character to be the only black player in a match. You've got to be even stronger to be the only black manager in the country. Tony had huge self-belief. His views on players was so passionate that many times we stayed up till the early hours, arguing about the relative merits of some talent on our radar. That's what I wanted. Absolute conviction.

Tony Collins doing another deal.

My pitch to him was simple and familiar. Promotion. Though with the warning that money and resources were tight, but not as tight as at Rochdale. A journalist friend of his in Manchester had a network of fellow reporters around the country who could provide extensive background on players. Looking at buying Ken Kendall from Kettering? Well, he's just left his wife and kids for a supporter. Another target, though pronounced fit, has still not shaken off that old knee injury. These unofficial background checks were a vital part of our own due diligence on potential signings. Tony was the master spy. He got information that wasn't on the player's CV. Information that could be crucial in deciding whether to invest or not.

By pre-season he'd put together a scouting network that covered most of the UK. He instructed his spies (coaches, journalists and club officials) to check on players, to make sure we were ahead of the competition, find that great player early and make the most of our limited budget. I soon made him assistant manager as well, which meant he had access to the boardroom on match days, something a chief scout doesn't get. It was in this rarified environment, pre- and post-match, that people talk, where information is revealed. So-and-so says that the top striker at so-and-so club is unhappy. That promising young full-back has fallen out with the manager and is looking for a move. Golden nuggets of information that Tony was expert at mining and passing on to me.

I had done a little bit of media work at Coventry, but when your boss is Jimmy Hill, opportunities are limited. He taught me that you must never antagonise the press as it creates a wall and makes communication difficult. We both lose. Make it as friendly as possible, mutually beneficial. He had a post-match press room, which was unusual at the time. It was another innovation that helped him benefit from his media contacts by creating a convivial atmosphere for thirsty reporters.

So, after home games, towards the end of that first 1967-68 season, I began the open-bar meeting in my office for all the journalists and the opposition manager. My secretary, Anne, served the drinks, reporters asked questions and swapped stories and rumours. The drink helped things flow. I was fascinated to know what the opinions were outside the club and of rival managers. A fixture was Roger Malone, the *Daily Telegraph* sports reporter and HTV match commentator, who would often take me to one side and quiz me about the team, players and the board. He was hugely knowledgeable and well-connected within the game. We built a great friendship and respect that still stands today. Peter Godsiff was the Bristol City correspondent for the *Bristol Evening Post*, another with whom I built a good understanding. He would come and see me every Tuesday morning and we'd chat about last Saturday's game, what went right, what went wrong, and plans for the next fixture. He was a great writer who went on to become the paper's sports editor. Today's press are much more aggressive and intrusive – more ready with advice on how a manager should do his job. Back then, we had more control.

Sometimes, youth team coach John Sillett sat in. After his hasty exit from Coventry to Plymouth Argyle, where his playing career ended, I brought him to Bristol. He was a loyal ally, an experienced professional, a great motivator and tactician.

Harry was looking to raise funds to compensate for the £25,000 the club had lost during the season, even though we had that good cup run and a record 2,000 season ticket holders.

If we had been relegated, I would have probably been fired. Then it might have meant the wholesale-selling business full-time.

As it turned out, Harry invited the squad for an end of season party at his Chew Magna country house. The last time the players were all there was to protest at Fred Ford's sacking.

I wondered if things had turned out differently, whether they would have done the same for me.

The end of the season meant player contracts had to be negotiated, all with the standard one-year deal. It was a procession of meetings with players. The chair opposite my desk was rarely cold. There were no agents at that time, fortunately. Even so, some of the conversations were unpredictable.

One morning, Chris Crowe, an affable Geordie who could play either midfield or up front, sat down. He'd been a first-team regular since Fred Ford signed him two years ago. And he'd played for England, once.

'Boss, I'd like more money. I think I've had a good season and deserve it.'

'But Chris, you're already the top earner. Even more than John Galley, who scored twenty-six goals.'

'I know that. But I reckon I deserve a rise.'

I'd done my homework. I had a system that prepared me. From the first match of the season to the last, I wrote a report on every single player. That was my Sunday night ritual in our house on Ormerod Road. The kids would be in bed and I'd settle down in the front room with a scotch, yesterday's game still fresh, to jot down my thoughts. It meant that I was ready for those end-of-season chats with an account of how each player had performed. Scanning all the match reports, it turned out that Crowe was less indispensable than he imagined. I had already weighed up the pros and cons.

'In fact, Chris, if we get the right offer, I'm prepared to let you go.'

There was stunned silence.

And I did. He was not the most team orientated player. Skillful but selfish, and with a very average goal average. So, he left for Walsall.

There was a standard response from each player after I'd been through their season, quoting from the reports, outlining their performances from months ago, how they had disappeared during the second half at Charlton, lost the ball that caused us to concede at Blackburn.

'So, did I have *any* good games, boss?'

Understanding every player in every game put me in a position of strength for these negotiations. They all knew I kept a record, so it wasn't me struggling to remember how midfielder John Quigley did at Birmingham City on Boxing Day. I knew he was poor, it said so. Alternatively, if there was a player that I wanted to let go, it wouldn't matter what his report said.

Quigley came in with the same request as Crowe. A Glasgow lad, he'd won the FA Cup with Nottingham Forest in 1959 but was not what I needed. He had plenty of talent but little energy. He got the same answer and ended up at Mansfield Town. Gordon Low, a solid wing half, needed more pace, which as a team we lacked, so he was let go. Tony Ford also. Jantzen Derrick was after a pay rise, so he went to Reading.

It wasn't easy telling someone they were not wanted, but that was the reality. Often, the rejected player would ring up clubs, be his own agent, sell himself for the next job. A tough call. We may have had enquiries about players from other clubs during the season, so I'd always pass those requests on and hopefully they could move on to another club. As everyone was on just one-year contracts, the scrutiny was more intense than today. Today, if you're on a five-year deal, that's the rest of your life sorted, whether you play or not.

In contrast, we had some bright young players coming through; Merrick, Tainton and Sharpe, all local lads. Tony Collins' reach and judgement also started working, laying solid team foundations. Limited funds meant strengthening through free transfers, buying smartly, and developing the youth. The club held all the power. Players couldn't leave without the consent of the chairman and manager. The player we *had* to hold on to was twenty-six-goal Galley, the second highest tally in a single season, just four short of Bristol City legend John Atyeo's total in 1955.

If I had compiled a personal report and grade for *my* first season in management it would have been B-, generally positive but with room for improvement. Avoiding relegation by just two places was too close for comfort. But I'd done what was asked – kept us up. The ship had been steadied. There were plenty of reasons to be optimistic about next season. Domestically, Maura and the five kids had settled well in the house in Stoke Bishop, all fit and healthy, and the schools were working out. Maura made friends so easily that she very soon knew the whole street.

With the job, came the profile. In Coventry it was not really an issue. Jimmy was boss, I was the boss's mate. But now I was in the full glare. The first necessary change in my lifestyle was that I stopped going to pubs. Hardly a radical life change, but as much as I liked meeting and chatting with supporters, it was often hard to relax and enjoy the evening.

'Oi, Alan, why aren't you playing Bob up front?'

'Parr needs help in midfield. The formations all wrong. Should be 4-5-1.'

'Rubbish keeper. Why not find someone who can actually *catch* the ball?'

All perfectly reasonable questions but a bit challenging when you're looking to enjoy a quiet drink with your wife in the Red Lion in Clifton. Pubs outside Bristol were OK, but nowhere in town. I was a public figure now which of course comes with the job, and I enjoyed it. Up to a point.

Initially, I watched games from the director's box, sat just along from Harry, in a lofty position at Ashton Gate, with a perfect 100% view of the whole pitch. But with no connection to the team.

I was literally just a spectator. So, from the Norwich City game in early December, I moved down to the dugout on the touchline. Now I could get a message across and be part of the match, though once the game has started, the influence a manager has by barking orders at players is minimal. But you can feel the game much better, even though the far corners of the pitch are distant, with 70% vision at best. Also in the dugout were the sponge man and a substitute, an innovation introduced just two years before.

For a 3 p.m. Saturday home match, players would arrive at 1 p.m. This felt rushed, so I suggested we had lunch together at midday in the club lounge. Anything to help team bonding.

Training began at 9 a.m. Monday morning; technical work with the ball. Players would then go home for lunch and return to sit through a post-mortem of Saturday's game. It was home defeats to mid-table teams like Norwich and Charlton that put us under so much pressure last season and needed analysis. Being Second Division, we were very rarely on TV so there was no evidence of any crimes committed on the pitch, just the report I had written the night before to highlight where players went wrong. The rest of the afternoon was physical: gym, sprints, practice games. We trained five days a week, unless we'd had a particularly good result and the players had earned a day off. Even then, many would still come in for light training or a massage, using the sauna I had asked to be built. Generally,

I wanted to give the players as many reasons as possible to be around Ashton Gate. I was in all day, every day and liked to see them there.

On Friday, to sharpen up before match day, we played five-a-side on the pitch, and shadow play, with no opponents. This exercise was to get the players used to the surface, working on marking and running with opponents, making the marker run forward or back. It was what Ron Greenwood called 'a run for him, then a sprint for you'. The daily squad training sessions were done in local parks like Greville Smyth and in sports grounds, but if we were playing at home the next day, it made sense to be at Ashton Gate. Preparation also included an exhaustive breakdown on the opposition using mine and Tony's research covering their danger men and how best to neutralise them, expected tactics, weak areas and recent performances. Knowledge is power, preparation key.

The only person unhappy with this Friday arrangement was the groundsman. He would get angry, outraged that the players wanted to train on *his* football pitch. The directors would haul me in.

'Why, Dicks? You know how long it takes to prepare the turf.'

'Yes, but do you want a good pitch and a bad team? Or a bad pitch and a good team?'

Of course, the groundsman wants his turf to resemble a snooker table on a Saturday afternoon, so doesn't want players ruining it before then. But those Friday workouts were an essential part of the preparation.

8

SEASON 2 – THE LEARNING CURVE

The one fundamental element that was missing from my game, that stopped me progressing from Chelsea to another big club? Pace.

I read the game well, had very good fitness, excellent ball control and passing ability – but lacked *pace*. Recognising the same in some of my squad, I hired a sprint coach in pre-season. If you can't outplay them, outrun them.

But before a ball had been kicked, there was a disaster.

The Great Flood in July 1968, where two months of rain fell in two days, tragically cost the lives of eight people and devastated thousands of homes across Bristol and north-east Somerset. A catastrophe that reminded us all of the power of nature. For a few days I went by boat to Ashton Gate, which was under water, causing damage to the offices and changing rooms. It was nothing in comparison to what happened to so many people and brought a moment of perspective. It is *only* a game.

Chairman Harry had given me a budget and with it I made the club's record signing – Bobby Kellard from Portsmouth for

£30,000. I knew him from Southend United where he began as a promising teenager who used to clean my boots. His arrival excited the fans so much that over 8,000 watched him in the friendly against Southampton. I knew exactly what kind of a player we were getting. He won the ball, kept possession, distributed smartly and had great stamina. The pocket battleship they called him, which was accurate, as sometimes he could be a destroyer. He upset the opposition, was a niggler, would lift us with his tenacity, winning the ball in midfield and driving the whole team forward.

Today, possession is seen as a tactical necessity, so a team that plays the ball across the back incessantly before finally moving it up the pitch is believed to be in control of the game. It makes me reach for my remote control. The game is about pace and energy. Of course, possession is important, but when a stat reveals that a team had 76% possession and yet only drew the game, you wonder if all that ball management was worth it. Kellard was my kind of player as he wanted to win the ball and move forward; to get on with it, with pace. His service to Galley and Garland was going to be vital.

The season started with a narrow defeat at Fulham, who had been freshly relegated. With Bobby Robson as manager, they had high hopes, though those hopes would be short-lived as he was sacked soon after. Bobby found out he'd lost his job, not from a phone call or in person, but by seeing a headline on a *London Evening Standard* notice board outside Putney Station – a headline that screamed 'ROBSON SACKED'. The equivalent today of being fired via Facebook. He went on to Ipswich Town and a great managerial career, taking England to within one game of the World Cup Final.

Seeing Bobby's treatment by Fulham, I was entitled to a degree of a paranoia. We had managed just one win from the first twelve league games, the lowest point being a heavy home loss to Cardiff, with John Toshack giving us a lesson in goal scoring which was usually taught by Galley. In November, we lost seven out of nine, including five consecutive defeats. We couldn't score in a Parisian brothel, averaging half a goal a game. Galley and Garland had lost their appetite, no matter how well Kellard fed them. Relegation form. Every home match the supporters told me with increasing anger and volume, their opinion. It was déjà vu. The weekly board meeting became increasingly grim. I was just waiting to read *that* headline on a *Bristol Evening Post* notice board.

A losing streak when you're a player is tough, but I found it much more challenging as a manager. The learning curve at Bristol was steep. Supporters were always there to remind me, of course, which is their right, but at home to Aston Villa it went too far. Walking down the tunnel, out to the dugout, for yet another must-win home game, some 'fan' leaned over the barrier and spat in my face. I lost it and went for him. Livid, I was just starting to haul him out of his seat when the long arm of the law intervened.

'Please, Mr. Dicks…it's not worth it.'

The officer dragged me back just as I was winding up to throw a punch. Another joined and my rage subsided as they escorted the 'fan' from the ground. Later, it made me think about what other jobs there are where the public feel perfectly entitled to scream, swear and even spit at you. Not many sprang to mind. It's another aspect that reinforces the isolation when things aren't going well. You must be mentally tough; to have the skin of a rhino. The officer saw me later to say that the supporter had been arrested, taken to the station and charged with affray. He missed Galley scoring our winner.

The League Cup provided a diversion with another trip to Elland Road. No punch ups this time, but we fought well, ultimately losing to a Mick Jones winner. Leeds United finished First Division champions that season, so it was no shame. I met Don Revie again, always finding it fascinating getting to know the top managers.

The optimism of pre-season was replaced by the backs-to-the-wall attitude of last season. Still, we maintained a good team spirit, with virtually the same line-up. Gordon Parr and Jack Connor, the central defensive pair, Kellard and Wimshurst in midfield, Galley and Garland up front. Though even this consistent team selection again struggled for consistency.

As always, we were on the lookout for new blood, Tony being key. As there were no specific timeframe restrictions for the transfer window back then, the search for players was constant. Before the manager's transfer dance began, Tony and his network of scouts would identify a potential target, make contact, and when we were sure he was interested, ask his club's permission to speak. Our scouting check system included the 'two matches away and one at home' principle. For any player being seriously considered, these were the quality match checks required. There were certain players who didn't travel well. Put them in front of 20,000 of their own fans, and all was fine. Put them in front of the Kop, they went to pieces. So, it was vital to check they didn't get travel sickness. Once that check was approved and I'd seen the player myself, Tony's spy network would supply the more personal kind of information that might be important.

The scouts we had covering the country just worked for expenses, motivated by the thought of being the one who discovers the next Geoff Hurst. So, for little outlay, we had a huge amount of intelligence on our targets. With his access to boardrooms on match day, picking up information, Tony could hold his own with anyone in football. He was smart, eloquent, hugely experienced and his knowledge was endless. This was confirmed in years to come when he was hired by Don Revie, Alex Ferguson and the FA for the England team.

It got worse before it got any better. November brought five losses in a row, scoring one goal. The 4-1 defeat at Middlesbrough drove Harry to call a crisis board meeting. It was so bad, I hauled the team into Ashton Gate on Sunday for extra training. We were poor in every department. Even the solid defence had turned soft.

During this dismal run, I signed Alan Skirton from Blackpool. He was from Bath and had played in the 1958 Bristol City team that reached the semi-final of the FA Youth Cup, so it was the return of a home-grown hero. A very quick winger, he spent seven years in the First Division with Arsenal. In fact, he was so quick, he'd often beat defenders by pushing the ball past them and running around over the touchline, to come back on to the pitch and carry on up the wing. Pace. It was always needed, especially now. It would also help to counter the reputation we'd acquired for tough and negative play.

Post-match drinks were now held in my office. The press had us as early relegation favourites. The longer the season went on, the more accurate this looked. No amount of free booze could make these meetings comfortable. The questions were rightly harsh; I was running out of ways to say, 'things will improve'. There was a period of grace when a new boss came in. After a year, this was now over. There would be around twenty reporters, some local, some national, all looking for that story for Sunday's back page. It wasn't helped by Harry having a tricky relationship with the local press, falling out with Herbie Gillam, sports editor of the *Western Daily Press*. Harry then decided to do an exclusive with the *Green 'Un*, the sports section of the rival paper, the *Bristol Evening Post*, annoying Gillam even more.

Before social media and Sky, you had to wait for the results on TV and radio at 4.40 p.m. on a Saturday. All games kicked off at 3 p.m., with ten minutes for half time and very little added time. The only match reports appearing on the day were in the *Green 'Un*, delivered at 6.00 p.m., which supporters would queue up for at newsagents. The reports usually had a lot of detail on the first half but little on the second, with journalists communicating by phone at half-time, then at full-time.

They all reported comprehensively, though, on the protest – calling for my head – by supporters outside Ashton Gate on a freezing Saturday in December before our game against Bury. We'd managed just two wins from nineteen league games. I was learning how to deal with the pressure – a crash course over the past year.

We beat Bury.

From *Dicks Out!* to *Dicks In!* within ninety minutes.

It kick-started a recovery. Galley found his scoring boots and in the next ten games we got five wins and two draws, including a 6-0 thrashing of Fulham. Garland, Skirton and Kellard gave the great George Cohen – the 1966 World Cup winner – a torrid afternoon in what was his last game for the Cottagers. It was our biggest league victory for eight years and helped send them down. We beat Bristol Rovers 5-0 in the Gloucestershire Senior Professional Cup Final at a rammed Eastville Stadium. For some supporters, it was our biggest win of the season.

The FA Cup third round sent us down a snowy A4 to the home of the World Cup winners Moore, Hurst and Peters: West Ham. We were about a mile from Upton Park, stuck in gridlocked traffic, with – as was required – the team list for the referee an hour before kick-off. So, I jumped off the coach, jogged to the ground and handed it in, to find that the pitch was more ice than grass. Old mate and manager Ron Greenwood told me it would be fine, and said they'd put some sand down. We didn't show the West Ham legends too much respect and were unlucky to lose 3-2.

Our match preparation became a well-oiled machine. Tony Collins would 'spy' on our next opponents and write a report on their tactics, key players, fitness, strengths and weaknesses. Some players would then be given specific tasks for that game. On a Friday at Ashton Gate, we would go through the required pattern of play on the pitch, against no opposition. But whoever we were playing, the principal was always to get the ball forward to the front men with pace and energy, push up the pitch. Players found it odd at first, playing without opponents, but warmed to it eventually.

Each player would be given responsibility to pick up a specific opponent at corners and free kicks. We'd go through tactics again on Saturday morning. Is it best to go down the flanks or be more direct? With 4-4-2 you work in pairs. Two strikers, two pairs in midfield, two down the flanks, two centre halves. At times a pair can hold up three. We imposed ourselves on the opposition. Later,

Terry Venables, manager of Crystal Palace, said he always hated playing us, as we were 'so strong'. Hard tackling, competitive and fit but within the rules. If you raised an arm, it was a foul. There weren't yellow and red cards until next season – 1970 – but a player could be sent off for 'serious foul play'. We gradually became a hard side to beat. Maybe not the most elegant, but effective.

Tony would come down to Bristol from Rochdale for a couple of days a fortnight to update me on new prospects. He became a good friend of the family, especially to my younger son Patrick, who called him 'Bony Tony', and he, 'Patch'. They remained life-long friends.

I was a tracksuit manager. My coaching background created the team's training programme – an amalgamation of the FA badges earned and five years implementing at Coventry City. It began with the basic principle that players had to be quick, both physically and mentally. Exercises for close ball control, throwing balls to each other in teams at speed, improving quickness of thought and awareness with a forfeit that anyone who drops the ball, drops and gives me ten press ups. The delivery had to be good. Speed of mind is as important as speed of body. Be aware of your surroundings. Form a picture of the game in your mind to understand where your teammates and the opposition are.

In the final fourteen league games, we had only three defeats and finished sixteenth. Since January, the goals had finally started to come. Galley was top scorer again, with eighteen, and the defence was tightening up. Progress.

Adding to the challenges on the pitch, this season had seen the first trouble off it. The visit of Cardiff City saw fighting in the Covered End, a taste of what was to come over the coming decade. While the hooligans were doing their best to cause

The Dolman Stand taking shape.

damage, Harry's dream of building a brand new stand to replace the Cowshed began at the start of 1969. It had an initial budget of £180,000, which quickly rose to £230,000. That could have bought me a top defender and a striker. And another striker. To help the financial knock-on effects of the project, Harry cleverly built a bowling arena under the stand, that raked in £12,000 a year.

The struggle between funding Harry's new stand and keeping hold of players was constant. To help the cause, sixteen houses the club owned around Ashton Gate were sold to players and staff. But when needed, Harry delivered. Bobby Kellard's previous club Portsmouth came in with a big offer and he was tempted. I told Harry we couldn't afford to lose him so he fixed it by buying Bobby's house on Hayling Island as he couldn't sell it and needed the money. Bobby's plan to live there and play for Portsmouth, money driving the desire to leave, resolved by Harry.

9

McBRISTOL

The search didn't stop just because the matches had. In the close season, with Tony's advice, I did some good business in the north east in the summer of 1969. Dickie Rooks was a courageous, tough tackling central defender who was brilliant in the air and who'd been a regular at Middlesbrough, so £17,000 seemed a fair price. Next, I convinced left back Brian Drysdale to move from Hartlepool to the south-west. Originally discovered by Brian Clough, he ended up playing nearly 300 games for us. Blessed with pace and strength, he wasn't tall but, as with some of the very best full backs, height is not a necessity.

Tony's scouting network in Scotland was growing. He organised several trial games in Glasgow, inviting all the promising players he and his contacts had discovered. One lad especially caught his eye, so much so that very early one morning we jumped in the car and seven hours later were stood on a touchline in Glasgow, part of a vast windswept park with over fifteen pitches, watching a lad called Gerry Gow play in a youth cup final. Despite the dreadful conditions, driving wind and rain, he was a force of nature. Tough, committed, uncompromising, skilful and with pace. He wasn't the biggest but was certainly the bravest. We looked at each other, thinking the same thing. Better act fast, Celtic and Rangers must be after him. Post-match, we tracked down Gerry's dad, Jimmy, a man built more of steel than flesh. Three-day stubble, barrel chested, he was a docker, and looked like all the tough blokes in south London I used to avoid.

'Hi Jimmy. We're from Bristol City Football Club and reckon your lad has some talent. Can we have a chat?'

He stared intently at me, narrowing his gaze like he was weighing up whether to shake my hand or punch me.

'McDevitt's, at six'

With that he was off. We asked around and discovered McDevitt's was a pub a couple of miles away in Drumchapel, where the Gow family lived.

At 5.55 p.m. we pushed the shattered glass door of McDevitt's open. It's a boozer that's seen better days, with drinkers who on seeing us walk in suited and booted, in business mode, immediately stop their conversations. Like a scene from a Western, the strangers in town are welcomed with intimidating silence. It was a tough old joint, sawdust on the floor. He was there already.

Jimmy gestured to a couple of free stools at the end of his table, which had at least eight people round it already. We sat. The room was still deadly quiet, suspicion running wild. No, we're not from round these parts. I offered the universal hand of pub friendship.

'Anyone like a drink?'

Within a few pints, they were our best mates. By 8 p.m. everyone agreed that our proposal for Gerry was good, though the details took till the small hours, and many whiskey chasers, to iron out. He would come down to Bristol a few weeks later with his parents and train with the first team. Our timing was good as we heard that Fulham, Newcastle United and Tottenham were also interested. Spurs went for Graeme Souness instead.

Looking to build on that result, Tony and I travelled to Edinburgh for another prospect called Steve Ritchie, who played for Scotland Schools. We visited the Ritchie's and sat around the kitchen table in their neat, terraced house with Steve and his dad. We did our pitch, selling Bristol, the club, the city and how we'd just invited a Glasgow lad down to spend a week with us. They both nodded. Then his dad piped up.

'You know his big brother is no a bad player hisself.'

Brother? Not heard of him. Mr Ritchie shouts upstairs. Down came a very slight and wiry youth. It looked like a gust of wind could blow him over, but he played for Scotland Schools as well. This was Tom.

We invited them both and their parents to Bristol, along with Gerry and his mum and dad for a week in pre-season to see how the boys shaped up on the pitch, developing a relationship with the parents and establishing trust. After all, their kids would be leaving home for the first time, moving 400 miles south. Tony and I would become substitute parents. At the end of the week, we signed all three.

Two weeks later, a smiling John Sillett warmly greeted them at Temple Meads Station as they arrived with their suitcases and dreams. Then he warned them in no uncertain terms of the very serious consequences if they weren't at Ashton Gate at 9 a.m. *sharp*, the next morning. You're professionals now, boys.

Though Tony's national scouting network was a smart way to find new young players, we had to be careful. Snatching regional talent, possibly denying local clubs, was a strategy that required some tact and caution. If Celtic or Rangers had known we were signing future First Division stars from under their noses, it might have caused yet another fight between me and the Scots. We built the foundation of our future team from Scotland. I'm amazed they still let us in the country, the amount of home-grown talent we had pinched.

There were few foreign players on offer in the early 1970s. Today, clubs are contacted by agents touting the great players they represent from Senegal, Iceland or Colombia. And maybe sometimes they are. Back then, it was homegrown only. No agents, no international scouting networks, no links to compilation videos on websites. You had to do your own homework.

Tony looked at hundreds of players every season, passing only a handful of the most promising on to me. He rang late one night, breathless with excitement, unheard of. The reason was a youngster he'd just seen play for Fourth Division Scunthorpe United. He insisted we meet at Ashton Gate first thing next morning. There was no time to waste.

At 8 a.m. he bounded into my office and hands me his report. 'He's sharp, brave and a brilliant reader of the game. Though a little lad, he makes up for it with fight and energy'. It's a five star review. I approve. Next, he's calling the Scunthorpe manager, Ron Ashman. After a bit of a dance, it's agreed the player could leave for £25,000. Coincidentally, this was the exact budget Harry had allocated for the next transfer.

'Let's get him.' I shouted. It sounded too good to miss.

But, when it came to the crunch, Tony was only 95% sure.

'Let's wait. I'll see him play just *once* more'.

'Ah, OK, if you're absolutely sure?'

With John Sillett and Tony Collins.

He was, and he told Ron we'd be back in touch.

Later that morning, Bill Shankly bought him for £25,000.

The lad packed his boots and left for Anfield, where he became the legend, Kevin Keegan.

The only thing more amazing than us remaining unbeaten in the 1969 pre-season friendlies was that a man landed on the moon. And it continued, beating Watford in the first league game, Galley getting the only goal. But then Geoff Merrick dislocated his elbow, closely followed by Galley injuring his ankle. *Once again, who's going to get our goals?*

By mid September, we had been on a troubling run of seven league games searching for a win. Last season's pattern repeated, we were jostling around the bottom of the table. The crowd got more restless, the board meetings tenser, and the press more questioning. I could see player's shoulders slump when the crowd got on their backs. As always, I continued to train them hard. Stick to the plan. We were only going to get out of this together.

And then it clicked.

We had only scored twice all season but in a three day period beat Norwich 4-0 and Charlton 6-0, part of an unbeaten six-game run. The press called it a 'remarkable revival'. I had been quoted wondering when we would score again. But Galley was back, scored half our goals. The 14,000 crowd that afternoon at Ashton Gate was increased by four who weren't fans of either team. Bill Nicholson, the Spurs manager, and three other First Division bosses had come to check out Galley.

Alan Skirton also got two, Chris Garland didn't score, but proved the perfect foil for Galley's heroics. Danny Bartley was flying on the left wing, creating and scoring. We were a different team. Same players, just with confidence. The mood around the club improved. Then it got even better. After a draw with Millwall, we scored five more, beating Birmingham and Hull, so were now mid-table.

John Sillett was doing good work with the youth team, challenging in both league and cup, bringing on potential first team players like Gow, David Rodgers and the Ritchies. Ashton Gate gates were averaging 19,000, so Harry was pleased. The bulk of club revenue came from attendances – no TV money, ground sponsorship deals or shirt sponsorship – but there was bingo and the lottery.

John Galley scores against Blackpool.

By early December, we'd made the top ten.

But it was brief. A post-Christmas nightmare saw us lose four in a row, including to Fourth Division Chester in the FA Cup. On a pitch made of snow, in sub-zero temperatures, I picked the best possible team. Though Kellard was suspended and Galley injured, we were level at ninety minutes, set for a replay to save face. In the second minute of injury time, they got a free kick and floated it into the box. We froze, they poked it in. The press called it a giant-killing. I wasn't sure it qualified, but it was certainly embarrassing.

The new year brought old issues. Lack of concentration, low confidence, poor decision making. And Galley was still injured. Despite putting a total of seven past Portsmouth and Blackburn in March, we then had zero wins in our final eight games. In the end, we were saved by the good pre-Christmas form.

Gerry Gow made his debut in the final game, at Charlton. I'd let him find his feet in the reserves before making the leap. The promise he'd shown as a ball winning, fearless, box-to-box midfielder had grown as he had – physically and emotionally – confirming our initial belief that this lad was special. He had such self-confidence, nothing and no one was going to intimidate him. At seventeen, he was not the finished article, but the potential was huge. Other players coming through like Peter Spiring and Ian Broomfield bode well. It was just a case of making sure they were all properly ready before seeing first-team action.

Charlton had to beat us to stay up. We were safe at fourteenth, so it was a tense afternoon for their new manager, Theo Foley. The smile on his face when we shook hands at full-time. And mine, as Gow had a strong debut.

Gerry Sharpe, along with his great work rate, was our top scorer with eleven goals, but how we missed Galley. Chris Garland got six and a call up for England U-23s, making his international debut against Bulgaria. We had finished a little higher in each of my three seasons, though at this rate, it would take another six years to get promotion. But it was progress. And Harry was happy the club had made its first profit for five years, though it was still in debt over the Dolman Stand, necessitating loans from the directors.

I signed a new five-year contract and asked the board to give Tony Collins and John Sillett three-year deals. They agreed. The transfer budget remained limited. Huddersfield Town, a club of similar size and financial standing as Bristol City, won the league by seven points. But then two big clubs, Aston Villa and Preston, dropped into the Third Division.

We ended the season playing Serie A team Juventus, in a friendly at Ashton Gate, which we won 2-1. Gerry Gow, not overawed playing a top European side, had an excellent game so was offered a new three-year contract and a raise.

Like so many, I was looking forward to World Cup 1970 in Mexico, with England aiming to retain the trophy. The contest became overshadowed by captain Bobby Moore's arrest after an allegation he stole jewellery from a shop in Colombia, just before the team arrived in Mexico City. It was a ridiculous accusation, that one of the most famous players in the world would steal a necklace. It was an unsettling start to a tournament that produced the famous Gordon Banks save, but even he couldn't stop West Germany beating England in the quarter-final. Many thought the necklace incident and an unfriendly reception from fans in Mexico played on the minds of the players. Mental strength and team spirit, those indefinable factors.

Post-World Cup, we arranged a pre-season friendly with West Ham, but Bobby had a threat to kidnap his wife and hold her to ransom, so he didn't play. Another disturbing incident for the great man.

There are so many examples of successful teams that have built their success not on money but on the attitude and spirit of the side; on character not cash. We were similar, with limited funds but unlimited spirit. A way to help strengthen that was to go on tour. So, every close season we went away. The first tour was in 1970 on a trip that took us to Sweden, Norway and Germany. Those concentrated ten days were invaluable, cementing the bond between players. It wasn't a new idea – I'd done it at Chelsea fifteen years before – but it was an important one.

10

FOOTBALL VERSUS MONEY

What does a manager need for success?

A strong, balanced squad, with key players staying injury free.

A supportive chairman and board, with funds.

A trusted back-room team.

A bit of luck.

But most of all? Time.

This was my fourth season, but if we had been in today's game, I would have been long gone. Wholesale distribution may well have been on my CV after 'Bristol City 1967-70'.

Fortunately, Harry gave me the time to build and shape the squad, *but* with the understanding that money is tight so players would need to be sacrificed to balance the books or contribute to the cost of the new stand. That was the agreement. It was the way the club had to be run to survive. And in exchange, it bought me time.

So, Bobby Kellard was sold to Leicester City in pre-season for £49,000 after being virtually ever-present the past two seasons. But, as Harry pointed out, it meant a £20,000 profit. Though not with us for long, Bobby left his mark on the club, and on the pitch. He once went in for a tackle with David Nish of Leicester so hard, that the ball burst. There was no money to buy a replacement for Bobby but Gerry Gow was ready to step up. I knew he was capable, despite the press branding me naïve to think that the inexperienced eighteen-year-old could ever fill Kellard's boots.

The Harry Dolman Stand opened, holding nearly 5,000, with a lower family enclosure and a tier above. It is still standing proudly today, though with some updates.

A pre-season article in a national newspaper speculated we would end up next season as the club with the top ground in the Third Division. The best part was the Dolman Stand, not the players in front of it. Relegation candidates in August. I suppose they have to fill the papers with something.

To warm up, we went to Holland, played against a couple of Dutch sides and West Ham, who were also out there. Results and performances were good. The players bonded on the pitch and later over 9% strength Dutch beer.

The start of the 1970-71 season continued the form, winning two of the first three games. We were fourth in the table. But in a now familiar move, we lost seven of the next ten. Autumn had us falling to four teams in a row, without scoring. Particularly painful was the four-goal thrashing at home by an ordinary Oxford United side. My programme notes for that game were full of optimism as a few days before we'd gone to First Division Blackpool in the League Cup and won.

We saved our best for the League Cup midweek games, beating Leicester then Fulham, making the semi-final with the same players as in the League but with a different mindset and energy. Maybe they were fired up by the knockout element. Why couldn't that form happen on a Saturday? If only we played our league matches midweek.

Mike Gibson had done a good job in goal for eight years, but we needed to find some cover. With limited money. During a training session, full back Ray Cashley volunteered to be keeper. For the whole morning, he stopped shot after shot after shot, had good positional sense and a strong pair of hands. John Sillett and I looked at each other thinking the same thing, so John tried him in the youth team. He was that good, the next step was as first team cover for Mike, and so this saved us buying a new goalkeeper.

The sports pages told the story of a club living way beyond its means. A lethal combination of huge bank debt (£120,000), low crowds and a high wage bill moved Harry to go public with the challenges we faced. The press eagerly reported his warning that 'the next few weeks were vital'. Yes, the club was at another tipping point. But we'd been here before. At least this time I had some crisis experience.

The perfect distraction was a League Cup semi-final against Tottenham – top First Division opposition with household names like Martin Chivers, Alan Gilzean and Martin Peters. The players were excited, the city was excited as 30,000 turned up; double the average league gate. There was something about playing under the floodlights midweek in the Cup that made us forget about losing here to Norwich a few days ago. The noise was deafening, supporters desperate for something to cheer

From the whistle we took the game to Spurs. It began at 100mph and got faster. Aggressive, motivated, disciplined, we put them under increasing pressure that finally paid off with

Alan Skirton stroking home past Pat Jennings early in the second half. It was the match when Gerry Gow confirmed he could replace Kellard, fearless in challenges, driving us forward. They stormed our defence but Rooks, Drysdale and Trevor Jacobs held firm until the dying minutes when Gilzean equalised. Frustrating, but there was a second leg at White Hart Lane the following week. It was a brave, spirited performance against top opposition. There was plenty of optimism for the rematch. Before this, though, it was the visit of bottom club Charlton, and a real chance to build on the Spurs result.

By half time we were 2-0 down.

I shared some uncomfortable home truths in the dressing room, about work rate, commitment and the need to be driven *every* game. I got the right response. Ten minutes after the restart, there was some neat work from Wimshurst down the left on the edge of the box, who floated the ball in for a stooping Rooks to bravely head home. Two minutes later, the equaliser came from a Sharpe penalty. But constant pressure didn't bring the winner. It was a chance to climb away from the relegation zone and show we didn't just save our good performances for the cup. It was a missed opportunity.

Over 5,000 journeyed up the brand-new M4 or took the train to north London for the second leg. The last time I was in N17 was to play for Chelsea in a 1955 victory. A semi-final offers so much to the winner, zero to the loser. Again, we weren't intimidated and had the better of the play in the first half. They lost their best defender, Mike England, early on which helped our cause, but we couldn't capitalise on it. The game was on a knife-edge, too close to call. In the eighty-fifth minute, Gerry Sharpe pounced in the box and whipped in a shot. From my position on the touchline, it was going in, and I was on my feet ready to celebrate. But the ball tantalisingly trickled a few inches past the outside of the post. Inches from Wembley.

All square at ninety minutes meant extra time, and they finally broke the deadlock, scoring twice. Our support was incredible that night and was so nearly rewarded with a famous victory. It was a great effort against the eventual winners and painted over the cracks of my inconsistent team. It offered some light relief from a league table that we were slipping further down each week. We had won just five league games since August and were deservedly bottom three.

11

PRESSURE

Being under pressure was becoming my default setting. Maura was great at diffusing it at home when I got too intense. Five children was a handful, another squad that needed guidance, which she handled effortlessly. I tried to be around as much as possible but in a job you never leave, switching off was part of the challenge. Christmas this year was different as we didn't play again until the second week of January.

Happy new year! Not really. Losing the first two matches of 1971 without scoring was bad enough but the biggest loss of the season was about to come. We faced Middlesbrough on a freezing, ice rink of an Ashton Gate pitch. Gerry Sharpe was sliding down the right wing, bearing down on goal, reached the edge of the area, when he was scythed down by Eric McMordie with a tackle that Avon and Somerset Police would file under GBH. The faces of the fans behind the goal, closest to the crime scene, were etched with horror. Some even heard the bone crack, it was that fierce. Gerry was stretchered to the physio's room and laid out on the treatment table. The bone was sticking out the back of his calf and he was moaning in agony. I'd never seen so much blood. I shut the door, didn't want anyone else to see the state he was in. Medically, we had our trainer Les Bardsley, with a 'magic' sponge, but nothing more. We had no doctor. Gerry's injury was so bad you didn't need to be qualified to know that his leg was broken. The ambulance finally arrived but they didn't operate until 11 p.m. that night. This delay was to be crucial. That we went on to lose the game was irrelevant.

Earlier that season, my old Chelsea teammate and now England manager, Ron Greenwood, came to a match at Ashton Gate. He wanted to size up Chris Garland but left with Gerry as the player he was most interested in for the national side. He was so quick, so skilful. If any player lived up to his name it was 'Sharpey'. A great reader of the game, he was a vital part of the team on and off the pitch with an infectious enthusiasm, wise cracking in the dressing room. After weeks in hospital – where an infection threatened amputation – he spent months recuperating. He missed the whole season but we were optimistic he would make a full recovery. The comeback was a reserve match early the following season, but he didn't even make it to half-time.

His career was over. At twenty-four.

Such a cruel twist for a player – and a great lad – who was still to reach his full potential. I kept him on at the club as youth coach, working with John Sillett. It felt like the least we could do. After this trauma, we made sure a specialist, who came to matches free of charge, was there to help out in any medical emergency. And the penalty for the crime? Red cards were used for the first time at the World Cup in 1970 but the FA waited until 1976 to introduce them, so McMordie received no punishment, adding insult to a career-ending injury.

At yet another emergency board meeting, there were a whole new line-up of recommendations on how to save the club money. We were once again one point above the drop zone but the agenda today was about staying solvent, not up. The first proposal was to sack Tony Collins.

He goes, I go.

That nipped it in the bud.

As I couldn't buy, I had to borrow. Brian Hill, a strong, reliable defender, arrived in March and made a difference. The loan from Coventry City was until the end of the season, and we paid his wages. I knew Brian from my days at Highfield Road. I wanted to sign him but he had to return in May.

The first win of 1971 finally arrived in late February against Millwall, nicking it 3-2. Galley, in and out the team with recurring injury issues was still top scorer, proving how dependent we were on him. Gow was becoming a natural leader, with Drysdale and Rooks strong at the back, but Sharpe was a real loss.

A big result came in mid-March, thumping relegation rivals Watford, 3-0, swiftly followed by a fiery West Country derby, beating Swindon Town.

Seven games to go. Five points from safety. Two games in two days. (Ask a team today to do that.) First up Luton Town, who, after successive promotions, were looking good to make it a hat trick, lying fourth from top, us fourth from bottom. The 18,000 crowd grew increasingly silent as they got their second through Malcolm Macdonald with Ray Cashley only having been in goal for a handful of games. It was one way traffic and could have been five.

It was a shell-shocked dressing room. I needed players to step up and take control of a game we weren't even in yet. Up stepped

Dickie Rooks, putting in a captain's performance. In one of our most remarkable forty-five minutes, we not only got back in the game, but won it. Three goals in seven minutes, two from a lethal Garland, gave us the most unlikely two points and turned the volume up as the players left the field to an elated crowd.

The very next day we were back at Ashton Gate, beating Portsmouth 2-0. Within forty-eight hours, the landscape had changed. We were now five points clear of the bottom two, with daylight between us, Bolton and Blackburn. Though the last five games produced just two points and a couple of sleepless nights, we were safe, finishing nineteenth.

According to the rumours, Harry was going to sack me.

If I'd had a pound for each time it was supposed to happen, there'd be enough to buy a new striker. I was slowly turning the ship around, but it seemed we'd got trapped in a tide that wouldn't let us move forward. It's part of the drama of football. How long should the manager of a struggling team be given? Today, chairmen are more trigger happy. The amount of money involved can cause knee-jerk reactions and many good bosses are discarded prematurely. The stakes are so high. Though the money was a fraction in the 1970s, the emotion was the same. No one wants to own a losing club.

The pressure had been relentless, heightened by the expectation from the previous season that finished so well. I was never a big smoker – only the occasional puff on a Saturday night with a drink – but recently found comfort in a Capstan. My habit wasn't helped by the Bristol-based Wills cigarette company sponsoring the club, so there were always packs of twenty lying around the offices. The smokers among the players saw this as a perk of the job.

Even though Harry was very cautious with the cash, the club was still paying for the Dolman Stand, losing £500 a week. But the books showed we'd made a £15,000 profit on the season, thanks to selling Kellard. In the past couple of years, some clubs had started to honour their best performer so we launched the Bristol City Player of the Year award. Quite rightly, the first winner was Gerry Sharpe.

At the end of the season, we all went on holiday. The squad packed sunglasses, swimmers and boots and we headed to Spain for a couple of matches in Catalonia, against Espanyol and Girona. I always made sure the trips didn't cost the club, with gate receipts paying for flights, hotels and beer. We always balanced the books, something I understood.

Among the many challenges of management is the routine but vital task of training. How do you keep it interesting on a freezing Monday morning in January, after another home defeat?

As I had passed the FA coaching badges in my early twenties, I was well-positioned. I could put the theory into practice at Coventry, so every element of coaching was covered. We had a physio, but I did everything else. Sports scientists, conditioning coaches, nutritionists and sports psychologists were not on the payroll in 1971.

Training with the ball we did shadow play, creating match-type situations where you run for the opposition then for yourself, understanding positional play to support each other. For the ball-training sessions, we had local parks like Greville Smyth and a sports pitch owned by the local gas company near Knowle, that we rented.

In that 1971 pre-season, we lost both striker Terry Bush and defender David Rodgers with knee injuries and after eleven years and over 400 games, Jack Connor retired. The average age was falling as youth team talent like Merrick, Cashley and Tainton stepped up to the first team. Tony had spotted yet another promising Scottish lad, Gerry Sweeney, who had been running the midfield at Morton after being let go by Celtic. We got him for £22,000. Running was the operative word. Sweeney really could run. He had stamina and was box-to-box-to-box-to-box, all day long. He could also play in defence. Another great find by Tony, the man the board wanted to sack. As the season progressed, the two Scottish Gerrys – Sweeney and Gow – were shaping up to be the engine room of the team. And goal scorers too, as they both proved in the opening match against Millwall. Then Galley got a hat-trick at Sheffield Wednesday and by early September we were top of the table.

Tactics were not confined to Saturday afternoons; I needed to be smart about how I played the board on a Tuesday morning. If they wanted me to sell a player that I couldn't afford to lose, just to bring in funds, I would try to disrupt the transfer process. One way was to simply not tell an interested club the player was for sale. This was possible as I did everything in management, including transfers.

'Dicks. We need to make some money. See if you can sell a player.'

'I'll see what I can do.'

This was how the conversation went. But not usually the player.

An exception was Chris Garland, who had started every match, and who agreed to move to Chelsea for £100,000 after a bid from their manager, Dave Sexton. I had mixed feelings

Gerry Gow in action.

about this. Chris was a great local lad who had been with us for five years, but they were a top First Division side and he'd be playing with Peter Osgood, Alan Hudson and Ron Harris. So, who could blame him? A taste of the big time. We didn't look like we were going to be joining them anytime soon. Of course, the person most pleased with the deal was Harry. He was so excited. He immediately did the calculation of how it would help the club's finances on the back of his cigarette pack. Losing Garland was tough. It left me with even fewer options, but I had no choice. I had to accept it.

The good results continued into the autumn, culminating in hitting five past Orient in late October. The gates increased, almost doubling from August. It was my first taste of a sustained period of success, with the crowd and the press not questioning my decisions. The word *promotion* was even heard around the club. Had we turned the corner? Team spirit was high and the new young players were fitting in well. There was now a nucleus to the team – Merrick, Drysdale, Sweeney, Tainton, Wimshurst, Galley, Rooks – playing regularly as we looked to maintain our top-three status.

But as the leaves fell, so did our league position. We lost the next four, conceding eleven, including a heavy home collapse to Carlisle United. This mid-season slump was now a fixture every season. Nothing had changed. The team was injury free. I'd even brought in Les Wilson from First Division Wolves as a defensive utility player. It's another reason why football is so compelling. Just when you think everything is in place, it collapses.

To confirm our decline, in December, we didn't score a single goal. Despite the challenges, we had a good family Christmas in Ormerod Road; five kids, my sister Joyce and endless friends and neighbours popping in. For the fourth year in a row, any prayers were aimed more to the gods of football, than Jesus.

In early 1972, we were managing to stay mid-table, again purely on the strength of our good start to the season. On a Friday in February, I took the team through the plan for the next day's home match against Charlton Athletic, one place above us, equally desperate for points. Tony had identified their danger man as Ray Treacy, a free-scoring Irishman who I asked Merrick to deal with. Losing tomorrow would be a blow, psychologically and points wise.

We'd only won at home twice in four months which was evident by the big gaps on the terraces the next afternoon. Harry wrote a rare MESSAGE FROM THE BOARD in the match-day programme, laying out the financial position of the club: a debt of £240,000. He justified the investment in the Dolman Stand by a prediction that the club would earn £45,000 a year from it, and three times that figure if we were promoted. It ended with a plea for everyone to get behind the team today and help in the push for the promotion to create history. And solvency.

The building of the new stand had not just been about a battle for funding. Bristol Council and the residents had been against the plan. The club had to fight hard to see the dream become a reality. It was a testament to Harry's conviction that he persevered in what was, for some, very unpopular.

From the kick-off we were in control against Charlton; Merrick was handling Treacy. We maintained a high tempo and eased to a 2-0 win. This set the tone for the remainder of the season. By March, we had rediscovered some consistency, winning nine of the remaining twelve games. It was the best run of my managerial career – a breakthrough for the team that included victories over top-five teams QPR and Sunderland. We finished eighth, a new high. John Galley got an outstanding twenty-two goals. The defence was the fourth meanest, an achievement recognised by awarding Geoff Merrick the Player of the Season award. The foundations were in place. If we could leap from nineteenth to eighth in consecutive seasons, what was possible the next campaign?

It also showed we had the character to tough it out when things weren't going to plan. But why were we there in the first place? We couldn't score. Goals dried up, even for Galley. The truth was that we were an average Second Division side. But with real potential.

Making that next leap was going to be about players. Tony never rested, driving 40,000 miles a year around the country in his quest for the next great prospect. He organised another trial match in Glasgow for young hopefuls, on a vast green landscape with the nickname The Hundred Pitches. It was positioned right next to Glasgow Rangers' Ibrox Stadium. On the top floor was a large office with a picture window that overlooked their pitch and the ninety-nine others.

There were no facilities for the thirty boys, so Tony cleverly booked a double-decker bus for the afternoon to be parked next to the pitch, for players to change in and leave their stuff, knowing it was safe.

As the game began, I noticed a large, burly figure staring intently down from the office window. He looked familiar. Tony confirmed it was Jock Wallace, the recently appointed Glasgow Rangers manager, who seemed unusually interested in our game. I didn't think anything of it and concentrated on assessing the talent. A couple of weeks later, I got a letter from the Scottish FA. It questioned our presence at the Glasgow pitch, trialling young Scottish players, when we were an English team. So angry were Glasgow Rangers, that they wanted their FA to introduce a rule to prevent English teams from 'poaching' young Scots lads. Paranoia? Not really. We had already found the Gerrys – Gow and Sweeney – and the Ritchie boys. Who would we grab next? But from now on, we had to be cautious. The English First Division was full of great Scots – Denis Law, Ian St John, Billy Bremner, Dave Mackay – we had to tread carefully to have a chance of poaching the next one.

There was always player movement. Mike Gibson left on a free after nearly 400 games as Ray Cashley stepped up to become the first choice keeper. The tireless Dickie Rooks, who we had only bought two years before, retired due to persistent knee trouble. He had been virtually ever-present and an inspirational captain. Away to Leicester City in the FA Cup, on a quagmire pitch in torrential rain, his foot got stuck in the mud, he twisted his leg and a bone in his knee splintered. Later it fused and effectively meant the end of his playing career. Today, the match would never have been played and a fine career wouldn't have ended prematurely. So, I made Geoff Merrick captain. He was still only nineteen, but with such a mature outlook, and commanding presence on the pitch, ready for the responsibility. Tom Ritchie and Peter Spiring were putting in some impressive displays in the reserves, and would soon be ready to add some more pace and energy to the first team.

The Monday after the season had finished, ending on a high putting four past Oxford United, I got the players together to announce the destination for our traditional post-season tour.

'Is it France, boss?

'Bet it's Spain. Again.'

'Money's tight, so we're off to Wales!'

'All wrong, boys. Iran.'

That shut them up.

The trip was personally approved by the Shah of Iran, set up by Alan Rogers (a contact of Tony) who, as adviser to the Iranian FA, suggested that it would be useful for their national team to play some foreign opposition. Plus, it would be good PR for a country that was certainly in need of some. The Shah had been in power since 1941 and ruled with an iron fist. His hard line, along with widespread government corruption and huge disparities in wealth, were overseen and facilitated by the secret police, the SAVAK. The more money Iran made from its oil, the more extreme the corruption and general misery overseen by the Shah. It was as much our mission to be playing the role of sporting ambassadors as a football team.

We were met at Tehran Airport by armed government reps and ferried in an ancient bus to a hotel in the centre of town, passing locals pulling hand carts, and donkeys laden with people and their possessions. It was a time warp in scorching 35°c, so reaching the air-conditioned hotel was a relief. The lobby was beautiful. Gold columns, marble floors and elaborate, colourful rugs my mum would have been proud of. We checked in and then met in the bar for a drink. A tall, beaming gentleman called Ali was our host. He explained that he knew the Shah personally and was going to give us the red-carpet treatment, and show us the finest aspects of the Imperial State. His warm smile instantly vanished when he noticed, at the other end of the lobby, the team ordering from the waiters.

'You allow your team to drink alcohol?'

'They deserve it. It's the end of the season, so we can let our hair down a little', I explained.

'But you are playing the top Iranian team in one day.'

'They are very fit lads. A couple of beers won't make any difference.'

He shook his head in disbelief but it had got the cogs whirring and he had an offer for us.

'We will double your fee for your first match, if you win by more than two goals.'

'Ok. I'll check with the lads.'

So I went over to the bar and explained the offer.

'If we win by two goals you all share £2,000.'

Their eyes lit up, glasses raised. I took that as a unanimous 'yes'.

The Amjadieh Stadium, the venue for our first match against a Tehran XI, had a capacity of 28,000. Unsurprisingly, not too many travelling Bristolians were amongst the big crowd. The conditions were unfamiliar to us. With the searing heat, and on a pitch that featured no mud, just dry grass, we managed a comfortable 2-0 win. Post-match, the team were pleased to have won but more excited about collecting their prize. Back in the hotel, beers being drunk, a beaming Ali arrived to 'congratulate the team on a splendid victory'. Before he could finish his praise, Gow piped up.

'Mr Ali, you owe us our win bonus.'

He smiled and shook his head.

'The deal we agreed was that if you win by more than two goals, then you will be rewarded. It was only 2-0.'

Maybe it got lost in translation and we all misunderstood, but it didn't go down well. Grumbles under the breath, dagger stares and a couple of players stood up as though they were going to take it outside with Ali. But, unlike a Saturday night in Glasgow, a couple of armed guards suddenly appeared and that was the matter closed. So, no international incident. We won the second game as well, with Peter Spiring scoring again.

That night, I got a message from Anne, my secretary, saying there was an offer from a couple of teams in Cyprus if we fancied flying over there. All expenses paid, it would cost the club nothing. So, we flew to Limassol and stretched our tour-winning run to four matches, seven goals and no one imprisoned.

I returned to Bristol reasonably content. Unbeaten foreign tour, eighth in the league, a team that was bonding, more balanced, more confident. Things were looking up. And then I got a call.

'Alan? Don wants me.'

'He does?'

'Afraid so.'

'And you're going to join him?'

'I am.'

Bloody Leeds again.

If they weren't beating us in the cup, they were approaching my partner, chief scout and assistant manager. Tony left the following week. Don 'Readies' Revie made him an offer he clearly couldn't refuse. I knew Tony wrestled with his decision, but in the end, it simply came down to the fact that when the biggest team in the country want you to be chief scout, how can you refuse?

I tried to hide my disappointment. I didn't blame him. Who wouldn't jump at the chance? But we had such an understanding – and the timing, just as *maybe* the team had turned a corner and could seriously mount a challenge for promotion. The squad was well balanced, much down to his network. Tony's quote in the press was concise.

'I'm leaving a good club, for a great club.'

He had a final swipe at the board, saying that 'City have a chance of growing towards a First Division side. But it can't be done on coppers.'

I spent a couple of days on the phone, calling Tony's contacts that I knew personally, explaining that I'd really like them to continue their good work. And some did. I promoted John Sillett to chief coach, with Ken Wimshurst looking after the reserves and ex-centre half Dave Merrington running the youth team.

12

OWN GOAL

On 16 July 1972, Maura discovered that I'd been having an affair with my secretary, Anne. I moved out of Ormerod Road.

13

REGRETS

News spreads fast, bad news faster, so when I arrived for pre-season, everyone at Ashton Gate knew.

It was all my fault and remains the biggest regret of my life.

I never helped Patrick with his football because I wasn't there. He says, 'Dad don't worry about it,' but when I look back, of course I do.

And Alan, Mandy, Michelle and Melanie growing up, missing their dad. What did they do to deserve that?

I still saw them every weekend, I lived within walking distance and they came to matches. I tried to do my best as father of the family that I no longer lived with and was no longer involved with on a day-to-day basis. But even the best is never enough.

And the pressure it put on Maura. Unforgivable.

To cope, you bury yourself in your work, which was what I'd partly been doing anyway for the past ten years. As manager, there's always another match to watch, another player to assess, another training session to take. It's all-consuming and will consume you if you let it. Yes, it happened to many families. But there are no excuses. None.

14

TOP FIVE

As if the universe was making me pay for my stupidity, we lose four in a row and by early September, are bottom of the table. The high, pre-season expectations, dashed.

We had been dependent on Galley for goals, four of the last five seasons he'd been top scorer. Now, he was struggling. So they came from an unlikely source, Peter Spiring, with five in the first seven games – as many as he got in the whole of last season. The winger had been at the club for four years but had not held down a regular place. He was now making up for lost time.

Life hadn't just changed domestically. Now Tony was gone, it was different at work. We had been a partnership for five years, become a tight team. I now had to rely on those in his network who would still give me information about new talent. But it was more than that. We would talk about every aspect of football, often late into the night. He was so knowledgeable and smart.

The significance of the timings of the separation from the two main people in my life in just a matter of a few weeks were not lost on me. Also, Tony and Maura had built up a very close friendship, which would remain.

I lived in Westbury with Anne, and the guilt.

Gow and Galley gradually took over the goal scoring as we finally started to win points. But in November, out of nowhere, Galley fired a warning shot. He said he wanted to leave, which came as a complete surprise. A few weeks later, he was off to Nottingham Forest for £30,000, leaving behind a record of ninety-two goals in 198 games, the club's eighth best of all time. A great loss. He'd almost single-handedly kept us up in 1968, and had been first on the team sheet ever since. Probably my best signing, he was desperate to move back to his roots in the Midlands.

Harry immediately approved the funds for a replacement, so I bought someone I had been keeping an eye on for a while, who I knew very well from Coventry City. Bobby Gould arrived for £70,000, a club-record signing. At sixteen, he was in the Coventry youth side and, of course, had won the Second Division title with me in 1965. Soon after, he was snapped up by Arsenal, followed by Wolves. Though shocked at Galley's departure, supporters were excited at the prospect of having this high-profile replacement at Ashton Gate. He was a sociable man. After I'd introduced him to the players and staff, he visited me in my office, looking uncharacteristically serious.

'Everything OK, Bobby?'

'Boss, do you mind if I play up to the crowd a bit?'

'What do you mean?'

'Well, you know, get them on my side. Be a favourite right from the off.'

'If you score a hat trick in the first game, that should do it.'

'But look at Derek Dougan at Wolves – the crowd absolutely love him.'

'He scores lots of goals, Bobby.'

'Fair point, boss'.

That's that sorted then.

By the end of September, we had clawed our way up to sixteenth and had settled in as a mid-table team.

Christmas was our traditional mixed bag. But going into the new year we looked reborn. A thrashing of Swindon Town started 1973 in fine style. We became a consistent top ten team.

Something had changed. The confidence was back. Maybe it was simply time these individual players had finally reached the point of being a *team*? It started to click in a way it hadn't before. Gow and Sweeney were driving the side, dominating midfield, breaking down attacks, setting up Gould and Ritchie – a strike force that would make us the league's third top scorers.

I still had lively discussions with the media post-match, but these were less charged now our position had improved. Over the seasons I'd built a good relationship with both the local and national reporters like Roger Malone, but there were occasionally moments when the press just pressed too much. Keeper Ray Cashley had got into a pub disagreement after the Sunderland game, ending up being bottled. I told him to stay home and recuperate, and to come in on Wednesday for training, if he was feeling better. A Bristol Evening Post reporter asked for his address, so he could go round and interview Ray, to hear his side of the story.

'Sorry, no. I want Ray to get better without any attention.'

'But you can't stop me, Alan. I just want to get the facts.'

'I can and I will.'

He saw it as journalistic restriction and stood up to make his point.

'I'm perfectly entitled to talk to the player. It's in the public interest.'

'More in your interest I'd say. The answer is no.'

He was fuming. Maybe fueled by the Glenfiddich, he really wanted the story.

The room went quiet. He sat down, still muttering something about restricting freedom of information. Ray was back four days later, his face still bruised, but fit to face Carlisle United, The incident was *not* back page news. Today social media would have sent it viral.

Ray still amazed me how he seamlessly moved from defender to goalkeeper. John Sillett used to say he was a natural; best pair of hands he'd seen. Ray became our first choice keeper for the next decade. You just had to be careful if you went for a pint with him.

Bobby Gould had been working hard at earning the fan's love, scoring four goals in six games, including a brilliant last-minute equaliser at Portsmouth in the FA Cup. It set up a home replay where we put four past them. There was a 17,000 crowd, 4,000 up on the average. Bobby was becoming a fans' favourite. Our reward was a trip to top First Division side Wolves. Some of the press predicted we may be the giant-killers of the round as most of our wins that season had been away. And it almost came true. A very tight game, we were every bit as good, with Merrick particularly outstanding. Sadly, Bobby Gould couldn't do that day what Derek Dougan did, and we lost 1-0.

Bobby was a character, one that divided opinion. In February, we were locked in a draw with bottom of the table Brighton, where a win would move us to sixth. As we prepared to take a corner, I see Bobby on the edge of the box pointing over to Gow and shouting something. Gerry instantly responds by sprinting over and punching him in the face.

With no choice, I had to get Gow off. Unsurprisingly, he was not pleased, but I remind my mild-mannered Scot that hitting a teammate during a match was not part of the game plan we worked on yesterday.

'Sorry boss, but you don't know what he said to me.'

'I don't want to know what he said to you. You don't punch a teammate. Ever. Never mind during a bloody match.'

He apologised to me and to the whole team after the game. His 100% commitment had caused a rush of blood to the head. Bobby stayed on but the players couldn't believe what he had said, whatever it was. And said it to Gerry, the fan's favourite, which didn't do Bobby's 'Mr. Popular' ambitions much good. It highlighted Gerry's passion and Bobby, well, he was just being Bobby. Despite the incident, we won.

Another Scot arrived in the shape of the quick right back, Donnie Gillies from Morton, swapping him for Steve Ritchie and £30,000. It kept up the level of Scots in the squad, but we still had ten Bristolians.

In March, Bill Shankly at Liverpool rang about Peter Spiring, who'd had a great scoring start to the season, but when Shanks called, I was open to an offer. It was well known he was a tough negotiator.

'I'll give you £50,000, Alan. Not a penny more, not a penny less.'

The dance had begun.

'Let me go back to the directors and check. There are a few other clubs interested, Shanks.'

'Oh, really?'

No there weren't. But it was part of the dance, my next move. I gave it a day, and then rang back.

'I've checked with the board and they are OK with the deal for £50,000'.

'Done.'

Dance over. Spiring never actually played a single match for Liverpool and left after just one season for Luton Town.

Central defender Gary Collier came up through the youth team and debuted in March, in a win at Luton Town. He was like a Rolls Royce, deceptively fast, with a smooth change of gear, sleek and made it all look effortless. He captained the team to the FA Youth Cup final and was quite a prospect at just seventeen.

Our run-in was tough, including playing high-flying Aston Villa twice, beating them 3-0 at home. A real mark of our recent improvement came away to Sunderland, a side also chasing a top-six finish. After fifty minutes they were two up and in complete control. Earlier in the season we would have crumbled, heads down and resorting to damage limitation. But a shift had happened and when Merrick headed in after an hour, it provided the spark for a comeback. Sustained pressure resulted in John Emanuel's perfect low drive from outside the box, sealing an important draw and, more importantly, a new team spirit. He was then called up by Wales for the Home Internationals – the first club player for fourteen years to be capped by his country.

We were on a roll, winning six of the final eight games. Revenge was sweet, putting three past Blackpool to avenge the defeat at Bloomfield Road by the same scoreline. There were two more at home, beating Preston and Hull to finish on a high.

Ray Cashley   Bobby Gould
BRISTOL CITY

Cashley and Gould.

Bobby Gould got ten in twenty games, with top scorer Gow grabbing thirteen, from midfield. We finished fifth. My highest ever. Harry revelled in record season tickets sales of over 4,000.

As the days grew warmer, so did the seat opposite my desk, as players filed in for the end-of-season contract negotiations. Or terminations. After seven years at the club, full back Trevor Jacobs went to Plymouth Argyle on loan. He ended up at Bristol Rovers. Central defender Dave Bruton – an occasional first team member – left for Swansea City, where he became a regular and the club's Player of the Year. This just showed again how it can take time to find where you fit in.

Les Wilson was a versatile player who I used mainly at right back. He had been with us for a couple of seasons. A spiky Canadian, he once banged on my office door late on a Friday afternoon, before barging straight in.

'Boss. Why aren't I in the team tomorrow?'.

'You're not playing well enough, Les. It's as simple as that.'

'You're just like Bill McGarrie.' he screamed, before storming out.

He had come from Wolves, where McGarrie was boss. He disappeared down the corridor, fuming. During the contract talks, Les was back in my office, though strangely this time he'd brought along his wife and baby daughter. I sat on the edge of the desk, with the three of them sat in front, looking up expectantly.

'Les, the club wants to thank you for your contribution to the team but if you would like to go and find another club, we won't stand in your way.'

Les looked increasingly pained as he processed my statement. So much so, that I wondered whether he would actually stand up and hit me.

'Look, Les, I know it's disappointing, but you can take your contract and find a new club. A player of your experience will soon be snapped up.'

There was just a death stare. He wasn't taking this well.

Suddenly, he lifted his baby, held her right up in front of my face and started to shout.

'Don't listen to the terrible man, Susan! He's telling lies! Bad man! Very bad man!"

I nearly fell off the desk. The wife sat there mortified.

He was a passionate man who Norwich City signed weeks later, but it wasn't long before he was back home in Vancouver. There was a clue earlier in the season when he physically 'man-marked' a reporter from the Western Daily Press, Herbert Gillam, in a Carlisle hotel bar. Having taken offence at something he'd written, Les literally stalked Gillam wherever he went. In the end, he had to be physically restrained.

15

PROMOTION?

In late September 1973, having won five of the opening seven games, Gould getting five goals, we are top of the table.

Perhaps we could go all the way this time, with a bit of luck and a good wind behind us. We had both against Hull City at Ashton Gate. Goalkeeper Cashley booted the ball from his area; it soared skywards over all the players, bounced into their box, high over the keeper who was caught ten yards off his line and rolled in. It's still the record distance for a league goal – ninety-five yards.

Maybe it was a sign?

We headed up the M5 as league leaders to face Hull City (again) and Middlesbrough in close succession, based in a Hull hotel for the three nights. We were poor against Jack Charlton's Middlesborough and deserved to lose against the team that would dominate the league. We had convincingly beaten Hull three weeks before, so I was confident we could jump back to the top of the table. But, in a scrappy game, they sneaked a win by the odd goal. The mood on the way back to the hotel was sombre. It was a long journey home tomorrow, so the natural next move was to the bar. Spirits gradually brighten after each pint. John Sillett and I, along with most of the team, retired around 11.30 p.m., leaving a hard core to continue.

A few drinks later, they're hungry. Answer? Break into the hotel kitchen and cook for themselves. It's no episode of *MasterChef*. The place is trashed with food all over the floor, pots and pans scattered everywhere, and cupboard doors smashed off. It was carnage. When the night porter came in to find out what was happening, he was met by a volley of abuse and vegetables.

I'm woken early by a frantic and desperate hotel manager, dragging me downstairs to witness the result of my team's night manoeuvres. Mortified, all I can do is apologise again and again to him and the kitchen staff who have turned up to find their workplace trashed. The night porter later wrote a letter that explained how in all his years in the job he'd never been abused like that. John and I get all the players out of their beds, packed and on the coach in record time. A shameful episode that embarrassed us all, and the club. The coach was guiltily silent. The five-hour journey felt like fifty.

Eventually, we arrived.

'Dressing room. Now,' John barked.

Heads down like scolded schoolboys, they tramped in and sat in a circle on the floor. John and I stood over them like avenging parents of feral, lawless children. I gave them both barrels.

'You're a disgrace. A disgrace to yourselves. To the team. To the club.'

You could have heard a pin drop.

'You're in the privileged position of being professional footballers. Your behaviour was no better than hooligans on the terraces.'

There was no response.

'Anybody who was *not* part of it can leave now.'

No one moves.

'Last chance. If you're not guilty, go.'

Still nobody.

'OK. You're all fined £20 each.'

There was silence. No one moved.

Finally, Ray Cashley stands which signals a general procession up and out of the 'courtroom'. When they'd all left, John and I looked at each other, thinking the same.

Now we've really got ourselves a team.

A team that stays together, no matter what. I didn't need to be Sherlock Holmes to know most of the culprits hailed from north of the border. I loved their desire, energy and commitment. Just keep it on the pitch from now on. But the group, under pressure, had *stayed a group.*

Five minutes later I'm in my office, when Bobby walks in.

'You can't fine me boss, I was nothing to do with it.'

He refused to pay the fine, whatever the team is doing.

For Bobby, it was the end. He'd had an uneasy relationship with the team after the Gow incident, and a few weeks later submitted a transfer request that resulted in a quick move to West Ham. He still refused to pay the £20 fine and even got the FA involved. He'd scored a goal every other game for us, and we made £20,000, so it was still a good bit of business. Six months after leaving, he would still be our second highest scorer.

The youth policy was now paying off, with Gary Collier in central defence and winger/full back Clive Whitehead both part of the first team. There was more balance and depth to the squad, and in periods where goals didn't come from a striker, the whole team pitched in. By the end of the season, we had fifteen different scorers.

As an average Second Division side, we were very rarely on TV. The players had no opportunities to see themselves, to have that perspective on their own performance. In a light bulb moment, I talked to John Pearce, who was the club's education officer, a great kid's mentor who lived opposite us in Stoke Bishop. He had the equipment to film matches, so we planned to start capturing the games. In November, John and his son Jonathan lugged heavy camera equipment up ladders to the gantry at Ashton Gate for the first time to record the visit of Crystal Palace.

Unsurprisingly, it turned out to be a brilliant asset, plenty to be learned from a frustrating home defeat. John came to the ground on the Monday to show the team the result, with some watching through their fingers. If I wanted a specific player filmed they would provide footage following, say, John Emanuel's movement in midfield. If I accused a defender of not picking up an attacker at a corner, and they disagreed, I simply pressed the *play* button. It put me in the unique position of being able to show my players exactly where they had gone wrong. Or right. At the time, a revolutionary idea, the first club in Europe to do it. And not one of Jimmy's! The Pearces traveled all over the country with us recording matches, becoming a vital part of the team.

The players hated seeing their mistakes and as Gow vigorously protested, no other managers in the league '*put their players through this ordeal*'. It allowed us to analyse and improve, however painful. It becamse the Monday afternoon ritual, reliving the best and worst moments. Invaluable.

That top spot in September had become twelfth by November. We gave our traditional Christmas gifts to the opposition, losing to lowly Oxford United, Luton Town and Orient in quick succession, gifting eight goals, scoring none. The low point was the 5-0 defeat to Oxford on Boxing Day, which was completely self-inflicted. The Scots boys had got together on Christmas Day evening and turned up hung-over. It was the second offence for Gerry Gow, so I stuck him in the third team for the next match. He wasn't just a box-to-box midfielder, sometimes he was pub-to-pub, once turning up for training in the clothes he'd been wearing the night before, his breath reeking of booze. But when he finally dragged himself onto the pitch, it was like a switch had been pressed from *stop* to *go* and he would become the hardest-working, sharpest player in training. Just not in the Oxford match. I read him the riot act. It never happened again.

There was trouble off the pitch as well. Hooliganism had become such a serious issue that FA President, Len Shipman, recommended bringing back the birch for offenders. We had only seen small incidents at Ashton Gate, but it was becoming an increasing menace throughout the 1970s.

Harry knew that nothing fundamental had changed, that there'd been no major injuries, but we'd lost the winning habit developed last season that continued into the first part of this. Then stopped. The final board meeting in late November – before he went on his annual winter holiday to the Caribbean – was frosty. But I'd experienced seven years of these awkward conversations. Of course, he was concerned, we all were, but it seemed to be just another demonstration of his continued patience with me. Expressing his disappointment, looking for something to pin this recent drop in form on, he would soon be lying on a balmy Barbados beach, so all I could do was reassure him that the new year would bring improved results. His look said, *it better.*

16

LEEDS' LOSS, MY GAIN

In early January 1974, our FA Cup run began by beating Hull City in a replay, with a winner from Trevor Tainton. Cashley was back from injury and made a big difference and Gary Collier showed his versatility by taking the right back role. The FA Cup was *the* glamour competition, with over twenty million tuning in for the final. For players and supporters, it had a very special meaning. In between, we had a visit from Preston and Bobby Charlton in his first managerial role. Next to us in mid-table, it was a thrill to welcome the new boss to Ashton Gate. He had brought in his World Cup winning teammate Nobby Stiles as player-coach. It was not a world class game; the 0-0 draw highlighting deficiencies in both teams. But at least it wasn't us that got relegated.

The fourth round of the FA Cup took us to Hereford United. Two years earlier, they had beaten Newcastle United with a famous thirty-five-yard rocket from part-time carpenter Ronnie Radford – a goal still shown on every FA Cup history highlights reel. Hereford were the lowest-ranked non-league side to beat top-flight opposition in English footballing history. We didn't want to be the next notch on their goal post. In preparation, I went to Edgar Street to see them in a third round replay, in which they beat West Ham. Their small ground was packed to the rafters, with a pumped-up crowd adding the twelfth man. It was going to be tough for us. And it really was. Not a match for the purists, we showed real character and ground out a 1-0 win thanks to a goal by Merrick on a muddy, quagmire of a pitch, more *Countryfile* than *Match of the Day*.

My recent signing from Norwich for £30,000 – a promising twenty-year-old striker called Paul Cheesley – was starting to fit in. A Bristol lad, he was quick, brave and most impressively for me, two-footed. Very few players had the ability to use both feet, so Cheesley's skill was a bonus. It always surprised me that so many could barely kick a ball with their weaker foot. It seems to be a basic necessity to have some ability with both. Of course, many great players enjoyed fantastic one-footed careers. David Beckham had the sweetest right foot in the world, no one cared about his left. So Cheesley was a rarity and also a straightforward lad who spoke his mind, which I liked. He fitted in effortlessly with the squad, quickly becoming big mates with Gow, Cashley and Sweeney. So nothing like Bobby Gould. We also bought my old Coventry City player Ernie Hunt, who, even though in extra-time of a long career, could still do a job up front.

In the fifth round, we were against the best team in the land. Again. There must be a sign on the A37 that reads: *BRISTOL TWINNED WITH LEEDS*. They were nine points clear at the top of the First Division, we were six places off the bottom of the Second Division. Leeds were welcomed to Ashton Gate on a run of twenty nine games unbeaten and as FA Cup holders. They played Manchester United at Old Trafford a week before, so I went to see just how invincible they were. Leeds completely dominated and were unlucky to only win 2-0, with Joe Jordan scoring and proving a constant menace.

Drawn together so many times, I was getting to know Don Revie quite well. As Tony Collins was working with him now, he had a very good understanding of our players and set-up. Revie famously prided himself on his meticulous preparation, which was one of the reasons Leeds were such a force. It was going to be a battle in the middle of the park with Gow, Whitehead and Sweeney versus Bremner, Hunter and Giles. The national press interest was huge, pitching it as the 'classic potential giant-killing'. I stoked this fire by arguing that it was possible to beat the best team in the land by mentioning Colchester United's famous victory over them in the cup, three years ago.

With Harry still on the beach, Robert Hobbs, the vice-chairman, sensed an opportunity to make a dent in the club's overdraft and reset the ticket prices in line with what Leeds would charge. So, it was £1.50 in the stands and 50p in the open end. It worked, with record receipts of £27,000. Nearly 40,000 crammed in, over double what we were used to, creating a deafening atmosphere. The demand was so great, we could have filled Wembley. Suddenly, Bristol was a footballing city. The local press were building up the match like no other since I'd joined. This was all fine, but my main concern was the league and our disappointing season, which journalists were nowassociating with the word relegation, not promotion.

Leeds settled more quickly and had the best of the opening, with Billy Bremner dominating midfield, putting them ahead just before half time with a thirty-yard strike. It could have signalled a collapse, but we showed real spirit and dug in, and when Gow played a wonderful ball that split their defence, Keith Fear brilliantly lobbed from the edge of the area to equalise. There were twenty-five minutes left. I thought maybe, just maybe. (I also thought, why have I transfer-listed Fear?) They pressed hard but we held firm, frustrated them; Merrick and Collier dealing with Mick Jones and Allan Clarke. We hit them on the counter and Gillies's close-range header brought a world class save from David Harvey. Then, their frustration boiled over; Gordon McQueen head-butted Fear, but we had done enough.

Three days' later, it was off to Elland Road.

The city's excitement reached a new level. There was a mad scramble for tickets. As the miners' strike was causing power cuts, the match would be played on a Tuesday afternoon, kicking off at 2 p.m. It seemed like half of Bristol were spending Monday working out an excuse why they couldn't be in work the next day. Our allocation was 8,000 in a capacity of 48,000. It would sell out, so I called Don.

'Are there going to be enough tickets for all our people, Don?'

'I'll see what I can do, Alan, but it's going to be tight.'

There was a convoy of cars up the M5, some escorting our coach. I just hoped they all had tickets, as a four-hour drive to not get in would be harsh. The traffic into Leeds was gridlocked, so we arrived at the ground just forty minutes before kick-off. I went to see Don to get the tickets.

'All gone I'm afraid, Alan. I've given them all out.'

'Ah. That's a shame. How will our lot see the match?'

'Why not walk them down to the front and they can push in on the terrace?'

Right. So we're going simply to barge in front of Leeds fans, in their ground, for a vital cup tie?

But a club official led our group to the front of the terrace and the fans good naturedly cleared a space for them to stand.

In the dressing room, the players were fired up. No sense of intimidation after coming so close at Ashton Gate. The underdogs have nothing to lose so let's play with freedom. Everyone knew their role. It was especially important for us to win that midfield battle, to have some control of the game. I told Ernie Hunt to mark Paul Reaney every time he surged forward. He didn't have the pace, but he had the brain to block his runs. Don dropped Joe Jordan, which helped, though the replacement was Allan 'Sniffer' Clarke.

They were all over us from the whistle. A relentless charge, attack after attack. It was backs to the wall, but we held firm. Their fans became restless, frustrated that this lower division team would dare challenge the mighty Leeds again. If it had been a boxing match, it would have been stopped after half an hour, the pounding we took. All eleven played their part, our young side gradually coming of age in the toughest ring. Trevor Tainton pulled a muscle midway through the first half and should have come off, but he wanted to carry on as a reshuffle would have upset the team's rhythm. Les Bardsley strapped him up and he lasted the full ninety-two minutes.

The momentum shifted. Gary Collier, still only eighteen, marked England's Mick Jones out of the game. Brian Drysdale took care of Hunter. We didn't allow them to play. We were constantly harrying, pressing, closing down, not giving them a moment on the ball. Sweeney made his right back role into what we expect from the position today; an attacking menace, adept at going forward as well as breaking up attacks. Gow was a tiger, giving Bremner a game. Two Scots locked in a midfield battle that took no prisoners, they just about managed to pull their punches. In the second half, we had decent attempts, with Gillies and Whitehead forcing the best out of Harvey.

On the hour, a Peter Lorimer cannonball flashed inches past our post and Jones had a goal disallowed for fouling Cashley. But we never looked rattled and were still prepared to attack, something they were not expecting. With seventeen minutes to go, Gow stole the ball from Bremner and fed Fear, who stroked a tempting ball into the box that Donnie Gillies ran onto, beating Hunter and stroking it past the flailing Harvey. Elland Road groaned.

We all jumped out of the dugout, higher than ever.

We couldn't, could we?

With ten minutes left, substitute Jordan powered a header that Drysdale somehow headed off the line. That was it.

We could.

One-nil to the Robins. Unbelievable.

Don, a real gentleman in defeat, warmly shook my hand despite what must have been painful and embarrassing. He told the press there were no excuses for his team and gave praise to a Second Division side with an average age of twenty-three, who outfought his prized internationals for a second time in four days. He ended with a warning for Liverpool that they were in for a tough game in Saturday's quarter final.

I was greeted in our dressing room by a shower of champagne. And mayhem. Gillies was the centre of attention, wearing nothing except a tartan hat and a huge grin. All the other players were hugging and singing, celebrating the biggest Cup upset in years. Through the bodies and booze, I spotted a well-known figure, beaming and shaking Tainton's hand.

'Hello, Shanks, how you doing?'

'Not as well as you, Alan!', Bill Shankly grinned.

Bold as brass, he worked the room, pumping the hands of every player. The cheek of it. I nearly kicked him out, but the lads were gobsmacked that this legend was personally congratulating them.

'Really, really, great to meet you, Shanks!', swooned the Scots boys.

The morning papers had been full of him questioning our chances, saying Liverpool were looking forward to facing Leeds in the sixth round. So, he came in to apologise to the lads. Apparently. But *we're* now playing Liverpool in the next round so really he just wanted to start the mind games. It takes some front. Tony Collins also popped in to congratulate us. He was genuinely shocked and pleased in equal measure that the team he had helped build had toppled his world-class new side. It was so good to see him.

On the coach on the way home, the players were flying, saying they deserved some champagne. I got the driver to turn off the M5 at West Bromwich and guided him to a hotel I knew, to continue the celebrations. As the bubbly flowed, so did talk of Wembley. Why not? This was our finest moment, so let's enjoy it and imagine what else can be achieved. Meanwhile, our odds tumbled from 500/1 to 25/1.

John Sillett and I had been drumming into the players the importance of avoiding reckless play. We often had a fatal inclination to compete without thinking, with a rush of blood to the head, forgetting the basics and the need to contain the opposition. The Elland Road result showed how far we had come in overcoming that urge. We were disciplined, had matured and hopefully could become an increasingly tough team to beat, no matter who we were facing.

Our upset made headlines everywhere, including the front pages of *The Times* and *Daily Mirror*, which carried a big picture of Donnie Gillies and the line THE MAN WHO KNOCKED LEEDS OFF THEIR PEDESTAL. *The Sun* even gave him his own column, headlined DONNIE GILLIES? I FEEL MORE LIKE DONNY OSMOND. *The Daily Express* headline shouted THEIR FINEST HOUR – CITY HEROES HALT LEEDS MACHINE.

Evening Post, February 19, 1974.

154

The press were unanimous. We looked nothing like a struggling Second Division side and they were asking why we couldn't play like this in the league. Good question. Gow and Ritchie were fierce in midfield, Hunt and Tainton supporting, with Fear and Gillies a constant threat up front. Why did it take the best opposition to bring out the best in my players? Another good question. There was a photo of me in the *Sunday Express* with the caption MIRACLE WORKER. The other story was that in a city of half a million people, they suggested that many didn't even realise that we had played, never mind won. The conclusion? Bristol was not a footballing city. Yet.

Billy Bremner wrote in his column in *The Sun* that we could 'do a Sunderland' and go on and win the Cup. He went through our team, comparing key players to members of the Sunderland side that completed *the* giant-killing act of recent times, when the Second Division side beat Leeds in the final. The Bristol papers praised the team effort and also calculated that winning the cup would wipe out 50% of the club's debt.

Walking into the local newsagent the next morning, seeing my picture splashed across a couple of the front pages of the national press, was a proud, if strange, feeling. Many reports mentioned how we hadn't taken any champagne to Leeds because we didn't think we'd need it. Well, I had packed it, just in case. Ever the optimist.

Also at Elland Road was a freshly tanned Harry, with his wife Marina, straight from Heathrow, back from Barbados. He said the result was a 'great homecoming'. When I arrived at Ashton Gate the next morning, there was an emergency board meeting going on. Straight after, Harry walks down the corridor to my office, pops his head in and delivers a short and sweet message.

'Alan. Don't believe all they are going to tell you.'

Then he was off.

'Good holiday, Harry?'

'What did you think of us beating the best team in the country?'

'Harry?'

But he had already turned and walked down the corridor.

I know he didn't do small talk but this was short, even for him.

So, I went to find Robert Hobbs, the vice-chairman, for an explanation. He was alone, still sat in the boardroom.

'Harry gave us an ultimatum before he went away and we've decided to accept it,' he explained.

'An ultimatum?'

'He said "If Alan Dicks is still here when I get back, I shall resign".'

I couldn't believe it.

'But we were hardly likely to fire you after the club's biggest cup win in fifty years, were we?'

So, beating Leeds saved my job.

And cost Harry his position as chairman, though he had talked about 'moving upstairs' before. The position would now pass to the quarry-owning millionaire, Robert Hobbs. Harry had prepared his move. A statement to the press quoted him as retiring after thirty-five years as a director (twenty-four as chairman), saving the club from extinction in 1960 by wiping out debts with a £55,000 cheque and the building of his new stand. An incredible legacy with just one regret – not being able to see his beloved club in the First Division. He was, and will always be, a club legend. Mr Bristol City.

But as I wasn't going, he had to, so it was upstairs to become the first president of the club.

The FA Cup sixth round against Shankly's Liverpool was in front of nearly 40,000, at an all ticket Ashton Gate, apart from a few freeloaders sat precariously on the roof of a house next door. From the dugout, the terraces were a wave of red and white scarves, songs ringing out, an electric atmosphere like we'd never had in my time. Sillett and I exchanged a look that said 'Maybe?'

Despite the blow of Captain Merrick pulling out a couple of hours before kick-off with a bruised foot, we started brightly, picking up where we left off from the Leeds performance. In between, we'd had a couple of draws and put five past Mill-wall, so were in the mood. Early pressure from Fear, Gow and Tainton threatened Ray Clemence's goal. Gillies blasted one just wide from thirty yards. We were sharp up front, stretching the meanest defence in the First Division with quick breaks and neat passing moves, plus dealing with all John Toshack and Kevin Keegan could throw at us. Half-time, honours even, we'd matched them in every department.

'We're going to win the cup!'

Bristol wit. Why not?

There was still little between two teams that were separated by thirty-six places in the league. But then, Keegan broke down the left, crossed into the box where Toshack pounced and drilled home. Still forty minutes to go against a side that had only conceded one goal in eight games. We pushed forward, Ritchie and Hunt probing.

A fifty-yard, inch-perfect pass from Fear found Tainton in the box, but his low shot went agonisingly wide. At the other end, Keegan was a constant menace. What if we'd signed him?

In the end, we didn't have quite enough. They sneaked it with that solitary goal. But it was no shame, as it turned out we lost to the Cup winners. Shanks was full of compliments post-match and looked forward to meeting us again, in the First Division. Praise indeed.

Helped by the attention of the Cup run, Gow and Gillies were picked for the Scotland U-23s. It is always good for the club to have international call-ups, giving a boost to the squad.

Our intensity dropped after the highs of the Cup performances, losing three of the next four. With just six games left, a result at Easter against Nottingham Forest was needed to stop the season collapsing into a relegation battle, something we thought we had left behind. A minimum of four points were required. It was the return to Ashton Gate of John Galley, who was not a regular and only on the bench. Strange to see. He averaged fifteen goals a season for us; this season Fear would be top scorer with eight. Paul Cheesley was improving, but aged only twenty, was not the finished goal scoring article yet. We had Merrick back and he and Collier were developing a good understanding. Forest had some fine players in Martin O'Neill and Duncan McKenzie, and were pushing for a top six finish.

The game was tight and nervy, with just 13,000 to witness neither side risking much, but we managed to keep hold of an early lead to take two vital points. There was no time to enjoy the win as we were at Sunderland the next day – another side challenging for promotion. We were up early for a five-hour coach journey, where a 2-1 win pulled us seven points clear of the drop.

Jack Charlton's Middlesbrough walked the league, winning the title by fifteen points. We finish sixteenth. After last season's fifth, the ambition was to challenge for promotion, not relegation. But we didn't have a fifteen-plus-goals-a-season striker. Gow quite rightly got the Player of the Season award.

A kind assessment of the season's performance would have been 'consolidation'. An honest one was 'regression'.

After the issue with Harry, a few weeks later there was another rift. This time with John Sillett. The youth team had an end-of-season tour of Holland and John was to oversee the squad, along with one of our scouts, Nick Knights from Cambridge. Sending Nick on the trip was a way to say thanks for all the unpaid work he'd done for the club. Fixtures were arranged, hotels and travel booked, when a couple of days before leaving, a stern looking John strode into the office.

'I want Peter to come on the tour. Not that scout from Cambridge.'

Elder brother Peter, with us at Chelsea, was now part of the coaching staff.

'But it's all arranged, John. We can't change it now.'

There was silence. Then he suddenly snapped.

'If Peter doesn't come, I'll resign!'

'Resign? Are you serious?

He looked me in the eye, confirming his position.

'So, you'd throw away all we've spent the past four years building, just because your brother can't come with you on a two-week tour?'

His face hardened. He marched off.

Persuasion didn't work, I even offered him more money. A couple of months later he was unveiled as the manager of Third Division Hereford United. I never found out if he'd got the job before his outburst. We'd known each other for twenty years and were close friends and colleagues. Football may be a team game, where great friendships are formed, but it's also a business where ultimately, it's every man for himself. The players would miss him. He was a popular figure, hard but fair, a great football mind and my right-hand man. In 1987, he managed Coventry City to the FA Cup, their only major trophy.

And I missed him on the end-of-season trip to Greece, where we played three matches, including a satisfying draw with Olympiakos, who had just won the league and cup double.

17

BACK TO FIFTH

No John Sillett, but I had full confidence in Ken Wimshurst taking over the reserve team and Don Mackay, ex-Dundee United and Southend goalkeeper, running the youth team. But it felt a vital cog in the machinery was now missing. We had a squad of thirty-two with, as always, promotion the expectation. Different chairman, same ambition. It was now my seventh time of asking, an ambition made just that little bit harder by the presence of Manchester United in the Second Division for the first time in thirty-eight years, odds on favourites to bounce straight back. So, there were probably two spots remaining, as the league had just increased the number of promoted/relegated teams to three. The bookies had us at 25/1, with consistency still seen as our stumbling block to promotion.

Where we were consistent was in our fitness. You knew when you'd spent ninety minutes with us. By combining this physicality, with guile and pace, we did well on a modest budget. But not quite well enough because so far, at the end of every season, there was still one thing missing. Would I survive another campaign without promotion? New chairman, Robert Hobbs, had been supportive but would he have the patience of Harry who waited seven years before getting the itch to sack me?

Away from the league, I'd had an idea kicking around for a while for a football TV game show. Maybe it was Jimmy Hill's influence; keep innovating. The programme would involve four teams of six players competing for a cash prize by showing off their football skills in a variety of entertaining games. Good fun, but more importantly, a way of helping raise funds for the club, contributing to our promotion push. With the club's marketing manager, we pitched the idea to ITV who commissioned a pilot episode of *All In The Game* in pre-season, to be held at Ashton Gate. We got six of our best players plus six each from Derby County, St. Mirren and Norwich City to compete in games like Beat-the-Wall, where five defenders stand on the goal line, attempting to stop the other team scoring. Good fun, but still testing the player's ability.

The show was filmed over a weekend in July 1974 in front of a good-sized crowd and was won by Derby, who collected the £2,000 top prize, with the other teams receiving £1,000. Initially, ITV couldn't believe that I'd get these clubs to compete, but I said if you pay the players and the managers, then they will come. And they did. It helped that the payment was in cash. The viewing figures were surprisingly good, so the talk was for a full series next season.

I called Don Revie to congratulate him on his appointment as England manager, succeeding Sir Alf Ramsey, showing that even if you win the World Cup, you will eventually be fired. Leeds then hired the brilliant and unique Brian Clough, who had previously publicly criticised the club, team and manager. A surprise appointment? It was like putting a fox in charge of chickens and was over within six weeks. A controversial figure, the best manager England never had, Cloughie was a one off. He had precisely what Jose Mourinho described as the single most important attribute required of a top manager – *charisma*. How to get the best out of players, the best of whom today earn a year's salary in a day. Clough had that ability in spades. He proved it with Derby County and twice European Cup winners, Nottingham Forest. Whenever I saw him, at matches or FA dinners, he would always give me a peck on the cheek, not a traditional greeting amongst football men. A week later and another great, Bill Shankly, retired from Liverpool after fifteen years, having transformed them from a mediocre Second Division side into one of Europe's finest.

I saw Cloughie at the City Ground on the opening day of the 1974/75 season, where we got a draw, and I got a peck on the cheek. By October, we were seventh and part of the pack that was already struggling to keep up with Manchester United. Our midfield was purring with Gow, Emanuel and Sweeney, plus I'd added Jimmy Mann from Leeds, on Tony's advice. He was another powerful presence with a cannonball shot. He once kicked a ball from outside the box that rattled the crossbar, then rebounded all the way back to the half way line. Jimmy played rarely for Leeds. He was desperate for game time and so became a replacement for Gow when he got injured, eventually becoming his midfield partner. Another great spy from Tony.

Bob Paisley was Shanks's replacement. He and Liverpool were welcomed by a 25,000 crowd for the League Cup third round with an optimism that we could improve on last season's cup result. A special atmosphere under the floodlights for a game that promised plenty, began with Merrick, who had scored three already that season, threatening to open the scoring with a drilled header that Ray Clemence just about parried away. Tainton's pace caused Chris Lawler problems in their defence and Gillies had a couple of attempts saved. They played like a draw would suit them, rarely getting the ball up to Keegan and Alan Kennedy, giving Cashley a quiet evening. As press reports agreed, there was no real difference between the sides, giving us hope for the replay a week later.

Hope that was quickly crushed at Anfield, 4-0. This time we did look like a Second Division side. It didn't affect our confidence. Three straight wins soon followed, then a visit from the red hot promotion favourites.

I was pleased to welcome Tommy Docherty to Ashton Gate. He had moved from Rotherham, via Aston Villa and the Scottish national team, to manage Manchester United. Even though they'd suffered the unthinkable, the club trusted him with the task of getting straight back up. Already eight points clear at the top, they'd lost just one game in fifteen, unsurprising with players as good as Alex Stepney, Sammy McIlroy and Lou Macari.

In my programme column, I praised the spirit at our club. It was the best it had been in my seven years and it felt like everything was finally in place for a real shot at promotion. I thanked the board for backing me when I needed funds, knowing that it was a constant struggle to keep the club solvent. And I ended with a rallying cry to the supporters. If we can all pull together on and off the pitch, maybe we could get a result today and start a serious challenge.

It felt like a familiar script, like something from a previous season, but the difference this time was that we had the team to do it.

Like us, United were a physical side, so it was a harsh encounter. Gow and Sammy McIlroy were stretching the legality of the 'full blooded' tackle. If these challenges had happened in the street, it would have ended up in court. Eventually, one from McIlroy proved too much even for Gow and he called for treatment from physio, Les Bardsley. Eventually, Gerry got back up and I assumed all was OK until a concerned Les returned to the bench saying that Gow's boot was filling with blood so he'd told him to come off immediately. But Gow, being Gow, refused and somehow carried on.

After half an hour, lively Tom Ritchie effortlessly dribbled around Lou Macari to set up John Emanuel's first goal of the season. They had plenty of second-half pressure but nothing Collier and Merrick couldn't deal with. It was a hugely significant result and justified the optimism of my programme notes.

The win over United lifted us to third. Tommy Docherty was not pleased, telling the press post-match that we were the most defensive side they'd faced all season, and the dirtiest. He was the sorest of losers. For us, it showed a new confidence and bode well if we could just manage to conquer the traditional Christmas dip.

In this mood of optimism, Robert Hobbs agreed a new £7,000-a-year contract for me that renewed every two years, at the start of each season. It meant if I was sacked, I'd still get a minimum one year's salary. A *genuine* vote of confidence from the board.

A run of three defeats ended with a win over promotion rivals, Aston Villa. The celebrations were overshadowed by Gow fracturing his foot – a terrible blow. Jimmy Mann could deputise, but the team were going to miss their engine. He was so important to us, but injury was somehow inevitable the way he played the game. Nobody gave more on the pitch – and he expected the same of his teammates. They would have to carry on the fight without him for a few weeks, which they did with a great win at Bristol Rovers, Keith Fear grabbing two. Fear was our joint top scorer that season but we needed another attacking option along with Ritchie and Cheesley, so I went for Hugh Curran at Wolves. He was a prolific goalscorer and just what we needed. The deal was in place, but at the very last moment he changed his mind and went to Bolton.

To maintain intensity in training, the squad did twenty-yard sprints. It sorted the fit from the very fit. Cheesley was so quick, he would outrun the rest of the squad and, as he neared the finish line, would turn to the rest trailing behind, and cheekily mime smoking a cigarette. At well over six-foot, he was built more like a rugby forward than a footballer. I had faith in him despite his average goal record. Four goals in twenty-four games is not the stat of a finisher. But his hold-up play was excellent and he was forming a partnership with Ritchie, who always found space to receive the ball. Plus, they were both good in the air, so our wingers could float balls in.

Our supporters didn't have to go far for their present that Christmas. In the first League derby for a decade, we went to Bristol Rovers, in front of 20,000 Bristolians, mostly in blue but with plenty of noisy red. They had the best of it for the first period and scored after Cashley parried the ball, the defence becoming statues. We were flat, uninspired and, missing Gow, deserved to go in one down at the break. I didn't pull any punches in the dressing room.

The wind blew in our favour in the second half, and we were a different team. Straight on the attack, confidence returned. Fear scrambled in the equaliser. From then on it was one-way City traffic. Mann coolly slotted number two in from the edge of the area. Then, a rare Tainton goal, a pinpoint shot into the top corner through a box crammed full of players. The icing on our Christmas cake was a ninetieth-minute Cashley drop kick that bounced into their area, finished off by a perfectly-timed Fear volley. Never had we played such a game of two halves. It took us up to fifth.

We maintained our top-six position throughout January, going into the final game of the month – a visit to Old Trafford. It had only been a few weeks since we made Tommy Docherty choke on his chewing gum. As we saw each other in the tunnel,

Presenting Paul Cheesley with an award.

he grunted something which could be loosely translated from the original Scottish as 'We're gonna give you a good kicking today'. They had maintained their place at the top, on a clear path to an immediate return.

Still without our Scottish midfield engine, in front of nearly 50,000 screaming Mancunians, we managed to hold our own, having now reached a level of confidence in even the most volatile situations. And we were still level approaching ninety minutes. But it got even better. In the third minute of injury time, Gillies found space in the box, turned and stroked the ball past keeper Alex Stepney. For Docherty to lose once to the 'dirty, defensive side' was unfortunate. But to lose twice? If there was a shade of anger beyond *very bright red*, he found it that afternoon. The top team was humbled by us, again, from which I took particular pleasure.

For us, the push was most definitely on. To prove it, we won six of the next eight, ending up on a very Good Friday winning at Southampton, climbing to the third promotion spot. We'd finally found how to win at home, and away.

With seven to play, it would be two from Aston Villa, Norwich City, Sunderland and us. But in a stupid piece of fixture planning, we had to play Norwich the very next day. We were on equal points, so it was absolutely vital to get something to stop them pulling away.

We lost.

It might have been because they hadn't played the day before. Or even in the previous week. Three days later, Bristol Rovers visted. Half the city about to have their Saturday night ruined – and it was usually Rovers fans. Not this time. In another feisty derby, we created chances but couldn't get the winner, so we had to settle for a point. Three games in five days had us running on empty.

Post-match press meetings kept an upbeat tone, though the '*p*' word heard now was promotion, not P45. The meetings could still be a place for frank exchanges of views and a way to get information on teams, players and transfers. At Burnley, the chairman would ban any journalist from the press box if he'd ever criticised the team in print. 'Banned By Burnley' became a literal badge of honour, and even, a tie. Banned reporters would have to buy their own ticket, stand on the terrace and take notes when reporting from Turf Moor. A referee who came to one of our meetings revealed that when he arrived for a match there, his changing room would have a table laden with sandwiches, cake, tea and a bottle of Scotch. But if during the game he gave a big decision against Burnley, he would return to his room to find the table stripped empty.

We were pushing hard for the third spot, helped by having Gow back. I'd had calls from Celtic and Ipswich Town about him, but he was committed to staying. Hobbs agreed and didn't force a sale. Although the money would have helped, it would have seriously affected our chances. By the time we went to Orient, we were looking for our third consecutive win to stay in the race. We started well, controlling the game against the mid-table side, when, as Ritchie shot from the edge of the box, boom, the lights went. Floodlight failure. As the teams came off, the groundsman got his toolbox out and turned his torch on. We fully expected the game to be abandoned but the ref restarted twenty minutes later, by then the momentum had shifted. They got one just before half time and no matter what we tried in the second half it wasn't enough.

The lights went out on our promotion. Should the match have been abandoned? Many in the press thought so. We went on to lose heavily at Sunderland, who finished fourth. Docherty's team were champions, losing only seven times, but twice to The Robins. We couldn't catch Norwich – that home loss so expensive – as they took the third spot. But still, we were three points off the First Division, the closest for a decade.

Finishing fifth was an improvement. But we had been here before, two seasons ago, failed to build and paid the price. The team was developing and the board comfortable with a no-sale strategy. For now. Gary Collier was voted Player of the Season. It was confirmation of how good our defence was – third best in the league. And what progress he'd made, still only twenty.

Post-season we went to Norway. We played four games, won them all, scoring eighteen goals. As some of the boys commented, if only we were in the Norwegian League!

18

NOT FOR SALE

Turns out I had as many lives as a cat.

Nine seasons at Ashton Gate. Despite regular calls for my head, I was still in charge and was the longest serving manager in the division. The average job expectancy was three years, so it proved my club was patient. Could I finally repay this loyalty? The bookmakers had us at 20/1 for promotion in this 1975/76 season. Despite the top-five finish last season, inconsistency was *still* the issue.

We had the perfect start, winning twice in three days against Bolton and Sunderland; scoring four, without reply.

Then we lost the next two.

It's why you never see a poor bookie.

As usual, I had negotiated all the player contracts so could keep chairman Hobbs and the board informed of every step in any potential buying and selling. Their policy was to let me know what amount they could raise, so defining what my budget would be. My experience in accounting and running my own business was invaluable. This knowledge helped with a club managing a continual overdraft, where money was a daily concern.

Ashton Gate training session.

Over the years, there were few players that I really wanted but couldn't get. The board would fund my targets. The most frustrating was Bryan Robson. Tony had heard from one of his contacts that he was privately unhappy in pre-season 1975, so we arranged to meet at a motorway services on the M5, to avoid prying eyes. After chatting, he was keen, said he wanted to come, things weren't great at West Brom where he faced competition for his place from, of all people, player/manager, Johnny Giles. Though only eighteen, I could see what a player he was shaping up to be. The deal looked like it was done. The board had approved the fee and wages, but at the very last moment he wobbled and decided to stay and fight for his place. I always wondered what a difference the future England captain would have made.

The core of the team we'd built had bonded through seasons of matches, training and foreign tours and had forged a strong spirit. Our issue was goals. Fear and Gillies were top scorers last season with nine each, but we were the top six's lowest scorers by a distance. Cheesley had plenty of potential but hadn't quite found his feet yet, his understanding with Ritchie still developing.

They would be opponents in training sessions during hotly contested Scotland versus England five-a-side games. Less popular still were the old shadow play exercises. Here, the team is on the pitch, playing in their positions, with a ball, but no opposition. It taught an understanding of how to dictate the play and get used to covering each other. The connection between the players was improving, with an intuitive instinct growing. It took time but was now beginning to pay off. They were noticeably more in tune with each other – covering, running, finding space – displaying an instinct and connection.

By October, we had fought our way into the top three, getting four at Oldham Athletic, where the Ritchie/Cheesley partnership was starting to fire. Next, we were blowing away York City with Cheese getting a hat-trick and Ritchie the fourth, putting us top of the league. And all captured by *Match of the Day*. 'The Robins look like potential promotion candidates', raved Jimmy Hill on the show that night, being completely impartial! The press praised our new-found consistency.

All the attention brought its own set of challenges. Suddenly Bristol City players were on the radar. Arsenal wanted Merrick and Ritchie for £250,000. Huge money, especially to a club like us with significant debt, struggling to stay solvent. I told the board we couldn't afford to lose them. They replied we couldn't afford to keep them. I argued that we were going for promotion, not liquidity, and that I needed those players. Money was tight and some of the directors were keen to sell, thinking of the bottom line and not the top division.

Hobbs updated me on the precarious financial position. We had an overdraft of £200,000, losing £1,000 a week. Despite the encouraging season, our gates were only averaging 12,000 where a figure of 16,000 was needed to break even. I knew if we didn't go up, players would have to go.

Adding to the board's trials, there was a club takeover bid from a group of Bristol builders to deal with. So, each director was asked to increase their investment, which didn't play well with everyone. As a result, there was a line-up change, as not all were prepared to put their hands in their pockets. Again. The takeover was successfully repelled but, as usual, it was money making the football club go round.

A few days later, Hobbs marched into my office to reassure me that Merrick and Ritchie wouldn't be sold. To help the financial situation, though, the board wanted me to visit the club's bank manager at Lloyds in Park Street, to take him through potential revenue opportunities.

The manager greeted me warmly, and ushered me into his office.

'Very nice to meet you, Mr Dicks.'

'You too. Have you been to many games?'

'Rovers, I'm afraid.'

'Ah.'

'So the directors are putting in an extra £10,000 each?'

I nod.

'But haven't you got players you can sell? That would be a simple way to sort the cash flow issue and balance the books. The directors advised that you've done this previously, to support the building of the new stand?'

I nod again.

'So, are there plans to raise new finance that way?'

'No.'

'Is there interest from other clubs in any of your players?'

'No.'

'That's a shame.'

'Yes, it is, isn't it?'

Sensing there was nothing left to say, I stood; he shook my hand and escorted me to the door. As I walked back down Park Street to my car, I 'realised' that I'd forgotten to mention the £250,000 Arsenal had offered yesterday for Merrick and Ritchie. Shall I go back and tell him? Well, my car is on a meter. And I've no more change. And he obviously missed the *Evening Post* article where Peter Godsiff revealed it all.

Most football clubs were run by successful local businessmen. All seven directors were local people with mostly local businesses, though one had a mushroom farm in Israel. As I hadn't sold two of our best players, to raise funds Hobbs smartly asked fans to buy season tickets early for next season. We were still in the top two, so they did, to the tune of £66,000. This kept the bank manager calm, and I kept my players.

An early Christmas present came in a phone call.

'Alan, I'd like to come back. Since Don left, it's not been the same'.

'You're absolutely sure?

'When can I start?"

Tony Collins re-joined as assistant manager on 5 December and I couldn't have been happier. The only requirement was that when manager Don Revie wanted him to do the occasional scouting job for England, I would let him go. So, for the World Cup qualifiers that season against Italy, Finland and Switzerland, Tony would visit the countries, analyse the training facilities, hotels, pitch condition, etc. Just doing what Tony did best – spying.

We then beat Fulham and York City, where Ritchie got a hattrick, maintaining second place in the table, just behind Sunderland. It had become an early two-horse race, with West Brom, Southampton and Bolton the chasing posse.

Just before Tony returned, I drove to Plymouth to watch Paul Mariner, an exciting young striker who was banging them in for Argyle. I'd been given a brand new Datsun 280Z. It even sounded fast. I bombed down the M5 like Niki Lauda, with my thrilled young son Patrick, in the passenger seat. A few lightning miles down the road, he pointed out in rather a high and excited voice that we were doing over 100 mph. I didn't even notice. As we went under a bridge, he pointed out the policeman with a speed camera.

'Er...Dad?'

Reading his expression, it was time to slow down. The terror etched on his little face was a clue. Sure enough, a few moments later, I saw the dreaded flashing blue light appear in the rear-view mirror and was pulled over.

The traffic cop looked at me knowingly.

'I'm very sorry officer, I'm off to look at a player and we're late for the game.'

He broke into a broad grin.

'It's really not your day, is it Mr Dicks?'

'What do you mean?'

'I'm a Rovers fan.'

They were everywhere.

For some reason he let me off with a warning. If it hadn't been for Bobby Robson winning with a bid of £220,000 to take him to Ipswich, we might have had a chance with a striker who six months later was playing for England.

The highlights of the Christmas fixtures were putting three past Hull City and ending the year winning at Portsmouth, which took us to second. Our concentration on the League in the new year was helped by being knocked out of the FA Cup by First Division Coventry City, but not without fielding our strongest team and losing to a cruel own goal.

Learning from last season's fixture pile up at Easter, in December I asked Plymouth Argyle if we could bring forward our April match to late January. They agreed. It resulted in a drab, goalless draw, but did get us a point and another game out of the way. You could do that then. Clubs were more flexible, there was less red tape, and few live TV screenings dictating kick off times.

By early February, Ritchie was lethal, scoring against South-ampton, the winner away to Orient and primed for the visit of

Nottingham Forest where Brian Clough was now manager. We meet pre-match with a peck on the cheek. It was early days for him and Peter Taylor at the club. It would be another season before they got promotion and then go on to win the European Cup two years in a row. Not too early to beat us 2-0 though. That famous side was taking shape with Ian Bowyer, John McGovern and Frank Clark in place. Taking a team from the depths of the Second Division to being crowned the best in Europe within four years was unheard of, and never to be repeated.

Oldham and Luton Town were comfortably beaten, then it was West Brom at the Hawthorns. Now promotion rivals, it was

With Captain Merrick.

potentially them or us. The game was supposed to be played in late February but was cancelled at the very last minute because nine of our players, and I, had flu. It was rescheduled four weeks later, under the lights, with many of our loyal supporters making the trip, yet again.

Though promotion is rarely decided by one single game, if there was a 'four-pointer', it was this one. Promising another full-blooded physical contest, the midfield battle would be crucial, though no one could risk a red card – Gow or Giles. We began strongly, had less possession but offered more threat, and eventually Sweeney tucked one home just before half time. The second half was a defensive master-class – or just desperate resistance – as they threw everything and everybody at us, with the last twenty minutes a nail-biter as they hit the bar, the post and we cleared off the line. But, we held out. This was a team that had become as strong mentally as it was physically. We went top with nine games to go.

It was the biggest win of the season. The supporters were incredible that night. In the minority of course, yet for some periods it felt like a home game. The players appreciated it so much that they waved at packed cars full of fans as they beeped their horns, driving past our coach on the way home.

Now we were on our way.

Then we stalled. A frustrating goalless draw at home to Fulham.

Up next was a trip to Roker Park, Sunderland, for a top-of-the-table clash. The club hadn't been able to say that for a few decades. Don Revie had written to Cheesley asking him to play for the England U-23s against Hungary. A great honour, but it clashed on that Tuesday evening. The lad was torn. Club or country? So, he put it to the team. They all agreed, saying it was well deserved; he had become a top striker and should go and represent his country. This just convinced him he should play against Sunderland.

Further proof of the spirit in the squad.

It turned out it wasn't 'Cheese' getting his sixteenth of the season but full back Sweeney who opened the scoring, setting up a historic and crucial win against a side that hadn't lost at home for over a year. We were relentless, chasing and harrying, dominating to such a degree that even the famous Roker Roar was reduced to a whisper. A perfect performance maintained for eighty-six minutes. Then they equalised. Really cruel. There was no time for regrets, though, as three days later we were on the coach up to relegation candidates, Carlisle United. We didn't help their cause by taking both points, courtesy of a Gow penalty. We were still top.

Five matches left and we trekked north again, to mid-table Blackpool, who had nothing to play for. They beat us. We looked off the pace, lacking in energy like it was us who had one eye on the summer holidays. Why, when we were this close, did we play like that? There was no answer in the dressing room post mortem. It was a long journey home, with plenty of time for me to apply my maths over the permutations – a daily obsession. With four games left, three from seven teams would go up. We were on forty-nine points, top of the table, one point ahead but having played an extra game. Next up we had Chelsea at home, one place beneath Blackpool.

It wasn't about motivation. The players wanted it as much as me, the supporters, the board and the city. It was about sticking to what we'd done all season that had got us to this position and keeping our nerve. Ashton Gate was noisy, nervous and expectant. Pre-match, I reassured everybody. We're here because we deserve to be. And it was a good performance, the energy was back, the highlight being two more beauties from Ritchie. But we still only managed a draw.

In the post-match press chat, reporters questioned how I could show no emotion in such a tense situation. I feel it, I don't show it. I'm not going to suddenly start running up and down the touchline, screaming at players. As one reporter commented; cool, calm and collected. The last three games would test that like never before.

Who would like to trip up our promotion charge the most?

On Good Friday afternoon, we were in a packed Eastville Stadium against a Bristol Rovers side just above the relegation zone. Now Brian Drysdale was back from injury, we had a full strength side. It was always going to be tight; they were organised at the back, so even Ritchie couldn't find a way through despite plenty of pressure. It was a goalless stalemate. Very frustrating but, fortunately, other results went our way and left us needing two points from the last two games. Both were at home. West Brom and Bolton were a point behind, just ahead of the chasing pack of Notts County, Luton and Southampton.

Sixty-five years. That was the number that kept being repeated in those days leading up to the visit of Portsmouth. The pressure of history, decades of underachievement, thwarted ambition, dreams of a return to where the club always thought it *should* be. Relegated in 1911, desperate to return ever since. Two world wars and a man on the moon, but still the club was not back in the top flight.

I had worked, planned, kept my cool and my job for nine years. Now perhaps the faith shown in me could be repaid in the best way possible. Could I afford another failure? I'd managed this club that had ambitions way beyond its budget, to reach this point. But now the *only* way to finish this season was with promotion. Anything less would be seen as failure. Expectations had been raised. Now there was so much further to fall.

Press articles cast me as one of the 'quiet men of football'. Maybe now I'd have something to shout about. Fifth last season, top three since October. It was the culmination of nine years' work in one night. No pressure, then.

Well actually, yes.

The biggest pressure I'd ever felt.

19

THE PROMISED
LAND

Our preparation was the same as ever for the evening fixture against Portsmouth on Tuesday, 20 April 1976.

We'd done some light training the day before, and run through our opponent's strengths and weaknesses – the most fundamental being that they were already relegated. But sometimes this is when a team can be at their most dangerous. The pressure is off, players are prepared for the drop, the crushing disappointment has now sunk in. Ian St John the ex-Liverpool striker – one of the foundations of 'Shanks' great side of the 1960s – was manager. They had veteran George Graham in midfield, in the twilight of his great playing career, and a young Chris Kamara in defence, at the start of his. The rest were young and relatively inexperienced.

Nearly half our team were ever-present the whole season: Cashley, Merrick, Ritchie, Gow, Tainton. Seven of the side were Bristol boys. It had taken a long time to reach this point. Finally the stars may have aligned.

I wore my same lucky suit, drove the same lucky way to the ground, but this time had 'good luck' on the way. On a warm afternoon, my car window down, there were shouts of 'Good luck, Dicksy!' as I drove past. Would it be our lucky day?

The players began to arrive three hours before kick-off and relaxed in one of the club lounges. Well, they tried to. Outside was constant chanting and singing, fans building the atmosphere, little realising the state the players were in. We had a laugh and joked around, with the Scots boys as always at the heart of it. It was an attempt to mask the nerves. But even they had worry behind their smiles. Tonight, was *the* night.

I saw Harry before kick-off. He'd just had a major operation and was still recovering but it was great to see him at his club, at a match he'd waited for longer than most.

It was a warm spring night that would turn into the hottest summer on record. The noise from the 27,394 increased the temperature. As I shook Ian St John's hand pitchside, he smiled, wished me well, maybe seeing in me where he aimed to be in a few years, if they gave him time, which they didn't. In a year he was gone. My pre-match dressing room talk was brief and to the point. There wasn't anything to say they didn't know already. Tonight was about calm, clear heads, carrying on the way we had played all season. I took my place in the dugout, had done all I could, so no fingers were crossed.

It was a dream start.

'Cheese' flicked the ball on to Clive Whitehead on the edge of the six-yard area, who caught it perfectly on the volley and drove it home into the top left hand corner. After three minutes.

The place erupted.

That should settle the nerves. Now we can relax and build. But despite the goal, the players let the occasion get to them and we looked nervous on the ball, playing more like a team afraid of relegation. The weight of history was pressing down, subduing their natural tempo and energy. Even Gow and Sweeney were quiet. Their minds controlled their bodies tonight like I hadn't seen before.

Half-time couldn't come quick enough.

The tension on the pitch transferred to the terraces and though the East End Stand had sung their hearts out, it wasn't doing its usual job of lifting the players. The half-time team talk was simple – relax. We were forty-five minutes away from the First Division. The effort was 100%, but composure 50%. We'd forgotten how to play our natural game. Something that for forty games that season had been instinctive, had now gone AWOL.

I was the calm manager. Ron Atkinson, Frank McLintock, Tommy Docherty were all heart on the sleeve, emotional, shouting, gesticulating and pumped up bosses, charging up and down the touchline. But even I was challenged that night. It was the longest-ever forty-five minutes. A second-half stalemate driven by tension and fear meant there was more movement on the terraces than on the pitch, as the supporters inched closer and closer.

We just couldn't get that second goal to kill the game, the closest being Cheesley hitting the bar. Portsmouth only had one shot all match and we were never in trouble. But we were nervous for ninety minutes. A game of this importance was never going to be a classic. It was, as Fergie would famously say, 'squeaky bum time'. Lucky I wore my brown suit. It was one of our poorest per-formances of the season but for once, nobody cared. The crowd kept inching closer to the pitch with every boot out of defence. We ran the clock down in the most risk averse half of football.

Finally, finally, the sweetest sound. The final whistle. I'm not even sure if we played ninety minutes as, by then, the crowd had reached the touchline. It was a starting whistle for mayhem. Uncontrollable, delirious mayhem. A pent-up sixty-five-year-wait mayhem. A wave of relief and joy like I'd never experienced washed over me as the supporters flooded onto the pitch and carried the players shoulder-high in a moment that still makes me shiver forty-seven years later. Homemade banners were raised everywhere, to the players, to the team and one even to me: ALAN DICKS IS GOD. Blimey.

In the chaos, for the only time, I turned into *emotional manager*, hugging the players one by one, often in competition with several supporters. Gow, Tainton, Ritchie, Cheesley, every single one of them had been a vital part of the whole team. With all the many moving parts of the side, we didn't have one that didn't fit perfectly with the rest. I felt so proud to be working with such a special group on and off the pitch, who committed to the task, put in the hard miles at training, and bonded so well into a unit that was strong enough physically and mentally, to get us over the line.

I saw Harry up in the stand, proudly beaming like a man who had just seen his life's dream become a reality, something he thought would probably never happen.

Through the mass of bodies, I managed to make it up to the boardroom, and shook hands with Hobbs. Forgetting all the usual decorum, he hugged me like I'd just scored the winner. Then the directors, the staff, anyone and everyone. The champagne flowed and we all grinned like schoolboys, while pinching ourselves that this moment had really, finally arrived.

The FIRST Division.

Bring on Leeds, Liverpool, Arsenal, Manchester City. Bristol was finally back on the football map, the red half of the city once again a home for top-flight football.

I went down to the dressing room where Hobbs had laid on bottles and bottles of champagne. Singing, cheering, drinking, hugging, joyful mayhem. The lads were spraying the bubbly over each other. Players were wearing grins wider than the suspension bridge.

The scene on the pitch was also bedlam. Thousands of supporters were crowded around the Williams Stand celebrating wildly, with no intention of going anywhere until their heroes had reappeared. The noise was deafening. It was a special sound the club had waited so long to hear.

We all jostled at the front of the stand – players, the board, fans. Bubbly was still being poured over everyone. A microphone stand was set up. I took hold and the sprawling crowd went quietish. I was scanning the sea of delirious faces to see if I could see my children, Patrick, Melanie and Michelle. I took a deep breath and, not being one for impromptu public speaking, launched with something from the heart of an 'unemotional manager'. Like playing the game itself, I kept it simple. 'I'm a very proud man tonight. It is one of the most marvellous moments of my life.'

It seemed to cover it quite nicely and was met with a roar so loud to have been heard in Highbury, Anfield and Maine Road. We were on our way. I had worn the same lucky suit for months. The players had filed onto the pitch in the same order and had insisted on wearing the same number on their shirts. Don't underestimate luck. And luckily, we had avoided any long-term major injuries.

We all piled back to the dressing room, where the flow of champagne continued. Someone suggested it should flow over me. So, I got sprayed by players. Moet all over me and my lucky suit. A bit disoriented, wiping it from my eyes, I was led over to the other corner of the dressing room.

And chucked into the bath.

Fully clothed, splashing around, surrounded by laughing, naked players. The photo of me beaming in the bath went the equivalent of viral in 1976 media terms. Most national papers and all the local newspapers printed it. It was a perfect expression of the joy and relief felt by thousands that night.

The only shame was that Tony Collins was away at Blackpool versus Sunderland, checking on a prospect. Always the super-spy, I missed celebrating with him. The journey would have been so much harder if he hadn't been with me. John Sillett, now Hereford manager, had returned for the match. His team had just been promoted after winning the Third Division title

In the bath – and the First Division.

in his second season, but he said this night was even more emotional. He'd played a big part as the youth and then first team coach for six years. The crowd cheered him that night like he'd never left. Between us all we had created a special combination of youth and experience which means, hopefully, it can only get better.

The player celebrations went on all night, quite rightly. There was still one more match to play, at home to Notts County four days later, on Saturday. It would decide whether it would be us or Sunderland who would be crowned champions.

I think there must have still been some alcohol in some bloodstreams because what should have been the icing on the cake turned out to be a stale affair. The County players formed a guard of honour for the team as they filed out onto the pitch. The crowd carried on from where they had left off on Tuesday night. We had achieved our ambition, but the final part escaped us, losing 2-1 and it felt like the morning after the four nights before, with a listless performance. I was disappointed we couldn't finish top but with Sunderland winning that day we couldn't claim the title anyway. We would have always had to settle for second place, on goal difference over West Brom. For the first time ever, the supporters didn't care. They had their victory.

These were the players I'd put my faith in for years and it had been repaid. No manager could ask for more. We used just sixteen players in forty-seven league and cup games. Try doing that today. The Cheesley/Ritchie partnership with thirty-three goals sealed it, plus the second meanest defence in the league behind them, conceding just thirty-five times. The Player of the Year honour for the 1975/76 season was not given to an individual, but to the whole squad. The board kept their bonus promise, with players awarded £1,000, and me £5,000.

My profile had never been so high. The national press rumour mill worked overtime. With other clubs apparently circling, a couple of back pages proclaimed DICKS: I'M STAYING. Arsenal were very interested, amongst others. I publicly stated I was happy. Why would I leave now? But it was flattering, of course. Much was made of my past. The lamp salesman, the insurance man, and the record of previous seasons – fifteenth, fourteenth, nineteenth – when you put it like that, it's a miracle I survived.

I was the friendly manager. Tough, but with an easy-going nature. *Could I cut it in the toughest league in the world?*

Rival managers and local figures, all had a good word to say, even Michael Cocks, the local MP. City had put the city on the map. *The Daily Express* said:

'It is sixty-five years since the capital of the West, famous only for the suspension bridge, ship builder Brunel, cigarettes, chocolates and sherry last saw First Division soccer. Now the city could genuinely be known for something else.'

We had made our own luck by always maintaining a great work rate. We never stopped running for every ninety minutes. Managers said they hated coming to Ashton Gate as they knew it was going to be relentless. It sounds so simple. Get eleven players to run for ninety minutes and you'll be successful. *Is that all we need to do?* Well, you won't win anything if you don't do that. Liverpool and Manchester City have built their recent supremacy on this basic strategy. If you don't run, you don't play, as one manager threatened. It's the foundation you build on. We were very fit, tough and good without the ball. Always working and always closing down, difficult to play against. Mistakes are made in football (and life) through pressure, laziness and lack of preparation. That much I'd learned in a rollercoaster nine seasons.

Robert Hobbs was splashed on the front page of the *Bristol Evening Post*:

'If Alan Dicks wants a fund for footballers, he will get it. Going into the First Division means a lot of extra detail to be worked out – extra turnstiles, more cloakrooms for people on the terraces, things like that. The overdraft has been reduced from £230,000 to £150,000, the lowest for years. We've trusted Alan's judgement in the past and will continue to do so.'

On the Monday after Notts County, we had an open-top bus parade which left Ashton Gate and headed for the south of the city, through Bedminster and Redland. I couldn't resist requesting 'Tickets please!' as the double-decker glided away with the players packed on the top, revelling in the moment. The streets were lined with supporters of all ages, waving scarves and banners that read ALAN DICKS RED AND WHITE ARMY, as thousands celebrated, some with typical Bristol humour, as we saw several mothers dressed in up in their children's full City kit.

Finally, we made it to College Green in the centre of town, for a civic reception in the Lord's Mayor's room. It was then out into the sunshine as the squad stepped onto the stage in front of thousands of fans, taking it in turns to say a few well-chosen words. Mine were simple as ever:

'We will remember this for all our lives. We couldn't have done it without you.'

The 1975/76 promotion squad.

The planning started the morning after the Portsmouth win, through a haze of Moet. Thoughts and ideas that I'd been kicking around for years could now finally be put into practice. With increased club exposure and regular TV and media attention, our profile as a club and as a city would be hugely increased. We had to leverage that. I felt confident if we managed to keep all the key players, we could hold our own in the First Division. The unit we had built was strong. Plus, there would be money to bring in new blood.

The end of season May Ball was held in a huge marquee on the pitch with players, officials and supporters celebrating like never before. The manager always makes a speech. Unsurprisingly, I was honest and straightforward, talking from a position of strength now, revealing how close I came to the sack two years before but now looking forward to the challenges of top-flight management. Money had always been tight, so half our promotion-winning squad had not cost a penny. Captain Merrick gave a great speech from the player's perspective and chairman Hobbs ended with a rallying cry that we would 'defy the knockers and stay up'.

Team morale was higher than ever as the plane took off from Bristol Airport, carrying us to the post-season tour in Spain. As always, I had one eye on the cost, so our travel agent – who organised all the pre- and post-season tours – worked to my rule that so long as there was no expense to the club we could travel.

At the Alicante hotel reception, I bumped into Bob Paisley, who was staying with his Liverpool squad, to celebrate winning the First Division title. What are the chances? So, we had two days of chatting, joking, drinking with and picking the brains of one of our toughest opponents for next season. Bob and his assistant Ronnie Moran were very generous with their time and advice when I quizzed them about what to expect. No trade secrets were given away, but it was good to hear the thoughts of people with such experience. Their season also went down to the wire, needing to win their final game to clinch the title from an overachieving QPR. Bob was a relieved man. No matter what level you played the game, the emotions were the same.

It was good to hear how seasoned champions think, and it gave me plenty of food for thought as I pondered the challenges ahead. From my sun lounger beside the swimming pool, my mind raced with ideas as a couple of our Scots lads pushed a Liverpool player into the pool. That's the spirit. It was going to be an interesting season.

20

ROBINS IN THE TOP FLIGHT

Before the biggest season of our lives kicked off, I had a TV programme to make. The first series of *All In The Game* was filmed on a boiling hot weekend at Ashton Gate in mid-July. Eight clubs battled it out for the £2,000 prize, for which they each sent a six-man squad of their best players. So, we had the likes of Billy Bremner and Norman Hunter from Leeds, Steve Coppell and Sammy McIlroy from Manchester United and Trevor Brooking and Frank Lampard from West Ham, twenty-five internationals in all. It was presented by Dickie Davis, with commentary from the great Brian Moore. In an entertaining weekend, the final was won by Derby County beating Norwich City, proving unbeatable in the 'Over The Wall' and 'Soccer Skittles' games. My hope was that it would become a TV format adopted in other countries, bringing in extra revenue for the club. We made £30,000 just from this weekend.

Our pre-season was the Anglo-Scottish Cup, beginning in scorching 34°c heat, with wins against our Second Division promotion rivals West Brom and Notts County, but going out to Nottingham Forest. It was a useful warm-up for the main event.

The excitement was rapidly mounting in a way that's only possible when you've waited sixty-five years for something. Our first match in the First Division? Arsenal away. The winners of the historic league and cup double five years before, and one of the giants of the game. Perfect. We were the new boys from the West Country, trundling up the M4, invading one of the temples of football. We had arrived, and Highbury was a fitting place to start our journey. The history, tradition and trophies. The expectation of the press, TV and every pundit in the land was that it would be a formality for the Gunners; a home win guaranteed. It suited us, meant the pressure was off.

Walking up the marble steps and through that famous Highbury entrance hall, watched by the bust of Herbert Chapman, was a thrill. It seemed fitting to start by playing a team that had been in the top division for 105 consecutive seasons. And one that had just spent £330,000 on Malcolm Macdonald, making him the most expensive player ever, who would go on to score twenty-nine that season. It was also an Arsenal debut for their manager, Terry Neill. He had to follow in the footsteps of Bertie Mee, who had resigned after a decade in charge, and who had masterminded the famous double win. Unusually, I was asked to write a column in the matchday programme, a courtesy few clubs offered. A proud moment, my piece talked about the challenge of visiting Highbury as a baptism of fire, but good preparation for trips to Anfield, Old Trafford and Villa Park.

Pundits presumed that I would inevitably sacrifice entertainment, to ensure survival. The skill gap that exists between the two divisions needed to be bridged, which would mean that we'd be set up *not to lose*. Park the bus. Do anything to stay up. My principles remained the same around fitness and team spirit, to play the game simply and effectively. But the bottom line was if fans were bored, they would stay at home. We would lose with a negative playing strategy. Money was, as always, a major factor, as I revealed in the article that our entire first team had cost around 25% of the amount Arsenal paid for Malcolm Macdonald. The piece ended with the challenge for us, that we work towards being a club that can compete with the likes of Arsenal, to be a permanent fixture in the top league.

As no new players arrived pre-season and I had sold John Emmanuel to Newport County, I picked the same team that finished the final game of last season. ITV's lunchtime *On The Ball* programme had a feature on us, where I spoke about our team spirit and determination not to be the whipping boys of the league, and to hopefully establish ourselves, quickly. There were questions about Arsenal's pursuit of Richie and Merrick last season. Would we have gone up without them?

Our midfield squared up against World Cup winner Alan Ball, supported by internationals Pat Rice and David O'Leary, all part of their double winning side. Plus, Macdonald up front, alongside the great playmaker, Liam Brady.

As the August sun beat down, the whistle blew on an Arsenal team that started as if they were still on a Spanish beach. This was echoed in the stands where 6,000 Robins fans outsung the 34,000 Gunners. We showed no fear, dominating the early stages, the most likely to score with a succession of piercing attacks. A long free kick from Collier was nodded on by Cheesley, dinked by the lightning-fast Ritchie, just inches over the bar.

Tom Ritchie attacking at Highbury.

Next, Whitehead's cross to 'Cheese' in the box, which was headed against the base of the post. Jimmy Mann effortlessly glided around George Armstrong, fed Cheesley, who forced yet another fingertip save from keeper Jimmy Rimmer. In the second half, we turned up the heat. 'Cheese' was the scourge of their defence, finding space and heading against the bar this time, on the hour mark. Moments later, Ritchie broke from the halfway line and was stopped on the edge of the area by David O'Leary, but he quickly retrieved it by the corner flag, laid it back to Whitehead who floated one into the box. 'Cheese' soared above O'Leary to head a bullet home past a static Rimmer. Highbury turned into a library.

Apart from the 6,000, who went mad.

We had arrived. It was a fearless performance in every department. Whitehead had the measure of Rice, Gow ran Ball ragged, Macdonald was totally eclipsed by Cheesley (surely now another England call-up from Don?).

The final half-hour and we were pushing for a second. They were shell-shocked. History was repeating itself, as bizarrely this was the same result as the last league meeting, in 1915. We weren't intimidated, or in awe and were never second best. Highlights on ITV's *The Big Match* the next day proved we had come, played and conquered. The team in red were embarrassed at their performance and manager Terry Neil said as much in his post-match interview. Underestimating the new boys was a mistake and gave us back-page headlines and a confidence and belief that, yes, we did belong in this league.

On the coach journey home, the mood was like promotion night, and I knew when we reached Bristol, the celebrations were going to be long and liquid. Well, they'd earned it.

Our second First Division match was against Stoke City in three days' time, and after Monday morning training we had the team video playback session of the Arsenal game in the player's lounge, though this time recorded from ITV. It became the players' video of the year, even more popular than *Rocky*.

It was the first home game in the First Division for sixty-five years. The red side of the city couldn't wait, with the excitement and expectation increased even more after the Arsenal result. Everyone I met in the town was my new best friend, shouting out of car windows and stopping me in the newsagent. There was one supporter, who, as a boy, had been at the match in 1911 when Bristol City were relegated to the Second Division after losing to Everton. He revealed that he never thought he'd live to see his team back in the top division and that he was one of over 32,000 who crammed in that night as we looked to carry on from where we left off at Highbury. My FROM THE MANAGER column in the programme was not about the team but the fans, how their support was vital to us now, maybe more than ever.

Stoke City were wary after Saturday's victory, so came out fighting, creating a frantic opening. With twenty minutes gone, Cheesley – threatening their defence – went up for a ball Whitehead had put into the area. Goalkeeper Peter Shilton rushed out and clattered into him as he headed the ball over the bar. Cheesley then landed very awkwardly, ending up in a tangled heap.

He looked in pain, but Cheesley was a big, strong lad, so I wasn't worried.

But when he came off, the reality kicked in. It was obviously serious from the pain he was in and a few days later we found out just how bad. X-rays revealed both ligaments were torn, the cartilage that surrounds the knee ripped and a bone in his knee was chipped. Today, that kind of multiple injury means surgery, with an expected return to full fitness within a few months. Not then, it was far more serious. No blame was made – Shilton was just trying to shake him up having seen how dangerous he was against Arsenal. But the outlook was not good. The worried faces in Ashton Gate that evening were testament to the severity of the situation.

The stretcher that took 'Cheese' off also carried our hopes of goals. He and Ritchie had formed a great understanding and were vital to the team. 'Cheese' was the complete centre forward; receiving the ball, backing into his marker, showing for headers, chest downs and layoffs. He made tireless runs into the box waiting for the cross and was always ready for passes played down the channels.

Three months later, he made a comeback against Birmingham City, but sadly his race was run. Just twenty-three years old. Tragic. A huge loss, both on and off the pitch, 'Cheese' was such a character in the dressing room. Here was another of our top players whose prospects had ended before they'd even really begun. Gerry Sharpe first, now 'Cheese'.

Career. Ending. Incident.

Thank God that's not a phrase you hear very much these days.

They would have both gone on to play for England.

Within a few days, the club had gone from an incredible high to a cruel low.

Despite the trauma, we remained unbeaten in the first six games, putting four past Sunderland and sitting comfortably in fifth place. A great start that no one dared predict, rapidly turned into a run of five consecutive defeats, scoring just one goal. I knew that we'd really miss him but didn't realise how much. It would be over two months before we had our next win, as the hunt for a new striker became more and more desperate. And then Ray Cashley pulled a muscle taking a goal kick, so now we were without our top scorer and our keeper. I gave a chance to John Shaw, another Scot, who we got on a free transfer from Leeds and had waited over two years for a first-team chance. Then Gerry Gow had an Achilles problem that meant an operation, and he would possibly be out for months. Plan as much as you like but you can't plan for injuries.

Then the cavalry arrived in the shape of Norman Hunter.

With Tony Collins' help, Norman arrived from Leeds United in late October for a fee of £40,000, after over 500 appearances and countless winner's medals. He signed a three-year deal at thirty-two, still with plenty to offer. After Don Revie left Leeds, he wasn't happy and had started looking for a move and, of course, there was plenty of interest. So, we had to act fast. It would be a coup if we could pull it off. Tony was the intermediary, so soon I'm sat opposite Norman in a hotel near Leeds.

'What would make you come and play for Bristol City, Norman? Tell me what you prefer. Is it money in your pension?'

'Don't need it, full up.'

Don Revie was a big fan of paying in to players' pensions.

'OK, so what do you want?

He thinks.

'I'll match whatever you're on. Plus 20%'.

'You will?'

I nod.

'OK.'

Deal done. He signed, there and then.

Norman was known as a hardman but was so much more than that. With one of the best left foots in the game, he was a superb passer and read the game so well, like he knew what was going to happen next. Plus, he was a leader on the pitch. Don Revie had christened him the 'greatest sweeper in the world,' which I couldn't argue with. And he was obsessive – 24/7 only one subject occupied his mind. An example of this intense level of commitment was when we were returning from an away game, with some players winding down with a card game on the coach. Norman was invited to join in. He considered it for a moment, then pushed the cards off the table, sat down and insisted everyone talk through how the match went and why we had lost.

Suitably, Norman had a tough debut at Derby County, where he had some previous, having been sent off a few years before. The crowd gave him constant grief and we lost 2-0. This was our sixth defeat in a row and we'd plummeted to twentieth place. It's a relegation battle, Norman. In November. Did he question what he'd done? No chance. In fact, to prove his commitment to the club, and the city, he opened a sports shop in Whitchurch, south Bristol. A great character and professional, I knew we had something special. We were going to need his rare talent.

His home debut was against Coventry City, and though we only drew, it stopped the losing habit of the past month. Norman made an immediate impact. His mere presence on the pitch lifted the team, with his marauding runs from out of defence, driving us up the pitch. A true leader.

Precarious just above the relegation zone loosened the purse strings of the board. I asked for a further £50,000 to buy thirty-year-old Peter Cormack from Liverpool, a Scottish international who, at various clubs, had played in almost every position. We had met in Spain in the summer, on the end-of-season tour, and I thought then he would be a good fit. Like Norman, he had priceless First Division experience and was a great athlete; tough and versatile. I needed them to bring their knowledge and understanding of the division to the team, with our lack of top-level experience really showing.

They made the difference at White Hart Lane. We arrived on a nine-game winless run, with Spurs just one point above us in the bottom four. It was Cormack's debut, with Norman in central defence, Merrick replacing Drysdale at left back. I knew Geoff wasn't thrilled by the move, but he was such a good professional that he just got on with it, putting the team before himself. Late on, Cormack fed a beautiful crossfield ball to Merrick out on the left, who guided it to Fear to poke home a last-minute winner. It was the one highlight of a drab game that didn't thrill the millions watching *Match of the Day*, but it did for us.

At the following Tuesday's board meeting, the mood was brighter, so I thought I may as well just come out with it.

'I need £110,000 to bring back Chris Garland.'

'But we've just spent £90,000 on Cormack and Hunter,' argued Hobbs.

'Yes, but we haven't replaced Cheesley. I need a goal scorer. Leicester City are prepared to let him go.'

There was silence.

'And he's now an established First Division striker.'

Still, silence.

I'd sold him to Chelsea five years ago for £100,000, where he scored regularly, including in the 1972 League Cup Final. He'd been at Leicester City for a couple of seasons but told me he was keen to leave. Most importantly, he had the experience we needed.

'OK. We'll see if the numbers work, Alan.'

They did.

Garland's homecoming brought over 30,000 to Ashton Gate for the visit of Norwich City and inspired a 3-1 win. Up to eighteenth.

It was short-lived. We lost three of the next four and welcomed in the new year as one of the favourites for the drop. The press were already sharpening their pencils for early obituaries. I'd grown used to pressure but now it was more public. There was a huge increase in press and TV exposure. Opening a newspaper became a risky move.

Next up, Manchester United away. We were against a team revelling being back after doing their time in the second level – they were on a winning run, banging in nine goals in the past three games. We had new keeper John Shaw still settling in. Forgetting to read the script, Fear caused a few cups of Bovril to be spilled after only five minutes, by scoring. We rode out the rest of the half and went in one up. There was an energy and confidence in that dressing room not seen for a while. Normal service was resumed though when they equalised and despite a strong and brave performance at the back, we couldn't stop Jimmy Greenhoff's late winner.

At the final whistle, I went down to the touchline to congratulate Tommy Docherty. It had been a tough match, we put up a good fight, but this was a team that went on to win the FA Cup and finish sixth, so it was no disgrace.

'Well done, Tommy. You were too good for us in the end. Well played'.

And, as is traditional post-match between managers, I offered him my hand. He point-blank refused to shake it, blustering in his thickest Glaswegian,

'You're not a football team. You're just a bunch of fuckin' parasites!'

Apparently, he didn't like that we played tight at the back, with men behind the ball, making it difficult for them. Our first season, playing at one of the biggest and toughest grounds in the country, we were set up precisely *not to concede*. Despite winning, Docherty seemed to take this tactic as a personal slight. He gave me a look like I was something stuck to the bottom of his shoe, turned his back and stormed off down the tunnel.

I was stunned. He had a reputation and we'd had some lively exchanges in the past, but this was the worst behaviour I'd ever experienced, from *any* manager. After checking on our dressing room, I went to the plush boardroom upstairs, still seething.

'Hard luck, Alan, you didn't make it easy for us,' was the warm greeting from the legend, Sir Matt Busby. We chatted briefly. He was a true gentleman. I moved over to the table, laden with food and drink. Docherty walked in. He shuffled over and stood a few feet away as he chose his drink. I calmly put my glass down, stepped over and went to shake his hand but feinted, moved my hand up to grab him by the neck and pushed him up against the wall. The surprise caught him and, for once, the gobby man had nothing to say.

Docherty's face turned increasingly red.

'You don't *ever* talk to another manager like that, you rude little man.'

The boardroom had gone eerily quiet.

He spluttered an apology, something about the heat of the moment. I loosened my grip. He tried to retain some dignity. I addressed the room.

'Thank you very much for your hospitality.'

Strangely, no one in that room even commented, as if they weren't surprised that Docherty would be subject to an assault by a fellow manager, in his own club's boardroom.

Three months without a win ended in late January as Arsenal were on the receiving end of a double, with Cormack's two brilliantly taken goals. His much-improved performance could be traced to our conversation a week before.

'Boss, I really need £5,000.'

'Really? You getting divorced?'

'No. Had a wee flutter. Or three.'

I asked the board. 'He owes £5,000 and needs a salary advance.'

'Owes who?'

I didn't reply.

'We have to know where it's all gone.'

'A bookie. Can you advance his end-of-season loyalty bonus?'

They did. He could repay immediately. With those two goals and some good performances, the weight had clearly been lifted. If only all lapses in form could be fixed so simply.

Newcastle United at home was a below-par performance from many. Sweeney missed a penalty, though Garland did get the equaliser, finally off the mark on his tenth appearance. Goals were still rare. We went to Sunderland, a fellow promoted team and now fellow relegation candidates, who ended a twelve-game winless run, scored their first goal for three months and won 1-0.

Losing five of the past eight, we were in a rut, so I tried a change of scenery. Torremolinos for a four-day break before a must-win game against Manchester City turned out to be just the ticket. Chris Garland got the only goal and we were comfortable against the side that would finish runners-up. There was no problem with team spirit and commitment, but we were still finding adapting a challenge. The gap between the divisions has always been a huge leap to make. The pace of the game, the speed of thought, the skill; it all takes time for players to adapt and to raise their game. And I was learning all the time, as well. With every new situation, there's an opportunity to take something from it, whether it's playing as a schoolboy in Scotland or a visit to Anfield in the First Division.

It was a false dawn, we won just one of the next nine games. The confidence was now visibly fading. We were a team on the back foot, struggling to score, missing the Ritchie/Cheesley formation. The pair had built such an instinctive understanding, the goals came naturally. It was not so seamless yet with Garland, plus the quality of defenders had improved. Now they were sharper, tougher and smarter. With a significant overdraft and money still owed on previous transfers, I had no funds to buy.

Bottom of the league, we faced QPR. It didn't feel like we deserved to be there, a view held by the much of the press, who noted our work rate and determination, that we just needed the breaks to go our way. PLUCKY BRISTOL was a headline that began to annoy me. In the previous match, we'd come back from 2-0 down against Derby County to draw, showing that fighting spirit. But I wanted us to be more than an overachieving new-to-the-big-time club. We had to establish our place at the top table.

A single Gary Collier goal was enough to get both points against QPR. That night, at the Trevor Tainton testimonial dance at the Dragonara Hotel, everyone had a spring in their step, having lifted us off the bottom.

Decent draws with high-flying Leicester and Aston Villa anti-climaxed in a 3-0 drubbing at Birmingham City, dragging us back down to twenty-second. Easter loomed. If we were to resurrect our season, now was the time to start. Tottenham were coming to Ashton Gate for a potential winner-stays-up match, with a defence that was the worst in the league. With us, the second worst.

It was nerve-wracking and definitely not a beautiful game, with 27,000 biting their nails until a penalty converted fearlessly by Cormack gave us hope. We were still bottom but only two points adrift, with nine games left, with a run of four away games, including Stoke City and QPR, also in danger.

Journalists hit more nails in our coffin with each match we lost. 'Gutsy Bristol out of the top flight for sixty-five years but only staying for a season' was typical. Post-match press chats were themed around one word – 'survival'. There are only so many ways I could explain that 'we were optimistic we'd still be in the First Division come May'. Of course, the players read the papers, saw us on TV and any chink in my armour could sow seeds of doubt. We all had to remain cool, calm and collected, most of all me. At least on the surface.

Norwich City needed points too, for absolute safety. Cormack scored again and we looked like getting the point to keep us in touch with the other twenty-one teams, when they forced a late winner. Next up, was Stoke City, away, on a wet Monday night, a real test of character even when you're doing well, never mind in trouble. Garland and Ritchie were on target to secure us a vital point.

Despite the crisis, everything stayed the same. The training schedule, the pre-match approach, the 'lucky' suit. Our fitness levels hadn't dropped, just our heads, so it was vital to keep the team spirit up, making training hard, but fun. The Scots boys were great at keeping it light, with the dressing room banter and joking so important for morale. To get through this challenge, more than ever we needed to have that team spirit and the confidence and trust in each other that got us promoted in the first place.

Away to relegation rivals QPR felt like Christmas Day at Easter. Tom Ritchie got the winner, a result that provided hope. It was our third away win of the season and all of them in the capital. Now the bottom four teams were separated by just one point. Other results were crucial, so Coventry City winning their first game in thirteen was significant and lifted them above us.

Next, Elland Road, a ground with some good memories. Not this time. We got off to the worst possible start, keeper John Shaw spilling a soft shot, which they converted. The sort of mistake that happens when you're desperately fighting relegation – those everyday balls suddenly becoming unplayable. It's called *no confidence*. He was usually so solid, a sign of what the whole team were feeling. Eddie Gray sealed our fate late on, meaning we were still propping up the table. To add further pain, all five clubs above us picked up points, though we did have games in hand, though one of which was against Leeds, again.

Now with five games left, we needed a minimum of two wins. It was between us, QPR, Stoke, Spurs, Sunderland, West Ham and Coventry – three out of seven would be relegated. Not great odds. Even Bristol bookies had us favourites for the drop.

A week after Leeds, I welcomed Tommy Docherty to Ashton Gate. He shook my hand before kick-off, though couldn't actually look me in the eye. How much did I want us to beat Manchester United today? I couldn't begin to count the ways. We had a noisy, capacity crowd lifting the team, many of them wondering if they'd soon be back to watching Carlisle United and York City. We *had* to get something from this match.

In keeping with the recent history of our meetings and given our desperate situation, it was even more feisty and bad-tempered than usual. Chris Garland got us off to the perfect start after six minutes with a bullet header. But it was like stirring up a wasp's nest, as they swarmed around our box. The second half was just warming up when Gary Collier conceded a debatable penalty that Greenhoff converted. Now we really needed to keep our heads. A point would do, a loss unthinkable. But the simmering tension quickly reached boiling point when Gow and Sammy McIlroy, who had been at each other all game (as before), were sent off for fighting. Not just handbags, it was proper, full-on punches that only stopped when players pulled them apart. Uncompromising midfielders, neither giving an inch, they finally crossed the line. Marching down the tunnel, Docherty jumped up and went after Gow and told him what he thought of him. Wrong person. Gerry gave as good as he got and barked back until I got there and pulled him away, before he repeated his Bobby Gould punch. I was sorely tempted to shake Docherty by the throat again for insulting my player. The temperature on the pitch now cooled enough to let us get a draw.

That point still left us rooted to the bottom for the fourth successive week, two points adrift. Four games to go and the next visitors were Leeds, for the second time in ten days, though this time without the suspended Gow, so Jimmy Mann stepped in. Otherwise, it was the same team, the same must-win.

I knew the reality. If we went down, I'd be fired. Hobbs and the board had kept their side by giving me £200,000 for players. In return, I needed to keep the club up. We go down, so does my career. In rare quiet moments, away from the ground, I imagined life without it. A decade in the city, my family here. Where would I go? Have coaching badges, will travel. But of course, I wasn't ready to leave. We had to stay up, I wanted more than one season of this league – a chance to see how far this

BACK ROW (LEFT TO RIGHT): K. FEAR, D. BARTLEY, P. SPIRING, G. MERRICK, T. TAINTON.
MIDDLE: R. ROOKS, C. GARLAND (now Chelsea), M. GIBSON, J. GALLEY, R. CASHLEY, G. PARR, D. MERRINGTON.
FRONT: G. SWEENEY, G. GOW, T. JACOBS, B. DRYSDALE, K. WIMSHURST.

Above: Bristol City, 1971.

Below: Bristol City, 1973.

BRISTOL CITY

Back Row (L to R): Windhurst (Trainer), Emanuel (now Newport), Gillies, Cashley, Rodgers, Collier, Ritchie, Alan Dicks (Manager).
Front Row (L to R): Fear, Tainton, Drysdale, Merrick, Gow, Sweeney, Mann, Whitehead.

Bristol City, 1975.

Bristol City, 1977.

BRISTOL CITY

Ashton Gate, home of City since the turn of the century, has a capacity set at 39,000 with seating for 7,577. The new Dolman Stand, flanking one side of the ground incorporates an indoor bowling arena and refreshment rooms. Inset: City manager Alan Dicks.

Ashton Gate.

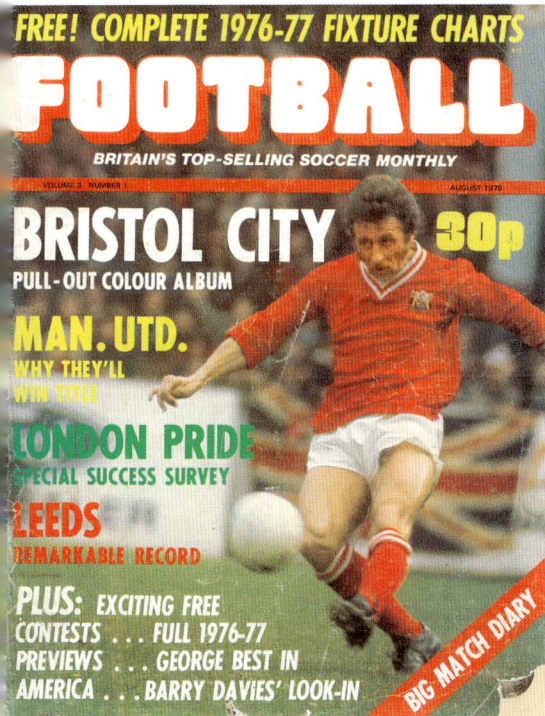

FREE! COMPLETE 1976-77 FIXTURE CHARTS

FOOTBALL

BRITAIN'S TOP-SELLING SOCCER MONTHLY

VOLUME 3 NUMBER 1   AUGUST 1976

BRISTOL CITY
PULL-OUT COLOUR ALBUM

MAN. UTD.
WHY THEY'LL
WIN TITLE

LONDON PRIDE
SPECIAL SUCCESS SURVEY

LEEDS
REMARKABLE RECORD

PLUS: EXCITING FREE
CONTESTS . . . FULL 1976-77
PREVIEWS . . . GEORGE BEST IN
AMERICA . . . BARRY DAVIES' LOOK-IN

30p

BIG MATCH DIARY

GERRY GOW
Bristol City

On the front cover.   *Gerry Gow.*

FULHAM

ALAN DICKS
Manager of the Cottagers

PRO SET

Above: *Al-Rayyan SC, Qatar, 1989.*

Left: *Fulham, 1990.*

Carolina Dynamo, USA, 1997.

Chelsea Old Boys' reunion, 2005.

Above: *The kids, 1989.*

Below: *With Maura and Patrick, 2000.*

The full squad, 2014.

Tash and Hal.

Patrick & Wilmary.

The sunflower man! 2023.

club could go, to create an established First Division side, to be a First Division manager.

Under the floodlights, on a balmy early summer evening, with four critical games left, we faced Leeds. In-form Garland got his third in five, scoring the only goal of another seemingly endless ninety minutes. It lifted us off the bottom, replaced by Spurs. All season we had never been outclassed by anyone, yet found ourselves almost out of the league.

Three matches in seven days that would decide our future. There were so many stats, it's lucky I'm good with numbers. First up was a visit to Middlesbrough. I arranged to see my brother Ronnie post-match and jokingly told him I hoped we could give him a miserable afternoon, though I knew he wanted the best for me and my team. He didn't need to worry as the game had little to concern anyone, certainly not football fans. The teams cancelled each other out; us so cautious not to give anything away and missing Garland, them happy with their mid-table position. The one bright note was Tottenham were confirmed as relegated. Two places left.

The final home game was against the champions, Liverpool. Fixtures can be cruel but then maybe as they were already crowned, their motivation levels might drop just a little. They also had the FA Cup Final five days later, so no one would want to risk injury. Billed unsurprisingly in the press as 'Top versus Bottom,' but with the points only meaningful for one. Our biggest crowd of the season at just under 40,000 squeezed in under the floodlights to witness – if we couldn't get at least a point – our final home match in the First Division.

My programme notes made a point of thanking the supporters for their loyalty (average gate 25,000) and the disappointment at how, despite good team performances, the results had not gone our way in part due to our failure in front of goal and some untimely injuries. The crowd generously applauded the champions when they ran out, a team packed with world class talent; Ian Callaghan, Alan Kennedy, Emlyn Hughes and Ray Clemence. They also had the European Cup Final the following week in Rome against Borussia Mönchengladbach, so they were chasing the treble. We couldn't match them in experience, skill or ability, but we could in spirit. The press still had our situation as mission impossible. After drawing with Manchester United and beating Leeds, we now had to prevail against the best of all.

After half an hour, they scored. But we didn't panic and a neat passing move finished with Garland equalising just before half time. The more the second half continued, the less focused Liverpool seemed to be. Their dreaming of the Wembley Twin Towers reached new heights, allowing Garland to steal in again with fifteen minutes left to get the winner. He had made the difference.

It turned out to be another classic bit of club history created under the Ashton Gate lights in an electric atmosphere. We held out for the win and with Spurs losing, it meant we were not just off the bottom, but out of the relegation zone to nineteenth. Stoke City joined Spurs in going down.

Fans ran on the pitch in a premature celebration, but with the relief that at least our destiny was in our own hands. The recent results and performances against the three top sides had been impressive. There was a post-match celebration, but unlike the night against Portsmouth a year ago, the fat lady had not yet sung. We had to go to Coventry.

Sunderland played at Everton. One out of the three of us would be the final team relegated. *None* could afford to lose.

Thursday 17 May 1977, a day remembered forever by Bristol City, Coventry City and Sunderland.

And English football.

21

THE GREAT ESCAPE

Boss. Gaffer. Dicksy. AD. Call me what you like.

The person in charge, in control.

Up to a point.

The list of uncontrollable parts of the football manager's job is long. You can prepare your players to within an inch of their lives, yet so many aspects are unmanageable. Injuries, fixture congestion, the board, refereeing decisions, weather, etc, etc. Elements out of your control.

And fate, of course.

It felt like fate had led me to one of the biggest games of my life, at, of all clubs, Coventry City. Jimmy Hill had returned two years earlier as managing director and was now chairman. That night, the stakes couldn't have been higher for both of us.

Coventry and Bristol, along with Sunderland playing at Everton would decide their own fate, both games kicking off at 7.30 p.m. that Thursday evening.

On the coach up to Highfield Road, we had an escort of Cortinas, Vauxhalls and Rovers with red and white scarves hanging out of the windows. It seemed every available coach in Bristol was full and on the M5. Apparently, even a judge at Bristol

Crown Court let the jury leave early to allow time to get to the match. The excitement in the city, which had been rising since the win over Liverpool, was now reaching fever pitch. 'The Great Escape' was the theme. Considering we were rock bottom of the league for over two months until just a week ago, according to the press, escaping would be worthy of Harry Houdini.

Crucially, we hadn't lost in four games. The team spirit was good, though it didn't help that Merrick was still not over his ankle injury that kept him out of the Liverpool game, but he came, nevertheless. Reaching Highfield Road, the roads and pavements were jammed with as much red and white, as sky-blue. Over 15,000 had made the trip, so the scene was chaotic. Huge queues snaked round the narrow streets around the ground. As the players got changed, Jimmy Hill visited the dressing room and explained to us that the police had advised him to delay the match by ten minutes to let all the fans get in the ground. I'd never heard that request before, so it was very unusual, but I agreed as it seemed sensible given the size of the crowd.

We had to stay focused and not let the importance of the match weigh too heavy. The fact it had taken sixty-five years to get here, and now the next ninety minutes would decide whether we were going straight back down. Sunderland kicked off at Goodison Park knowing their superior goal difference meant all they had to do was draw against a mid-table Everton side with nothing to play for. What they didn't know was that we kicked off ten minutes after them.

The noise when the teams finally ran out was deafening. It sounded like we were at home, our supporters out-singing the Coventry faithful. My son, Patrick, sat next to me on the bench in the dugout. We had been through some nail-biters in our time, but this was the most danger our fingers had ever been in. We just needed to get a good start, settle, hopefully get an early goal that we could build on. As we kicked off ten minutes late, there were still fans coming in, adding to the 36,000.

The last time Coventry City were in the Second Division was in the 1966/67 season, when Jimmy and I guided them to the top flight for the first time. A decade later, they had become very familiar with a relegation battle.

After fifteen tense minutes, Tommy Hutchison struck the first blow. There was still plenty of time to recover but we looked nervous, couldn't settle, were missing Merrick and our usual spirit. A Tainton shot was cleared off the line, but we never really looked like equalising. Relegation was the elephant in the dressing room at half time as I called for focus and calm. On the way back out I bumped into Coventry manager Gordon Milne in the tunnel who mentioned, with a smile, that a draw would be a good result. I agreed with him, knowing it was the understatement of the century.

Back on the bench, I looked out at my team and knew we had the character to get through this. Gow, Hunter, Sweeney, Ritchie – strong players, physically and mentally. As they used to say, 'Good men in a blizzard'. But some schoolboy defending in our area after just seven minutes allowed Hutchison to drill in his second. We have thirty-eight minutes to rescue our club. Are heads going to fall or will it lift us? I got my answer ninety seconds later when Sweeney found Ritchie with a long throw down the touchline, crossed to the far post to Gillies, who nodded down perfectly for Gow to sweep it home from twelve yards for his first of the season. What a time to get off the mark. Now we have a chance.

Coventry looked concerned for the first time. We turned the screw, pushing forward, our tails now up. They had everyone behind the ball and were defending deep. Any deeper and they'd have been on the Nuneaton Road. Our fans turned the volume up as the ball bounced kindly for Gillies, hovering in the box, and he volleyed it into the far corner. With eleven minutes left. 2-2. Both teams had what they wanted. What now?

How were we going to play out the remainder? As usual, Jimmy had the answer. His latest innovation at Highfield Road was an electronic scoreboard, so he thought now he'd make good make use of it. He ran down from the directors' box to tell the scoreboard operator to put up the final score from Goodison Park – Everton 2 Sunderland 0. So, the message was clear. Do nothing. Keep the draw, and keep everyone safe and happy. Apart from Sunderland.

The final ten minutes were among the most unusual ever played in the English league…or in any league. The ball was passed around across the pitch, never going anywhere near either goal, or even penalty area. Coventry would knock it to each other in their own half. Then it was our turn. After a few minutes, Chris Garland shouted to me from the half way line.

'They're not playing the ball up to me, boss!'

Chris hadn't worked out the ramifications.

'Don't worry about it.'

'But *boss*!'

It had turned into a pre-season kickabout on a beach in Spain; the most relaxed match I'd ever seen. The fans were cheering every pass, understanding what was being played out. There was no need to park the bus, as there was absolutely no oncoming traffic. Bemused referee Ron Challis finally blew the whistle on the least competitive end to a match. The fans were delirious. The players hugged each other, knowing they would be meeting again next season, before disappearing down the tunnel in the strangest post-match scenes. *Everyone* was happy. How many matches end with *both teams 'winning'*?

In the chaos, I shook Gordon Milne's hand.

'Good game Gordon. Fair result all round.'

'Exactly Alan. I say well done to both teams.'

Everyone knew Jimmy and I were friends, had worked together for years. Some smelled a rat. We had fixed the match. Cost Sunderland their place in the First Division. Cheated the system. The media had a field day putting forward endless

Post-match 'cuppa' with Coventry's Gordon Milne.

conspiracy theories. Ultimately, it was the catalyst for a new FA ruling that all games on the last day of the season had to kick off simultaneously. Jimmy innovating again, even though this time he didn't mean to.

But, in truth, it was unprecedented. Never before had any of us in all our experience, been at a match where the kick-off had been delayed, never mind for so long. Someone remembered a kick-off three minutes late because a linesman became ill and a replacement had to be found. But never ten minutes. Police advised against delaying matches just because the crowd weren't all in the ground. If fans were late and missed the start, tough. Start the game at the appointed time. How did 7.30 p.m. become 7.40 p.m.?

Was it a smart tactic by Jimmy, planning ahead, convincing the referee to delay? It seems very unlikely he would have that influence. It must have come from the police with safety concerns, but we never had confirmation either way.

But whatever, it was *the* great escape. Odds-on favourites for relegation for months, yet unbeaten in the final five games. Twelve points from the last ten matches, two down with thirty-eight minutes left of the season, and we avoided the drop by *one* point.

Unsurprisingly, Sunderland lodged an official complaint with the FA, who held an investigation, the upshot being a strongly worded letter from Alan Hardaker, Secretary of the Football League, to Jimmy 'reprimanding the club for their actions'. It was a slap on the wrist. But what could they do? Ask every team to replay their last game of the season? Jimmy got most of the flack in the press, which was water off a duck's back. Since then, Sunderland fans have taken any opportunity to target him. At a

Fulham versus Sunderland match (when Jimmy was chairman of Fulham) in 2008 – over thirty years later – they colourfully reminded him of that night. Long memories, football fans.

To match the drama on the pitch, the next day chairman Hobbs announced that anyone wanting to be a director could buy themselves a place on the board for £25,000. It didn't go down well with the members. He was voted out as chairman, with Stephen Kew his replacement. I liked Hobbs, he'd supported me with transfer funds to build a team that could compete and survive in the First Division. Just. We had plenty to do before next season. I didn't want to be on the same rollercoaster and would need Kew to be similarly on side. But the boardroom battle wasn't over. It rumbled on into the summer, with Hobbs mounting a charge for reinstatement that eventually failed. On the plus side, the club had experienced the best gates ever, with an average crowd of 24,000. Compete in the top league and they will come.

Time for the end-of-season reports. There were two defining factors that affected our returning season to the top league; one terrible, one great. Paul Cheesley's injury robbed him of such a promising career and us of one half of our scoring partnership. First on the list for next season was to buy a striker to replace him. Apart from Stoke City, we were the lowest scorers in the division, with Garland and Ritchie getting seven each. The huge positive was the arrival of Norman Hunter. His experience, football brain, and motivational and inspirational presence on the pitch lifted the whole club. He was rightly voted Player of the Season and would be so crucial for the next campaign.

For my personal report, I'd achieved the most important objective. But coping with the increased spotlight had brought its own personal challenges. I improved gradually through the season, adapting to the higher profile. Now, I was expected to regularly speak on TV, and give interviews to the local and national press. It became another part of the job. My post-match journalist's room continued to be a useful way of keeping my enemies, and friends, close. Despite today's media training, with so many pundits, it's unsurprising that some of them can't cut it. Just because you had a good career on the pitch, doesn't mean you'll have one in the studio. No amount of training will turn some great ex-players into great pundits. I spoke quite naturally on TV, and was very happy talking about football, but you must know your limitations. I was not so comfortable when it went off topic and not great at making speeches. A comment about the game, player or next match was fine. Just don't ask my opinion on anything else.

The post-match press conference was a good training session for me. Journalists were – and continue to be – hungry for a quote, but it is important to choose your words carefully. There was once an Everton manager who famously revealed in our post-match chat; 'When we went one down, I was sick as a parrot. But when we equalised, I was over the moon.' Some managers after a disappointing result could overreact; some even stormed out if they didn't like yet another question about their job stability.

Post-match, win or lose, I'd answer in the same manner. If a reporter asked a leading question about the result or my short term job prospects, I'd never get heated or rude, I just answered the question, so rarely made the back page headline.

A master of the art was Bill Shankly. Charismatic, unflappable and smart, he came from a poor Scots background with four brothers who all played professionally. His motivational team speeches were legendary.

'Remember, you are playing for these people who work in a factory all week. This is their one piece of heaven if you can provide it on a Saturday.'

When his team arrived at a ground, he would always send out one of his staff to check the pitch pre-match and peek into the home team's dressing room. When he returned, the question was always the same.

'Well, what did they look like?'

'To be honest, boss, they looked a bit stressed.'

He'd say this whether he'd seen the opposition or not.

'There you go, lads. I told you they were worried about playing you!'

They did this every match.

His side won ten major trophies in as many years.

22

CUP WINNERS

With Queen Elizabeth's silver jubilee in 1977, it was a summer full of all kinds of celebrations.

Including one for Tommy Docherty's sacking by Manchester United.

I had another weekend of filming *All In The Game* before the season began – it was now the third series. The venue again was Ashton Gate, in front of a good-sized crowd in the sunshine, who saw us knocked out by Manchester City, the eventual runners-up to Leicester City. So, there was more income for the club, and still the potential of lucrative franchise deals.

As a sign of how the club relied on the fans beyond Saturday afternoons, a message was sent out for anyone who could donate their time to help smarten areas of the ground that looked worn out. A few fans volunteered and gave the all the offices a fresh lick of paint. Amazing support.

We were in the Anglo-Scottish Cup. After getting comfortably through the early rounds, we travelled to Glasgow to play Partick Thistle in the quarter final, losing 2-0, though still with the home leg to come. Before this though, was the small matter of the opening match of the First Division at home to Wolves which we lost, conceding three – all self-inflicted individual errors, a hugely disappointing start.

To fill the very large hole left by Cheesley, who had just had his third ultimately unsuccessful knee operation in ten months, I signed a local lad – England schoolboy and youth international, Kevin Mabbutt. Just eighteen and full of promise, his dad Ray had played over 400 times for Bristol Rovers, and his younger brother Gary was also a great prospect. Kevin had been a midfielder in the reserves until Ken Wimshurst moved him up front; a position from which he had been scoring regularly. I gave him his first-team debut against 'Cloughie's' Nottingham Forest, where we lost to a late goal.

Our first point of the season came at Leicester City. Two days later we beat Stoke City in the League Cup for the first win, Mabbutt getting his debut goal. Disastrously, Chris Garland damaged his cruciate ligaments at Norwich, which led to a cartilage operation and him being ruled out for the rest of the season.

One striker in, one out. We were already looking for a replacement – in September.

The programme for the West Ham match had chairman Kew sending a message to supporters, promising to heal the rifts in the boardroom. It was our first league win, beating a side that included Trevor Brooking, Frank Lampard and Bryan Robson, even though they would struggle all season. Tom Ritchie got a couple and Mabbutt his third in three. It was a relief to finally be scoring again.

We went to top of the table Manchester City full of confidence. I had an interesting start to the fixture, reading the programme notes about 'today's visitors'. The article didn't bother with the usual player-by-player analysis and team stats, but instead focused on a blow-by-blow account of my salary since starting at Bristol City, current earnings and potential future remuneration. The financial theme was continued with details of the cost of our recent signings and how much players like Joe Jordan, who we were rumoured to be looking to sign, would cost. It ended by finally getting around to football and the fact we were yet to score an away goal that season. This remained the case as we lost 2-0. *The Guardian* report described us as 'worryingly lightweight'.

October was my ten year anniversary at Bristol. To celebrate, we were back on the train up to Scotland, this time to face Hibernian in the semi-final of the Anglo-Scottish Cup, having seen off Partick. Our Scots boys loved to go back home, especially as First Division players, giving a chance for friends and family to see them, and to wind-up the opposition. Maximum wind-up was achieved during the Hibs game when Peter Cormack headbutted one of their defenders. True, the game was more physical in those days, but an on-the-pitch headbutt was rare. It was a match that began with wild tackles and reckless challenges and went downhill from there. He was swiftly joined for an early bath by Hunter, for a challenge that could be classified as ABH. Yellow and red cards had only been introduced a year before and were still quite rare, so to get two in one game, for the same team, was unusual, and concerning.

We lost our discipline but somehow managed to draw the game with just nine men. Cormack apologised, but I gave him and Hunter a roasting. That lack of self-control could – and should – have cost us the match. My team was always physical, but never, ever to resort to this level of behaviour. Hardly lightweight.

The chairman of Hibernian branded us the 'Butchers of Bristol'. The press stoked it further and splashed it large across the back pages when he pronounced that his team refused to play the return leg. We were so 'reckless and dangerous' that Hibs should be awarded the tie, and go through to the final.

So, we put in a compensation claim for lost revenue from the 'cancelled' match. With this, and pressure from the Scottish and English FAs, he finally agreed to the second leg being played. The Ashton Gate crowd were expecting another bout, but I'd been explicit to the players about our behaviour. The club's last piece of silverware was the Welsh Cup, forty-four years before, so let's keep our heads, focus on a clean win and make the final. The preparation wasn't ideal, losing three League games in a row without scoring, but when it came to Round Two, we won an orderly contest, scoring five, with not a word from the ref.

I was still trying to bring in players while fending off bids for ours, including one from QPR for Merrick. He was unhappy being at left back to accommodate Norman. I sometimes had Gillies there, so Geoff was a target. But of course, I didn't want to lose him.

St. Mirren were the opposition in the first leg of the Anglo-Scottish Cup Final. The media interest was low (unless we started a fight), but we were still playing for silverware, even if it was one of the lesser-known pieces. Their manager, eight years younger than me at thirty-six and in his first job, was Alex Ferguson. In two years, he had transformed a mid-table team into a title-winning side, with an average age of nineteen. Already a great talent spotter, he had the confidence to give unproven youngsters a chance, with incredible effect (see also the Class of '92). His pithy programme notes mentioned the high quota of Scots at Ashton Gate (seven) and highlighted Peter Cormack, not for his pace and attacking threat, but for his headbutt at Hibernian.

We had a dream start, with Gow opening the scoring in the first minute on a quagmire of a pitch. With fifteen minutes left, a sweet Cormack strike, with his foot, put us in the driving seat. Though with a few minutes to go, they got one back. Fergie was bullish, with everything to play for. But we went into the second leg at Ashton Gate two weeks later in pole position. Just.

The nine games it had taken to reach the final helped improve our league performances. Winning any game builds confidence, and that was reflected in the steady improvement, and a creep up the table to sixteenth.

I proposed to the FA that future winners of the Anglo-Scottish Cup should get a place in the next season's UEFA Cup, with an expansion of the competition to sixteen clubs from each side of the border. It would increase its profile and give clubs an added incentive to take part. They said they'd get back to me. I'm still waiting.

Six of the St. Mirren team had visited in July for the *All In The Game* recording, but it was going to be anything but light-hearted fun tonight. Never wise to underestimate any team of Fergie's, they went ahead after an hour. We levelled through a neat Mabbutt finish, but with just ten minutes to go, their pressure paid off and they scored. But the referee disallowed it for a foul on keeper John Shaw and we held firm to draw, meaning we were the cup winners on aggregate.

Fergie was livid. On the final whistle, he ran over to the ref and gave his uncensored view on the disallowed goal verdict, claiming his team had been cheated out of the cup. I led him to my office and tried to get him to cool down with a glass of wine, but he was raging. Every time we met over the next twenty years he remarked: 'You beat us in that final, Alan. But the result was wrong. It was never a foul.'

Here was a sign of the man's desire to win at all costs, whatever the match or tournament. Fergie was a winner and one of the greatest managers of all time. We've always had a good rapport, whether meeting as opposition managers or at industry events like the League Managers Association dinner. But he always remembers me by that game nearly fifty years ago. If I saw him tomorrow it would still be, 'Oh, Alan, you beat me in that bloody final!'

He would go on to win more trophies than any other manager – but I denied him his very first one.

We won the cup! (My only one).

Being an unemotional manager, I stood on the touchline playing the game in my mind. But some, like Fergie, wear it on their sleeve. I was more restrained, some would say detached, but I felt it as much as any other boss. I just didn't show it. I didn't bullshit. There was a trust there that helped forge that team spirit, creating an atmosphere at Bristol in the dressing room, in training, where players could be themselves, where they could feel comfortable enough to focus just on their game. We were honest with each other. The only time I was economical with the truth was with directors when I wanted money for a player, or didn't want a player to leave.

Cloughie was also uniquely brilliant, and after we'd narrowly lost at The City Ground, he invited me for a drink. So, I went to find him, down the tunnel and along the lino-floored corridors, eventually reaching his office. A quick look inside the darkened room revealed it was empty, so I turned to carry on the search. A booming, disembodied voice came out of the darkness.

'Come in, Alan.'

'Er... sorry?'

'Come in, lad.'

So, I pushed the door open and there, just visible, sat in the far corner of the room in the pitch black, was a figure. I approached.

It was Cloughie. He was at his desk with a bottle of scotch and two glasses, which he began to fill.

'Sorry, Cloughie, I couldn't see you,' I said.

'That's the point. Don't want any annoying directors popping in.'

I bumped into him next at a League Managers Association dinner, where after he'd given me a peck on the cheek, he asked after my brother Ron, who had been a teammate at Middlesbrough.

'Lovely man your brother, Alan.'

But Ron was not a huge fan of his. He said that Cloughie would shout to him on the pitch, 'Just give the ball to me and I'll put it in the net'.

He would say it *all* the time. He would talk to the rest of the team like they weren't doing anything, that *only he was*. In Cloughie's eyes, it was a one-man team.

But what a team he was.

Played 274 games, scored 251 goals. The best manager England never had. Gareth Southgate came up through the FA – youth, U21, U23, a company man, and a natural fit to be England manager. Cloughie wasn't. They were unnerved by his maverick, unorthodox approach – attributes that were never part of the FA job description. In a classic example, in his first manager's job at Hartlepool, he often drove the team coach to away matches. He was a one-off.

Goals were again our problem. Solid at the back, but up front we didn't score away from home until three months into the season. Young Mabbutt had grown well into his role, with three goals in his first six games, but he and Tom Ritchie needed help. Tony Collins was constantly on the lookout for a new striker.

I made a proposal to the board that the club recognise the invaluable contribution Tony had made to building the team that won promotion. It was one thing they all agreed on. So a testimonial was organised, Bristol City versus an England XI, managed on the night by my old friend Ron Greenwood, now England manager. There were some top players on show; Tony Currie, Paul Mariner, Stan Bowles, Trevor Francis. A good-sized crowd at Ashton Gate (including Elton John) saw a ten-goal thriller, with us winning 6-4. It was a fitting celebration for Tony's thirty years in football, and he got a nice cheque at the end of it. As a thank you, each player got an onyx table top cigarette lighter.

Welcoming Leeds United in early October, not the formidable side Don Revie managed, but still with top players, Hunter got the winner. His scoring record averaged one goal a season, but they always seemed to be vital. He hit this one so hard his boot flew off and followed the ball into the goal. The fan's banner famously said NORMAN BITES YER LEGS, but he was so much more.

He was the template for our transfers. The principle of buying a seasoned pro with First Division experience to support our youthful and relatively inexperienced side that was still finding its feet in the top division. Enter Joe Royle, an

Norman loses his boot scoring against Leeds.

Everton, Manchester City and England striker. He would not only provide the goals we lacked but would also be a mentor to Mabbutt. There were eyebrows raised at the deal by the press and some at the club, that Joe's best days were behind him now he was pushing thirty. Even chairman Stephen Kew, who always left the football matters to me, wondered out loud whether this was perhaps 'too high risk'.

Joe wasn't getting a regular spot at his City, so I promised he would get one at ours. Also, he was an old friend and England colleague of Norman's, which helped. Of course, it was a gamble. The critics called for a younger, more long-term addition to the squad. A striker of that age could well end up firing blanks. To reduce the risk, I got him on loan. I gave him his debut at home to Middlesbrough, knew that Joe would be a presence up front, add weight to the attack, and use his intelligence and experience from thirteen years in the top division. Fingers crossed.

It was a biting cold, late November afternoon when he ran out in the red and white for the first time. We were fired up, having won the Anglo-Scottish Cup three days before, and from the whistle overwhelmed Boro in every area of the pitch. We always looked in control and won 4-1.

And Joe? He got all four.

He showed what we'd been missing since Cheesley's tragic injury. He had four chances and took them all. He was lethal, using both feet and his head. I'd signed Roy of the Rovers. Or Joe of the City.

After the game, Gerry Sweeney had his very own special celebration of the win, which he shared with the team in the dressing room. He knelt down on both knees in front of Joe, looked up, hands locked together in prayer, and in deep Glaswegian cried: 'The Messiah has arrived! The Messiah has arrived!'

And it did feel a little like a miracle, with four goals on his debut. He added another dimension to the team. His hold-up play, positioning and reading of the game were first class. Every Sunday back page splashed the story with a similar theme; 'Career rebirth. City's saviour. Back from the dead.'

The fans went mad, petitioning in their thousands for the club to make the deal permanent. So we paid £90,000 for him.

I remember the feeling relaxing with a drink later that Saturday night. I had found him. The player that could not only help keep us up, but to grow into this league, get established. Maybe he was our Messiah.

Maybe.

Joe didn't score again for another *seventeen* games.

Seventeen.

His all-round contribution on the pitch was excellent but that four-goal debut hung around his – and my – neck for three months till he finally got number five. It wasn't lack of commitment, he was 100% focused and getting in the positions to score, but lacking the killer finish. As the drought continued, the flood of questions rose.

By the time we beat Ipswich Town with a brave goal from Don Gillies, earning a broken nose for his courage, we were unbeaten in nine and showing confident mid-table form. But in a two-week period pre-Christmas, we gifted wins to Derby, Birmingham City and Nottingham Forest, and slid back into the bottom three.

Welcoming Third Division Wrexham to Ashton Gate in the FA Cup – a side that had knocked us out of the League Cup earlier in the season – was an opportunity to get revenge, and goals. We'd managed just four in the past eight games. It worked. We got four. Unfortunately, so did they. And then thrashed us in the replay. It was a role reversal. Being on the receiving end of a giant-killing didn't do much for morale. The cup can be a salvation or a curse.

Results improved as we got further into 1978, despite Gary Collier – who had been ever-present since the beginning of last season – damaging his knee at Old Trafford, keeping him out for the rest of the campaign. We got a decent point there and his replacement, David Rodgers – a big lad in the Jack Charlton mould – scored the winner at West Ham next. Completing the double over Leeds United with a 2-0 away win was a boost and took us to eleventh in the table. Again, the vital factor in our performance was the physical commitment, keeping the pressure on for ninety minutes, with Hunter, the two Gerrys and Tainton at the heart, providing muscle and energy, as well as skill. This committed approach had always been part of the collective spirit we had built the team on. But it was about to become a problem.

Trevor Tainton was sent off for kicking out at Chelsea's Steve Wicks when we were 3-0 up. He was provoked, but when you're winning so comfortably, it brings unnecessary pressure. His short fuse lit the touch paper as a full-blown brawl started, with a group of players grabbing shirts, pulling and shouting. It was proper handbags, like Hibernian all over again. How we didn't have others joining Tainton in the early bath, I don't know. It escalated from that Chelsea game, with Sweeney seeing red against Birmingham City and Gow at Ipswich Town.

Manager of the Month.

Three players sent off in seven games. Had I lost control? The FA thought so. We were slapped with an £800 fine, a result of accumulating 200 disciplinary points. I protested that the player's committed performances were about their undying dedication to the cause. Some of the press painted us as an uncultured, workmanlike team. The physical side overshadowed the skill and energy.

We went to Spain for a few days to turn down the temperature. Settled in at the hotel one evening after a day's training, Sweeney, Gow and Royle are at the bar. As I walked past, Sweeney had a question.

'Boss, can you give the boys some more money?'

He looked toward Gow, who'd clearly drunk all his expenses already.

'You've all had £10 off the club to spend, that's it. Tell you what Gerry, why don't you give him some?'

And I carried on walking.

He thought I was going to be dad, with bottomless pockets, giving the kids spending money. But in a way, that's part of what a manager was. There were no agents, social media advisers or PR people then. Just the boss.

Despite only two wins from the last eleven games, we avoided the drama of last season, finishing seventeenth. A goal difference of -4 with teams around us being around -23, proved we still had a solid defence. The last game of the season was against Coventry, again, but no controversy this time as we were both safe. Favourites to go down in August, we could now prepare for another season in the First Division. I used those final match-day programme notes to wonder why we had such a poor disciplinary record. Self-control needed working on next season. Norman was voted Player of the Season again.

Physio Les Bardsley left after twenty-one years to set up a private practice. We would really miss him. He had become an expert physiotherapist in athletic injuries, treating not just footballers but tennis players and cricketers. We organised a testimonial against a Bobby Charlton XI. All gate receipts (after expenses) went to Les. Dave Merrington also had a testimonial, though he'd only been with the club three years. Tony Collins had one. Me? Not yet, after ten years.

23

FIRST ON MATCH OF THE DAY

The ten weeks between each season seems like plenty. But it goes in a flash. I lie on a beach for a week but don't stop thinking, going through potential signings and formations, planning and calculating. This summer had World Cup 1978 in Argentina. For the second tournament in succession, England hadn't qualified. We prided ourselves on being a force in the world game, but the reality was different. Ron Greenwood's team couldn't find its way out of the qualifying group, losing on goal difference to Italy, but he kept his job, the FA giving him more time as he'd only had a year. Stick with the manager. Now there's a policy I support. It paid off when England qualified for Spain 1982.

During our 1978 pre-season tour of Scandinavia in July, I gave the captaincy to Gerry Gow, which of course didn't go down well with Geoff Merrick. He had been a brilliant leader for seven years, but we knew we were not going to be using Geoff so much this season, so it made sense to pass the armband on to a player who would be a regular. Gerry would still be applying his blood-and-guts-keep-fighting-to-the-end policy, but now with the remit to encourage others who weren't pulling their weight. Actually, this was pretty much what he had done from day one, anyway. For this third season, we felt we could go into matches on equal terms, with no inferiority complex. We needed to be mentally, as well as physically, fit.

And this mental fitness also included each player's contract with the club. Anyone unhappy with their deal will not be 100% focussed on the pitch.

Seven players refused to sign new contracts, the core of the side. As First Division players it became a big news story. I'd offered them better financial terms than last season, but it brought a lot of issues to the surface. Don Gillies asked for a transfer after I dropped him for an Anglo-Scottish game. Even Captain Gow was dissatisfied.

I asked him not to speak to the press. He didn't, but his wife Julie did. She revealed to the *Bristol Evening Post* that Gerry's gripe wasn't just about the money; principles were at stake, and he was set on leaving. Gerry would keep handing in transfer requests until he was released. It took some handling to get everyone back on side. And some money.

With the small budget that remained, in keeping with our policy of signing experience, I bought Terry Cooper from Middlesbrough for £10,000. We had plenty of first-hand knowledge of his ability, playing against him as part of Don's Leeds side. He'd been a long-time teammate of Norman's, who helped smooth the move, along with me offering him a wage rise. Terry was a left back – and so much more. Incredible crossing ability made him a constant threat to defences, as we had often found out to our cost. In the twilight of his career at thirty-four, though a little slower, he still offered so much and proved it immediately when he smartly set up Tom Ritchie's winner at Bolton in our opening match of the season.

For England, in the 1970 World Cup match against Brazil, marking Jairzinho, the best right winger in the world, not to be intimidated Terry thought he'd let the player know he wasn't going to have it all his own way. Early on he gave him a standard warning elbow in the stomach. It nearly broke his arm. Not only was the Brazilian the fastest down the wing, it turned out he had a stomach made of steel. He ran Terry ragged and scored the winner. A rare example of him not being in control.

In pre-season we started our defence of the Anglo-Scottish Cup, hammering Bristol Rovers 6-1, before eventually losing to St. Mirren in the quarter final. By then, Fergie wasn't in charge to enjoy his revenge as the club had sacked him two months earlier. He took them to court, where the industrial tribunal had a surprising conclusion with the ruling that Fergie had, "neither by experience nor talent, any managerial ability at all."

In a trip to Bobby Robson's Ipswich Town, we kept the marauding Paul Mariner quiet, with Ritchie grabbing the only goal, which moved us up to fifth. In the match-day programme, BBC commentator John Motson wrote about the impact of older players in the division. He'd called me earlier in the week for my thoughts and pointed out in his column that Norman Hunter, with 621 league appearances, was sixth in the table of current players, but, crucially, that only he and Martin Peters were still first-team regulars. I told John about the times last season when we would strap Norman up, send him out to play ninety minutes, and then put him back in plaster straight after the match. His injury meant that for months he couldn't train in the week but saved his all for the weekend match, but you would never know.

Vice-chairman Graham Griffiths told the press that my transfer fund was £500,000. So I tried to bring in Gerry Francis, QPR's ex-England captain, who would have added such experience, but the deal fell through.

We needed to get something from a trip to Old Trafford to keep up the momentum. The goal ratio averaged one per game, which was solid but unremarkable. Mabbutt had fitted in well, grabbed a couple so far, but I wanted much more from him. He showed real promise and had a confidence beyond his years. When I saw him drive into the club car park in a gleaming sports car with his name written in big letters on both sides, I knew he had plenty of front off the pitch too. He explained to me that he was simply marketing himself, spreading the word about *Kevin Mabbutt, Footballer* to the wider world.

He sold memberships to his own fan club, which was very enterprising and twenty years ahead of its time. Though small in stature, he was great in the air and a good finisher. His confidence came from the training his dad Ray – ex-Bristol Rovers – had given him. Kevin had played for England Schoolboys and his brother Gary hadn't, so I offered Gary less money because he was younger and less experienced. His dad said if he doesn't get parity, he's not signing. So, he went to Bristol Rovers instead, before moving to Spurs where he played nearly 500 times, along with a fine England career. I should have pushed harder to get both brothers.

Kevin finally got the national attention he craved after that Old Trafford match. He scored early, quietening the noise,

Me and Norman.

extinguishing it altogether when he got his second on the hour. Manchester United got one back and we had to soak up some pressure, but with ten minutes to go Kevin wrapped it up, beautifully. One of only a handful of opposition players to score a hat-trick at Old Trafford, it won us the game, him a huge number of new fan club members and I'd found a new goalscorer.

This result also showed how we had grown as a team. In previous seasons, in a tough away match, we would have played for a draw; damage limitation, go for the point. This was our third victory on the road in eight games. Last time, that was our total for the whole season. And it was only October.

And then we faded, losing two home games. To prevent a hat trick needed a result against a Bolton team we'd already beaten, but they scored after three minutes. Royle and Tainton both came close as we dominated and, seconds before half-time, Mabbutt put one into the box that Ritchie met perfectly with his head. Royle got his first of the season, then headed his second two minutes later. The rout was completed by David Rodgers at the far post. This showed again how we had matured as a team. There was no panic when conceding early.

The great striker we lost, Paul Cheesley, had a benefit match against his first club, Norwich City, which provided some financial compensation for a promising career that ended way too early.

Unusually, we had a good Christmas run-in and were unbeaten in December, including a very satisfying home victory over Liverpool – a team that would go on to win the title by eight points and included Kenny Dalglish, Graeme Souness and Alan Hansen. We finally looked stable in the division. With any inferiority complex gone, now the talk was of a push for Europe, and not Torremolinos. There was a confidence around the club. We had survived, and finally arrived. After two and a half years, little Bristol City had found its place with the big boys. The Christmas cheer peaked when we thrashed Coventry 5-0 on Boxing Day in a club-record win in the division, with Royle getting a hat-trick.

New Year's Day. The snow and ice were so thick that all First Division games were cancelled, with the FA ruling that it was too dangerous to play. Except our match at West Brom. I protested that the league should be shut down when the conditions reached Arctic levels. The decision was left to either the referee or the home club and for some unknown reason, they decided it should go ahead. The back page of *The Sun* cast me as a 'moaner'. I was right to be, as they adapted better to the freeze and were more comfortable with the orange ball and frostbite. We lost. Post-match press reports revealed Adidas had supplied them with special 'snow' boots, with 150 rubber studs in each.

By then, we had decided to concentrate on the league by getting knocked out early in both Cups, each time by Second Division Crystal Palace, who were smartly managed by Terry Venables. This highlighted our inconsistency in what had been a consistent season. The reality was that the Cups were the best chances we had of silverware, so to go out tamely to the same team in both competitions was really disappointing. Discipline was still an issue. I had to drop Hunter after yet another run-in with a ref. His nineteen disciplinary points were one booking away from a three-match ban.

By mid-February, we were on a losing streak of five in a row, which dragged us down into mid-table having been in the top ten since August. We widened the net in our search for new talent, with the board saying 'spend, spend, spend' – even if it took the club further into debt. Tony went on a couple of trips to Europe to re-watch players from a list of potential signings seen on our pre-season Scandinavian tour.

The first we went for was Pertti Jantunen from the Swedish Second Division. He had twenty-six caps for Finland. Chairman Kew joined us in Malmo to seal the deal for £30,000 and make him the first Finn to play top level in England.

Kew and the board were publicly supporting a spending spree to counter the idea that we were a club reluctant to put its hand in its pocket. The club debt would increase but as we had discussed at many Tuesday meetings, if we didn't invest, increase our squad size and quality, Europe would remain a dream. Previously, chairman Hobbs had always warned against over ambitious spending. It was every club's vicious cycle. If you don't spend, and have a big enough squad, then relegation is a threat and, with it, reduced income from TV and gate receipts. Finding the balance was vital.

On to Amsterdam to finalise the signing of Geert Meijer, a 6' 2", swift, left winger from Ajax, multiple European Cup winners. They initially wanted £160,000 but after lengthy toing and froing, I managed to halve that fee. It proved a good bit of business for a player with plenty of top European experience. He made his debut in the win against Birmingham City and scored after only five minutes. In fact, he almost had a hat-trick, rattling the crossbar twice with his powerful left foot. Meijer's introduction offered us a different option and kick-started a run of four con-secutive wins that took us back into the top half of the table, including beating Chelsea, which helped relegate them three weeks later. I had mixed feelings about that.

It was a relief to get through the sticky patch and give the supporters something to cheer about, though I'd noticed that crowds everywhere had become more aggressive recently, including at Ashton Gate. The anger levels rose quickly when things weren't going well. The more we lost, the more aggressive they became. As the crowds were now up to 30,000, the rage increased in volume, gates twice what they were in the Second Division, where I was less aware of the threat. It was nothing like that when I played, with very occasional insults thrown from the terraces, though I found when playing you don't really hear it; just a collective white noise. The anger level had risen in a society increasingly more violent, reflected in the growth of football hooligan gangs in the early 1970s. When Manchester United came to Ashton Gate in 1974, following their relegation, they caused chaos inside and outside the ground. It contributed to the FA's introduction of crowd segregation, high metal fences and the caging of fans.

We ran out of steam in a tough final five games, with just one win. The European dream remained just that. Finishing thirteenth was respectable, though frustrating after spending much of the season in the top ten. The side was basically still the one that got promoted along with the senior, international additions of Hunter, Royle, Cooper and Cormack. I felt we had established ourselves and built some solid foundations for next season. As always, the team spirit was so good, with all the new signings fitting in. A big part of that was Gow, voted Player of the Season for the second time in five years, a driving force on the pitch and in the dressing room.

24

CONTRACT FREEDOM

America, a new end-of-season tour destination. I was in my office at 9 a.m., finalising tour details, when Gary Collier came in to collect his FA Cup Final ticket, which each player was allocated. We chatted about the 1979 final and who we'd play in the USA, then he left me to continue organising the arrangements.

At midday, chairman Stephen Kew arrived to discuss transfer funds, when the phone rang.

'Hello, Alan. It's Gordon Milne'. He was still manager at Coventry.

'Hi Gordon. How are you?'

'Yes, OK. Listen, I've got to tell you something. We've signed Gary Collier.'

'You what?'

'About half an hour ago. He's here, at Highfield Road.'

'But he was just in my office getting his cup final ticket!'

He must have jumped in his car and driven straight up there.

So, after seven years at his boyhood club, the Bristol lad, a crucial part of the team, had left without saying goodbye. Without saying anything.

And what about John Sillett, Gordon's right-hand man? We'd known each other for thirty years. He must have helped tempt Collier, grabbing one of my key players from behind my back. It left me feeling betrayed and became part of a radical move that changed the English football transfer system for ever.

Collier signed for Coventry City on freedom of contract. It was the most fundamental shift in player power since the abolition of the maximum wage in 1961 (initiated by Jimmy Hill), along with the Bosman ruling of 1995 (where players could move to a new club at the end of their contract without their old club receiving a fee). From May 1979, players were legally allowed to agree a pre-contract with another club for a free transfer, if the players' contract with their existing club had six months or less remaining. He was quite within his rights – just the way it was done felt wrong.

It wasn't like he was going to a better or bigger club. They finished just a few points above us. After the promising season we had, it was hard to stomach losing one of our most important players, especially like that.

Collier was the very first player in the Football League to take advantage of the newly relaxed regulations. A tribunal was called to set the fee. So, I couldn't even negotiate. I was powerless.

I only found out when it was too late how one of my key players drove up the M5 to sign for a rival club, initiated by one of my oldest friends in the game, for a fee well below his real value.

My instant reaction was to call an emergency board meeting.

I wanted Stephen Kew and the directors to approve me signing up every valuable player in our squad until they were thirty-five, when they could claim a Professional Footballers' Association pension. We were already one of the top payers in the league, with a weekly basic of £300 for most players, an amount only bettered by Everton and Liverpool. This new initiative would keep key players at the club for a longer fixed period and prevent any of them 'doing a Collier'. We would have the balance of power in negotiating.

Gary's wife went public in an interview with Peter Godsiff of the *Evening Post*, with a plea not to cast her husband as the villain. She claimed I'd ignored opportunities to sign him on a new contract during the previous year, and that he didn't leave for financial reasons, simply to further his career.

So, with full board approval, I offered Gerry Gow an eight-year deal on £350 a week. Tom Ritchie, Geoff Merrick and Clive Whitehead got the same, along with three others. It made sense at that time to find a way to secure the nucleus of the team that had risen together, to give us the best possible chance in the coming season. We had to stay in the First Division for this pay structure to be viable. So, we needed these players to stay. One beget the other. It was a risk, but a risk that I, and the board, agreed was worth taking to secure the future of the club in the top league. Crucially, we failed to include a clause to cover a relegation situation. Little did any of us know the future ramifications.

I left for the American tour with plenty to ponder. Over the years, we'd played in Iran, Cyprus, Turkey, Beirut, Egypt and all over Europe. It was a great education for the players. Annoyingly, my tour had to be cut short to attend the tribunal to decide what fee we received for Collier. They set it at £350,000. No negotiation, and £100,000 less than our valuation. What is it going to cost to replace him?

The next bombshell landed the day after the team flew back home. Norman Hunter stood in my office wearing a look that revealed exactly what he was about to tell me. His old Leeds teammate Allan Clarke had been appointed Barnsley manager and the first move he made was to ask Norman to be player-coach. I had already offered Norman a new two-year deal, which was generous considering he was thirty-six. Such a vital part of the team, it was essential to keep him. But it was futile. This was the time for him to start in management. I knew also that his wife, Susan, was keen to move back up north. All I could do was shake his hand and thank him for his inspirational contribution to the club over the past three years. Without him, we may well have not been looking forward to our fourth season in the top league.

It was a huge loss. In three seasons, he played 122 times, with a presence on the pitch that demanded 100% from everyone, driving the team on. He was often the difference between winning and losing. It was so sad when he passed away in April 2020, especially as I'd seen him just eight months before and he looked so fit. He was only seventy-six. A great footballer. A great man.

25

LONGEST-SERVING BOSS

Each season, the board and I drew up the players' incentive scheme, paid on top of their wages. It laid out the value of the bonus for each match, depending on the competition. There was a rising scale of payments for league position and number of points. The cups had a value for each round, peaking at £2,000 for each player, if we won either domestic cup. The Anglo-Scottish Cup was more modest, with a £50 appearance and £20 for the final.

Despite the disappointment of Hunter and Collier leaving, we still had a decent squad. To compensate, Tony Fitzpatrick arrived from St. Mirren, breaking our transfer record, paying £250,000. Fergie signed him at nineteen, made him captain and he went on to play for Scotland. Now twenty-three, he would give us more options in midfield, continuing the flow of Scottish talent to Bristol.

Expectations were high both in the club and in the city. The fourth season in the First Division, it was time to really establish ourselves. The excitement of playing in the top flight had spread far and wide. We now even had a big group of supporters from Cornwall who came to all home games. At last, growing into a bigger club, with a broad fanbase.

Team wise, the chink in our armour was now the defence. It was the one constant that had been the strong foundation. We might not score many, but we didn't concede many, but this area was now the weakness. Collier and Hunter were the backbone of the team that kept us up.

Remove them and risk the whole structure collapsing.

I had David Rodgers and Geoff Merrick (who missed the whole of last season), but we needed options. Roger Kenyon arrived from Vancouver, but it didn't work out. More cracks appeared with the realisation about Terry Cooper's game level. He'd struggled with injury and had only played a handful of games in his two seasons, so I had to break the news. How do you tell a legend he's not needed anymore?

We sat opposite each other at my desk and after the pleasantries, I just came out with it.

'It's not working I'm afraid, Terry.'

'I think you're dead right there, boss.'

'You do?'

'Yes.'

'Oh, OK. So, I'm going to have to let you go.'

'Completely understand, boss.'

'Right. Thanks, Terry.'

'No, thank *you*, boss. You're treating me better than Jack Charlton. He never spoke to me. Just didn't play me. I appreciate the honesty.'

A true gent. He didn't go far, just down the road to Rovers, then returned to Ashton Gate as player-manager in 1982.

Hull City expressed interest in Peter Cormack while I negotiated with Emlyn Hughes, who, after twelve incredible years at Liverpool, was looking to leave. Neither deal happened, with Hughes stating he wasn't going to live anywhere other than Liverpool, the seven-hour round trip being an issue.

The opening game of the season started on a high before a ball had been kicked, with marketing manager Tony Rance's bright idea of some pre-match entertainment in the shape of the Bristol City cheerleaders. This was the 1970s, after all. Things looked even better a couple of hours later when we found ourselves ahead against Leeds United, from a Ritchie penalty and a wonderful strike by Pertti Jantunen. They forced a 2-2 draw, equalising in the dying minutes, but it was an encouraging performance. The team looked well balanced, despite all the changes.

Off the field, the club won the Programme of the Year award and the FA announced that I was the longest-serving current league manager. It meant a photo shoot, requiring me to sit relaxed behind my desk. Fair enough. Except they put the desk in the middle of the Ashton Gate pitch. Not relaxing, just odd. The official list of longest-serving football managers in history, runs to fifty. I am just outside that list.

Of course, now there will never be anyone added above fifty, not in the modern game. The most recent entry is in 1954, for Bill Struth who managed Glasgow Rangers for thirty-four years. The longest ever was Fred Everiss, boss at West Brom for forty-five years, until 1948.

But the idea of a 21st-century club manager lasting twelve years at one club is science fiction.

I was interviewed by reporters fascinated about how, in the twelve years I'd kept my job, over 400 league managers had lost theirs. Only Bobby Robson, ten years at Ipswich, came close.

What was my secret? How had I lasted so long when so many hadn't? The axe was sharpened on several occasions, but never swung. It was the inevitable question posed by the media. The answer? Because Bristol City wasn't a club that demanded instant success, mainly as there hadn't been any for so long. Another theme of the articles was that now I had my reward for that longevity, it was a chance to establish Bristol City in the First Division. The hard work had been done, now we could consolidate and secure.

Let's hope that turns out to be true.

In the era of the great Brian Clough and Peter Taylor, I always mentioned Ken Wimshurst and Tony Collins as vital to my success – the team off the pitch was just as important as the one on it. Geography was also a factor, competing as a regional town, outside the traditional football powerhouses of London, Manchester, the East Midlands and Liverpool. In terms of top-flight football, we were a small club – with basic training facilities and a small trophy cabinet – but we'd learned how to punch above our weight and continued to do so.

It was a story the media liked. David versus Goliath. The rise of the small man. I was regularly branded 'the nice guy'. We were, I suppose, 'a nice club', just don't study our recent disciplinary record too closely. In the days of larger-than-life characters – Cloughie, Fergie, Paisley – there was Dicksy. I'd ended all these interviews on a cautionary note, saying that to maintain our place in the league was going to be the toughest challenge yet.

Training session at Ashton Gate.

Winning comfortably away at Aston Villa, clinched by yet another Ritchie penalty, he and Mabbutt were now building an understanding. Victory at home to Wolves, with their new signing Emlyn Hughes, who it turns out was prepared to commute there, meant starting September in the top six. And with yet another penalty from Ritchie, putting him in the record books with four in consecutive matches.

Injuries had resulted in all kinds of new formations as I was forced to put players in unfamiliar positions. Sweeney shuffled across from left back to cover each defensive position. Ritchie relocated to midfield, Whitehead to left back and centre half. They all did well in their new roles. It highlighted the team spirit, with players prepared to sacrifice personal preference for the good of the whole. The exception was Chris Garland, who was set on leaving as I hadn't given him a game yet this season. We disagreed on his valuation. I calculated he was a £150,000 striker. He threatened to take it up with the Professional Footballers' Association if we didn't reduce it, as he thought it was a price that would scare off clubs.

With a peck on the cheek, Brian Clough and Nottingham Forest arrived for a fourth round League Cup match. They were the holders, hadn't lost in three years, and would win the European Cup for a second season in a row. Against £1m Trevor Francis and with Peter Shilton in goal, we equalised with an incredible chip from Sweeney that forced a replay, which we lost 3-0. In-between, we visited Elland Road and put three past them, with Mabbutt getting a couple.

The father and son duo of John and Jonathan Pearce had now videoed over 400 first team, reserve and youth team games in the past five seasons – an incredible achievement. They were like the twelfth and thirteen on the team sheet, ever-present squad members. Through their expertise, we led the way in team analysis, so unsurprisingly other clubs followed, enquiring about our process, what equipment was used and how it was set up, keen to have the same facility.

We were the forerunners of an idea that benefitted all First Division clubs and many in the lower leagues. It was invaluable, with the final version about an hour long, only the highlights. Even if some were the exact opposite this season. Of course, Jonathan went on to become one of the most knowledgeable and respected football commentators, bringing his expertise and passion to *Match of the Day* and multiple World Cups.

A pattern emerged through an autumn of draws. Not a disaster, but eight out of twelve ending in stalemate was not top ten form. In November, we welcomed Malcolm Allison's Manchester City, who had a similar issue to us with consistency. He was gradually rebuilding the team after a difficult period, but we didn't help him with a winner from David Rodgers, created with a piece of brilliance from Tony Fitzpatrick. It coincided with his call-up to the Scotland squad. At St. Mirren he was part-time. He spent his week painting and decorating. Now, he was a professional, he hung up his brushes, training and playing full time.

An article in the *Daily Express* titled MANAGEMENT PRESSURES began by listing all First Division managers and the length of their tenure. The nearest manager to me was still Bobby Robson; the next closest was seven years in the job. In the past two years, half the clubs had changed their manager. The piece highlighted how managers should be judged on many different criteria: size of club, financial situation, backing from the board, potential of the squad at the point of taking over. There was appreciation in the industry and the media for my achievement. It was something I felt very proud of but had little time to dwell on. We faced Spurs at home next, in early December – a team that had joined us in looking abroad for talent with the signing of Argentine pair Osvaldo Ardiles and Ricardo Villa. They had imported a different style of football and had transformed the team into an attractive and potent force.

A win was needed to lift us closer to mid-table than to the relegation zone. The biggest crowd of the season, 25,000, packed into Ashton Gate, high in expectation, but we let them down. Spurs were two up after an hour, with the Argentinians having a hand in both. Ardiles in particular went on some mazy dribbles and increasingly panicked our defence, eventually leading to a penalty. We got one of our own, converted by Ritchie, and though we pressed for an equaliser it was Glenn Hoddle who buried a header, along with our hopes. The defence looked vulnerable. Rodgers had just returned from injury and Merrick had a recurring knee concern.

As our league position fell, the bank overdraft rose, up to £400,000, with the cost of transfer fees and ground improvements.

The Spurs loss began a run of five consecutive defeats. On Boxing Day, we finally dropped into the relegation zone after losing heavily at West Brom. The mood shifted. The fact that I had taken the team up for the first time in sixty-five years was forgotten. I was now the man who might take the team down. The same people who not so long ago said I was God were now swearing I was the Devil – in so many words. The mood had changed so much that some were screaming at me even as I walked down the tunnel for the start of the home game against Aston Villa, the final match of 1979. These were obscenities even a south London boy recoiled from. Aren't I the man who delivered you to the promised land after years in the wilderness?

It's YOUR fault we're rubbish.

One even spat in my face, hitting me on the cheek. Sadly familiar, my response was the same. If a couple of policemen hadn't held me back, I'd have hit him.

Of course, criticise.

Shout your frustration, scream from the terraces, write letters to the Bristol Evening Post.

Chant in the Ashton Gate car park – 'Dicks out!'

But don't spit in my face.

26

THE END

I took a deep breath before walking into the first board meeting of 1980. The general air of doom and gloom meant I needed answers to often impossible questions. There was mainly silence. No one knew what to say. They had been supportive, but that support was running dry. There was no open disapproval, no criticisms of team selections or specific performances, but the silence spoke volumes. We'd been here before, but somehow, this time it felt different. The consequence of a poor season in the Second Division was excusable, but relegation from the First Division was unthinkable. In a way, I wanted some anger, some emotion. No spitting, obviously, but at least some passion. But I suppose there was nothing to say. Their attitude seemed to be that the ship was very slowly heading towards the iceberg. I pointed out there were still eighteen games left, and thirty-six points to play for. Let's not climb into the lifeboats just yet.

A factor that didn't help relations with the board was when Robert Hobbs left. Stephen Kew was not really a football man. He was a lawyer who liked the position and the title of chairman, the most important person in the room, but he didn't really understand the game like Hobbs did. Hobbs was a generous man, Kew less so. Hobbs instinctively understood people, Kew didn't. It meant a very different dynamic.

My traditional new year optimism was rewarded with an early January FA Cup victory over Derby County, scoring six. It was the perfect match, with the team almost unrecognisable from the group that that managed just three goals in the previous month. Confidence returned. But it was a false dawn. The next four games were all defeats, including a 3-0 home loss to Ipswich Town which sparked a supporter's demonstration in the car park, calling for my head. From the player's lounge, I heard it become more intense and hostile. The police eventually moved in to break it up.

The mood was also ugly inside, as Gow and I had a frank exchange of views. He gave nothing less than 100% on and off the pitch, and reckoned some were not pulling their weight, asking what I was going to do about it? There was a sense the team spirit that had carried us through so many challenging times over the past decade, was fast evaporating.

I dropped Merrick for the Ipswich game. We'd conceded eighteen goals in the last eight games, so something had to change. He'd been ever-present this season and I knew I'd bring him back, but we had to look at other options. Ritchie was also dropped, admitting that as he'd struggled to score for a while he should get his form back in the reserves, to win back a first team place.

Twisting the knife further, we drew Ipswich Town at home in the FA Cup to be played a week after their clinical win at Ashton Gate. I recalled Merrick and he and five others were booked in a heated match, though he showed real fight by staying on after a serious collar bone injury which would have retired most others. The team effort was tremendous – Fitzpatrick and

Garland especially – and we were minutes away from a morale boosting result when an error from keeper John Shaw, who minutes earlier had kept us in the tie with a brilliant point-blank stop, gifted Paul Mariner the winner. As Bobby Robson admitted after: 'Not sure how we won, they let us off the hook'.

It was the third consecutive defeat, with a match at fellow strugglers Stoke a few days later which ended the same way. We were now deep in the relegation pit.

The Tuesday board meeting went on into the small hours, with solvency the main issue. How could the club balance the books, especially given the struggle we were having on the pitch? Sell players while in a relegation battle? Immediately, I told them straight. Gow, Whitehead and Mabbutt were *not* for sale. They agreed. But everyone else was potential revenue, so calculations were hastily scribbled on notepads, working out how to prevent an increase in the overdraft without hurting the squad so much that relegation became an inevitability – though some of them thought it was anyway.

Of course, the club's only saleable assets were the players, and from where the board were sitting, anyone that could raise funds was fair game. We had to find a balance between keeping enough quality players that would preserve our status and selling to keep the bank manager happy. They had seen all the press articles putting a price on each of our players. With the transfer deadline just six weeks away, it meant that if we were going to wheel and deal, we had to start now.

They took a vote, then told me to begin right away. But it's so high risk. A fragile team needs strengthening, not weakening. I was being ordered to balance the impossible; to cut players without affecting the team's performance, stay up and stay solvent.

Tony Collins sat in my office and we talked though the permutations. The wage bill was over £10,000 a week. Who would we be prepared to sell and what would we get? The one thing we all agreed on was to try and get Gary Collier back as he wasn't a regular at Coventry and he could help fix our leaking defence. This wasn't a time to hold grudges. He was a great centre back who could come home to help save us. And he wanted to come. But money became an issue, so he had to stay. After all the drama with his transfer, it turned out to be a disaster. Soon, Coventry sold him to a team in America. Everybody lost out.

Speculation and rumours flew about as to which player was supposedly going where, and for how much? None of this helped the team focus. After we were thrashed 4-0 at Old Trafford, the slope got even more slippery. Players had to be sold but they must want to leave. You can't force a player out. Well, you can if you never play him, make him train with the youth team and generally make his life miserable. But the other big factor for Bristol City players was Bristol. It's a great place to live. A player may see an opportunity at another club, but does he want to move himself and his family? It's a complex process that often isn't just about football.

Tony and I received a one-page memo from chairman Kew, asking us to review, with the board, the future of the club given the alternatives of survival or relegation. They needed reassurance that we were ready for either eventuality. The list of players available to be sold was released. It basically included everyone who could command a fee, even those previously seen as unsellable. The situation had now reached crisis point. Now, no one was indispensable. I was about to lose the dressing room. Well, at least some of it.

Gow, Mabbutt, Whitehead, Ritchie, Garland, Merrick and Royle were made available. The contracts of Cormack and Meijer were cancelled – they both found new clubs. But no offers came in for anyone else. The press rumour mill reached fever pitch. Ritchie to Forest. Gow to Brighton. Royle to Norwich. But nothing happened. Of course, the season would be over in a couple of months when, if we were relegated, prices would be seriously reduced.

As we were in this turmoil, a comment by Tony Collins on Malcolm Allision's transfer strategy at Manchester City became back page news.

'He has undermined the whole transfer market with his big spending'.

Big Mal had splashed out an extraordinary £5m on players. Unheard of. It did however, set the tone for the club to this day.

Arsenal were title contenders, with both the FA Cup and the Cup Winner's Cup finals to come, so a trip to Highbury was even more daunting than usual. How we could have done with a result like our very first game in the First Division. Gow still had a knee injury which demanded a plaster cast and there was a chance he also would miss the Liverpool game on Saturday. Our physio, Bill Heather, warned that this may be a long-term, or even a career-ending injury. With Gow out, Mabbutt – who had been scoring for the reserves – would play, with Ritchie taking Gow's midfield role.

No-one expected us to get anything, so the goalless draw was a result. A precious point at Highbury. Now home to Liverpool. It was first versus twenty-first in front of 30,000, and twelve million watching at home. Both teams had been here before.

The title favourites versus relegation favourites played out as predicted when Dalglish swept the second past Cashley on the hour. Then they took their eye off the ball. We pushed forward and put Souness, Hansen and Kennedy under some pressure. Mabbutt poked home five minutes later, giving us a glimmer of hope, until they got their focus back, dominated the final twenty minutes, and confirmed game over when Dalglish got his second.

Manager Bob Paisley spoke encouragingly to me post-match, that my team showed great spirit, hoping we would be around for another fixture next season. Nine games to go. The safety points tally was thirty-five. We had twenty-two. A tall order, but not impossible.

There were just 15,000 to read my programme notes for the home game against West Brom. I revisited the theme of how important the supporters were at lifting the team. If only the other 15,000 had been there to read it. We drew.

Seven games left, every one a must-win. And that's just what we did away at Brighton, sealed with another nerveless Ritchie penalty. And the same at home to Bolton, who were already down, though the final minutes were nail biting as their sub, Sam Allardyce, pulled one back, meaning some desperate defending. We held out.

Suddenly there was real hope. Up next was a trip to big-spending Manchester City, only two places above us. We were poor, nervous, made mistakes all over the pitch, conceded three goals before half-time, and left empty-handed. No time to wallow. Three days later we had another cup final against in-form Middlesbrough, where two from Richie gave us two vital points.

Three games to go.

If we won two and other results involving Stoke and Everton went our way, we *could* be safe on thirty-five points.

So, Norwich City at Ashton Gate four days later, was whatever the next level up from 'must-win' is. The atmosphere was intense, with a dressing room desperately trying to stay calm. I gave encouragement, repeated the game plan we'd gone through the day before, with each player knowing their part. Then they were gone. Preparation over. It was out of my hands.

Norwich were virtually safe, but it didn't play out like that.

A nervous, jumpy opening quickly boiled over into an angry, nasty contest. Our anxiety proved costly as they went two up. We looked down in every sense, the crowd sensing the worst, but when Rodgers and Ritchie scored in quick succession, another great escape seemed possible. The songs started on the terraces.

The temperature on the pitch reached boiling point, with the match exploding when their striker, Justin Fashanu, head-butted David Rodgers. With blood running down his face, it sparked a huge melee involving fifteen players, earning Fashanu a red card. They had been niggling each other throughout the game, but nothing to justify this. It made no sense. We were the ones fighting for our lives, yet he resorted to violence. Maybe it would help us, playing against ten men with half an hour still to go. I was out of my seat shouting, waving and screaming them forward. Not cool or calm, the pressure finally getting to me.

Our fate was sealed by Martin Peters' late winner. Against the run of play, the best team lost. Now, not only did the last two games have to be won, we also needed other results to go our way. Our fate was out of our hands. My lucky suit needed to work harder than ever.

Now, it was on a wing and a prayer, to The Dell. Southampton had lost three of their last four games but comfortable in eighth, so we went with hope. The Scots boys as always firing up pre-match, instilled some spark that was quickly extinguished by conceding two early on. Mick Channon and Alan Ball inspired them to a 5-2 win.

Other results didn't go our way which finally sunk us.

We'd hit the iceberg.

I couldn't fault the player's effort, but in the end we had too much to do. Norwich was the killer blow. We won twice as many games at home as away, but couldn't manage it in the most crucial match of all.

27

DOWN BUT NOT OUT

Sixty-five years to get up.

Four to go down.

So many stats tell the story of that season, but the one that summed it up was the goal difference. Our foundation for success had always been the strong defence. The goal difference for the previous three seasons was -4. Now, it was -29.

We had become easy to score against, conceding an average of two goals a game. So with a requirement of always scoring a minimum of two, with the lowest strike rate in the league, despite Ritchie getting thirteen, meant we were always going to struggle.

Norman Hunter was a huge loss, especially being hot on the heels of Collier. If they had stayed, we might have been all right. *If.* But I should have focused on immediate replacements. That was the most urgent need, but Tony and I just couldn't find them. Deservedly, Geoff Merrick was voted Player of the Season, which was some achievement, given we had one of the worst defences in the league.

To general amazement, the board awarded Tony and I new five-year contracts. A journalist made the point that the manager of the team that had just won their second successive European Cup – Cloughie at Forest – had only been given a three-year deal.

We accepted the offer with very mixed emotions.

28

UNLUCKY THIRTEEN

Confidence is everything and I was confident. Had to be, always had been. We still had the core of a good team, one that had competed well in the First Division for four seasons, so there was no reason we couldn't bounce straight back. Today, the boomerang effect of clubs going up and down between the Premier League and Championship is common. Back then, less so.

Peter Godsiff wrote in the *Evening Post* about several clubs queuing up to sign Gerry Gow for £500,000. Aston Villa, Everton, Manchester City, Brighton. You name it, they all wanted him. Gow explained that his desire to go was partly inspired by the actions of others, including Merrick and Cashley also wanting out – Merrick having interest from Terry Cooper's Rovers.

After much haggling with manager John Bond, Joe Royle was off to Norwich for £60,000, to stay in the top league. Chris Garland wanted his valuation halved to attract clubs. Having played just thirty-six first team games in four years, he had a point. The club had hit the iceberg and people were jumping overboard, which I understood.

Chairman Kew wrote a long article for the *Bristol Magazine* where he looked forward to the new season and pondered how long it would take to bounce back, citing lack of goals as the main cause of relegation. He praised other managers like Bobby Robson and Brian Clough, who had publicly supported me while the vultures were circling. It contradicted the supporters, journalist and TV pundits, all with their own invaluable advice about where I went wrong and how I could put it right.

Plenty of short memories, Kew concluded, reminding readers of the sixty-five years out that I had helped end, urging me to go into the transfer market more regularly, noting a link between new players and increased attendance. I looked forward to the transfer funds. He ended with a passionate appeal to those who visited Ashton Gate only when the big, fashionable clubs were in town, to reconsider and come along for games against the likes of Grimsby Town and Wrexham. It was a very honest and open plea – a rallying cry to the city not to abandon the club just because Liverpool and Leeds wouldn't be coming this season. The city of Bristol deserved to have a top football club, but we needed the support of the community in tough times, as well as in good.

The team that started the 1980/81 season had six players from the promotion team four years earlier. I was loyal to that core group of players. Maybe too loyal.

Pre-season was a continuation of last season, with more underwhelming results. Joe Royle finally left for Norwich, leaving behind a tally of twenty goals in 112 games, after that four-goal debut. Our opening game at Preston got us a point, as did the next fixture at home to an impressive West Ham team that were run from midfield by Trevor Brooking, and who'd go on to win the title by thirteen points. We were a threat going forward and matched them in every department, so maybe some of the 13,000 crowd would be back for the much anticipated local derby in four days' time?

They weren't. A drab, goalless home draw with Bristol Rovers, who finished the season bottom, showed they were right. We lacked confidence and that game proved it. We were back to playing in a half-full stadium, even for the local derby. The spark had gone on and off the pitch.

After losing away to Watford, the pressure built. The confident start we desperately needed was not happening. That old team spirit, even though Gow was now back, was fading. Tony, Ken and I were still demanding the same levels in training and the routines were as challenging as in the First Division. But it wasn't working in matches.

Bill McGarry was sacked by Newcastle United at the end of August, with the season barely two weeks old. As if I needed reminding.

So, the home match against Swansea City on Saturday 6 September was vital – like so many others in the past thirteen years – despite being so early in the season. We'd only lost once in the league but had not yet won a game. This was a match that needed not only a result but a performance, to show the team had regained the confidence and spirit to challenge for promotion. That week we worked hard. The training on the pitch the day before was upbeat, encouraging, with a spark returning to a damaged team.

I was called from Friday training to join an emergency board meeting. Taking my seat, Stephen Kew declared that, after much discussion, the overwhelming decision of the nine-man board was that they wanted to change my role. I was to be moved over to run the fundraising side of the club, to help generate more revenue.

So, not to be the team manager, but the *fundraising manager*.

They had decided it was time for a younger man to come in and take over the running of the football side.

Younger? I was still only forty-six. Seeing my jaw drop to the carpeted boardroom floor, Kew pacified me with a holding tactic.

'We'll have another meeting about it on Monday, Alan'.

They were changing my job. *Completely* changing my role.

My recent new contract stated, as it had done for thirteen years, that I was in total control of all football matters – team selection, player transfers, player salaries. This five-year contract awarded just three months earlier, and literally just signed off by one of the board directors, stated that.

I returned to the training session, stunned.

'You alright, boss?' a couple of players asked.

'Do ten more sprints'.

Ironically, the front cover of the match-day programme for 6 September against Swansea City had a photo of me, smiling at a training session, with my arm round Donnie Gillies. I couldn't remember the last time I'd been on the cover. My programme notes explained an idea I'd had about whether it was time to rethink the tradition of playing all matches at 3 p.m. on a Saturday. Attendances were down for most clubs that season. It seemed a change in fixture times and days might freshen up the system. How about a 4.30 p.m. kick-off on Sundays? Imagine that!

To prove a point, less than 10,000 turned up for the Swansea game. I'd picked the core of the First Division side – Mabbutt, Cashley, Mann, Merrick, Ritchie. That indifference on the terraces didn't help those on the pitch as we looked for the confidence to take the game to them, and make our mark early. But, from the whistle, Swansea looked more composed, confident and skilful, like a team that would be chasing promotion, which they did, ultimately going up.

We went one down. So did our heads. No amount of touch-line management could raise the energy levels. There was no spark, no spirt and we were flat in every area. There was plenty of advice from those not playing, most of it based around one single thought: *Dicks out.*

We lost by a single goal, but it wasn't just the result. The performance was tame, uninspired and anxious. Hard to believe that it was basically the First Division side. A stiff Scotch provided no comfort that evening. We'd turned a corner down a dark alley with no light at the end of it. What was the answer? The past three results were bad, but we were OK in the league, mid-table. Be confident. Still many positives.

I was called into the boardroom first thing on Monday morning and fired.

One month short of thirteen years at the club.

They said they'd been talking to other candidates for the job and were genuinely surprised that I didn't bite their hands off at their offer of the position of *fundraising manager.*

Maybe I'd got too comfortable. After 611 matches, the final whistle had blown. I was lucky to get thirteen years, some managers don't make thirteen months. Jimmy Hill reckoned I stayed too long. But how many managers leave a club rather than being fired? Not many. Jimmy, and legends like Fergie and Shanks are the exceptions. Most are shown the door, as I was. Though not many last thirteen years.

I had taken the club to the First Division at a cost of just £117,000 and had stayed up for four years, while making a £9,000 profit on transfers. It added up, on and off the pitch. Until now.

The board publicly stated that the reason I was sacked was for 'not operating a more vigorous buying and selling policy.'

My new contract, which had been signed just three days earlier, meant they owed me £110,000. I accepted £50,000 as a cheque and deposited it at the bank. It bounced. I had £25,000 given to me and £25,000 put into my pension. So, I lost £60,000 because the club's financial situation was so dire.

Next day, at the Tuesday meeting, I explained to the board that last Friday, I had taken advice from my lawyer, who suggested I find a director who would sign a contract stating that my current salary should be continued. I found one and he obliged. Despite this explanation of the legal situation, Stephen Kew had just one line of questioning.

'So, Alan. Will you be taking the job?'

What, *that* job? The one I don't want, am not qualified for and have never shown any interest in?

The job of *fund raising manager*.

'My contract has been broken. I'm contracted to look after the playing side of this club and now you want me to have an administrative and financial role. So, I'll start to look for another job. Goodbye and thank you for your support over the past thirteen years.'

And that was it.

No outburst. No recriminations.

I walked out of the boardroom, down to the office, collected my things and headed to the car park for the very last time.

Cool, calm and collected to the end

I didn't even say goodbye to the players.

A few days later, some came over to my house in Henleaze for a few beers. I also had goodwill messages from many ex-players.

Achieving promotion was something very special, something I will always be proud of. But I do regret the knee-jerk reaction of signing the players onto such long-term contracts. And not bringing in a couple of central defenders when we needed options in the relegation season.

Tony Collins and Ken Wimshurst were made joint caretaker managers, losing the next three games. Bob Houghton then took over, with Roy Hodgson his assistant. Tony returned to Leeds as chief scout. He told me the Bristol board were considering bringing in a well-past-his-prime George Best, from Hibernian, in exchange for one of our youngsters and £1,000 per week.

Tony wrote an article in the *Sunday People* headlined OUR BOSSES WERE RULED BY FEAR. He said the reason Bristol City were no longer a First Division club and now bottom of the Second Division, was the 'skinflint' attitude of the board. He named their 'sell don't buy' policy during the relegation season as evidence. Yet despite their very tight budget, they were dazzled by the thought of George Best arriving and didn't question the inflated salary. And the failure to replace Hunter and Collier was not about available players, but available funding.

A few weeks later I got a call from an equally unhappy Gerry Gow, as ever wearing his heart on his sleeve.

'Boss, I feel like I'm in a game of tennis.'

'What do you mean?'

'The ball goes backwards and forwards, over my head, all game long. It's like I'm stuck at the net, in the middle, watching it fly over me.'

He sounded desperate.

'They don't want the ball played short. They want it long, so it doesn't go anywhere near the midfield.'

Bob Houghton had changed tactics to a long-ball strategy. Gerry was literally stuck in the middle.

So, I rang a few people, including John Bond, who had recently got the job at Manchester City. He had been in touch over the years, asking if I'd sell Gerry. He always rated him. I told him he was still a great player and had plenty to offer, not least his insatiable appetite for the game. A few weeks later he was sold to Manchester City and went on to play in the 1981 FA Cup Final against Spurs. He'd played 375 times for Bristol, was a true legend of the club, and an inspiration on the field and off. It was so very sad that he passed away so young.

I got a letter from Kevin Mabbutt thanking me for the support and advice I had given him, helping him to 'grow up' off the pitch. He was now at Crystal Palace, where he would finish top goalscorer in that 1981-82 season. It had a brilliant opening paragraph.

'Sorry I haven't replied to your letter sooner, but I have been busy scoring goals (at last).'

Not entirely true as he was City's top scorer in 1978-79 and 1980-81, but it was a gesture I appreciated, knowing that your influence as a manager could help a career grow.

A year later, my sacking and subsequent compensation deal was still a story. They formed part of the furore about Bristol

City's financial woes, a huge £700,000 debt. Club finances were as much a part of the back-page headlines as match results. For so many clubs, the balancing act of staying competitive and staying in business was as much a drama as anything that happened on the pitch. The end game was The Ashton Gate Eight, when in February 1982, eight players tore up their contracts to save the club from financial ruin. This selfless act is the reason the club still thrives today.

29

THE NEXT CHAPTER

After nineteen seasons, I needed a break from the game.

But I wanted to stay in the city and be near my children, so I joined a local company – Globesport Productions – that worked in golf and snooker promotion. The day to day work took me to events around the city and the country.

In Bristol, most were very kind and appreciative of the thirteen years, some full of advice about where I went wrong and how things could have been so different if I'd just picked *him* instead of *him*. One supporter, as I sat in my car at traffic lights, spotted me and decided to spit in outrage, though fortunately my window was wound up. Maybe it was *him* again?

Hero to some, villain to others. No problem.

I wouldn't change my professional life in any way. The personal life is another matter.

Invitations came in to play in pro-am golf tournaments, which neatly combined my love of the game with spreading the word about the golf promotion business. Putting and pitching, I suppose. With free time for the first time in so long, my handicap went down to seven.

I had an offer to manage Gillingham and went to meet them. They were in the Third Division but full of ambition and finance, with the great ITV commentator Brian Moore on their board. Could I *do a Bristol* with them? Maybe? But I wasn't ready to leave the city yet.

I saw the players occasionally. Our relationship was as colleagues, me their boss. And in some respects, a surrogate parent, especially to the Scots boys. Sat on the coach, returning from away games late on a Saturday night, I'd often be asked the same question.

'Boss? Can we go to Platform 1?'

No, not a train journey. A late-night drinking club.

Like most work places, there was a social aspect and a drinking culture. I never restricted post-match socials. That essential team spirit was often cemented in those evenings. And sometimes, nights.

And even after I was sacked, I was still 'boss'.

After leaving a club, it's the manager's strange privilege to have very conflicting emotions.

Rejected, so I don't care how Bristol do.

But after thirteen years, I was emotionally twinned with the club. It was, and still is, in my heart.

So come on Bristol!

I had no contact with Bob Houghton. And why should I. He was his own man, with his own staff. He didn't need advice from the previous boss.

I helped Globesport Productions run golf tournaments. The most entertaining was when the top snooker players swapped six holes for eighteen. The crowds would flock to see household names like Alex 'Hurricane' Higgins, Cliff Thorburn and Willie Thorn, when they spent afternoons hitting a very different kind of shot. Some were quite good, others less so, but they were helped by playing in a four-ball, paired with decent club players. For a Globesport tournament in Cardiff, I had to drive the 'Hurricane' from south Cornwall, which was over 200 miles. That was a strange trip. He was a lovely bloke and the most exciting and original snooker player, but as mad as a box of frogs. We had some weird conversations during that four-hour drive, many of which were only loosely based on reality. This tone continued during the tournament. After five holes, he'd not had much luck. On the sixth fairway, 150 yards to the pin, he suddenly dropped to his knees and played the shot from a kneeling position. The crowd went wild, the ball went inches.

During this time, an old friend – Bertie Mee, the ex-Arsenal manager – rang. Bertie had an unusual path to being boss, joining the club originally in 1966 as the physiotherapist, with no playing career to speak of apart from a handful of games for Mansfield Town before the war. Circumstances conspired to elevate him to manager shortly after arriving, with zero experience. It turned out he was a natural boss, leading Arsenal to the historic league and cup double in 1971.

He had a question. Did I fancy working in Greece? This was the first offer since Gillingham and I felt ready to go back, having missed the game and not coached abroad before. As the full extent of my Greek was taramasalata, I assumed that the universal language of football, plus a translator, would suffice. After all, I did eventually become fluent in Scottish at Bristol.

Piraeus is in the south-west of Athens, five miles from the centre and originally its naval port. When Greece ruled the world in 5 BC, it was where the ships set sail to conquer faraway lands. Roles are reversed now, with hordes of tourists descending every summer. Ethnikos Piraeus Football Club, formed in 1923, was one of the founding members of the Hellenic Football Federation. The most successful club in Greece is Olympiakos, and they are just down the road. Like Oldham Athletic being close to Manchester City. And their top goalscorer of all time was called Dimitrios Chatziioannoglu. 'There's only one Dimitrios Chatziioannoglu!', they bravely sang.

Christos, the owner, was a character. Large, hairy and prone to emotional outbursts, he had fingers in lots of pies – shipping, transport, manufacturing. And a football team, the essential part of every rich man's portfolio, whether he knew anything about the game or not. Which he didn't. But that was fine, so long as he didn't start advising on team selection. Which, eventually, he did. Matches were played in a neat little ground that held around 5,000, just a long throw away from the picturesque Bay of Phalerum and the crystal-clear waters of the Aegean Sea.

The league was basically split in two. There was Panathinaikos, Olympiakos and AEK Athens, 'the big three'. And then everyone else. The standard of football was English Second Division, apart from 'the big three', with the bottom four being relegated. Unusually, the Piraeus team I inherited, along with the Greeks, contained players from as far afield as Zaire, Yugoslavia and Germany. Yet from early on, I noticed there wasn't much team spirit, with little cliques in the dressing room. The league of nations this wasn't. With no money to buy, I decided to promote some young players from the development team into the first-team squad, which raised some eyebrows. The fans were fanatical, with football being more of a religion than a hobby.

It was refreshing to be out of the English game, and fascinating to be applying thirty years of coaching experience in a different culture. It's still the same game but the sensibilities and responses were less predictable. The most important person in the squad wasn't the captain, but the translator, Dimitris, who'd worked for Greek TV in England. I asked him to be truthful, to translate as they spoke, insults and all. If everything failed, use universal sign language. Scream and point wildly at the player, or manically wave your arms and twist your face like you're in agony. Jose Mourinho started as Bobby Robson's translator at Sporting Lisbon, and it didn't seem to harm his career.

My first season reminded me of the early years at Bristol City. We'd have a great result against one of the big three, beating AEK Athens, followed by a humiliating home defeat to Rodos, who were in the bottom three. Inconsistency – the same the world over. I kept the same principles in training, implementing routines to improve the physical, as well as the mental, which was met with a mixed response. The team were never short of surprises.

At the end of the season, we were at home to Apollon in a fierce local derby, like City versus Rovers. We were one up with five minutes left. From the touchline, I'm 'telling' the players to close the game out in a match we should have wrapped up by now. A win would take us into the top half of the table – a rare place for Ethnikos, like they were scared of heights – when suddenly, something very odd happened.

Apollon were frantically pushing for the equaliser when their attack broke down, with our keeper safely gathering the ball. Just hold it, slow the game down, wind down the clock. Their striker was standing in front of him to inhibit his kick. But, instead of the standard goalkeeper tactic of going round the player and booting the ball up field, he dropped it and violently pushed the striker onto the scorched turf.

The referee pointed to the penalty spot. I shouted at our goalie, questioning his madness. He shrugged. In desperation I turned to Dimitris, who explained. 'We are not going to win today. It is time to help our neighbours.' Loosely translated, it meant the result had been arranged before kick-off. Our neighbours needed points. We obliged by handing them a draw.

I had an apartment on the harbour, with a fine view over the Aegean Sea and an excellent links golf course close by. Friends and I enjoyed many fine rounds. One memorable afternoon, my tee shot preparation on the fourteenth was interrupted. Setting up, I heard a shout in Greek from behind. Turning, we found a fleet of gold golf buggies with armed police drawing up, with one gun-toting officer gesturing for me to move away to let someone behind play through.

A buggy then pulled up carrying the President of Greece, Andreas Papandreou. He began to set up his shot. Now we understood the unusual golf course etiquette. He took a practice swing and, like a true socialist, sliced the ball to the left.

Piraeus did well that season, with no money and an ageing squad. We finished solid mid-table. It felt like a good time to leave, on a relative high. Our last game of the season was at home, with no relegation worries, so I drafted in some youth players. Post-match, I had a proud father present me with a case of retsina after I gave his lad a chance.

Christos revealed he couldn't pay the three months he owed me. Suddenly, he had a cash flow crisis, but promised faithfully that when there were sufficient funds, he would forward the whole amount to the UK. *Really?* He expected me to leave. So, I said I'll wait, that I was in no hurry. The apartment and car were paid for, so I stayed the whole summer playing golf, lying on the beach and enjoying the lifestyle with Anne.

Eventually came the call to go to his office. He was sat behind the desk with his feet up, his sprawling bulk spilling over the arms of the old leather reclining chair. With hands linked behind his head, maps of sweat were visible under his arms. He didn't speak. He just nodded, reached down, took a bundle of notes from a drawer of the desk and threw them towards me. The drachma flew everywhere, over the desk, onto the floor. For a moment I thought I'd leap over the desk, Clint Eastwood style, and pummel him. But then thought, let's just collect the cash and leave. After all, I'd had three wonderful, free months' holiday and didn't want to risk spending time in jail, which would lose me my hard-earned tan.

30

ARABIAN DAYS

I crossed the Mediterranean from Greece to Cyprus in late 1983, to manage Apollon Limassol, a First Division side with a history of domestic success and occasional qualification for European competitions. The previous season they had played Barcelona in the Cup Winners' Cup, managing a draw at home, soundly beaten in the Camp Nou. Today, they regularly play in the Europa League, though invariably exiting early.

It was short-lived. The political situation was volatile, and after a couple of months I was advised to move on. I was disappointed, as experiencing different cultures was becoming addictive. I got a call from an English agent who had a proposal. Would I like to manage in Qatar? The club was Al-Rayyan SC, the boss Mohamed bin Hammam, one of the guiding lights of football in the region. He went on to join FIFA as an Executive Member, a big influence on the awarding of the 2022 World Cup to Qatar. On the way, he was banned for life from all footballing activities after violating the FIFA ethics rules, running the money for Sepp Blatter. But, in 1989 he was the ambitious chairman of newly relegated Al-Rayyan SC. The brief to me couldn't have been simpler – promotion. Where had I heard that before?

With endless money flowing into the country's coffers from oil and gas, it was a very different set up to Greece or Cyprus. Or any club I'd ever been at. Al-Rayyan was the second biggest city outside Doha, the capital, which was only down the road in a country the size of London. It was rapidly changing from a desert into an urban forest of towering skyscrapers, hotels, luxury houses and Rolls-Royces. The club's training centre was better equipped than most English teams' grounds. From a state-of-the-art grandstand, I'd watch players go through their paces in the 40°c heat. Despite the high-end comfort, we were still in the middle of the desert.

Before the emergence of the petrol-based gold rush, Qatar was a poor pearl-diving country. Now, they had wealth beyond their wildest dreams. But what they had in money, they lacked in compassion and basic human decency, demonstrated by the way they treated their citizens and migrant workers. Yet despite all this conspicuous wealth, the football club had a more basic approach when it came to rewarding its players. My team was semi-professional, with their other job being as soldiers. It meant my disciplined training sessions worked well as an extension of their military life, but with match-day consequences.

During my second fixture, a decision by the referee was challenged by one of our players. He marched over and gave him both barrels like I'd never seen before, in any game. Anywhere. His face was pink with rage as he screamed his objections to the verdict. I waited for the inevitable red card. But no, the ref was subservient, bowing to our winger, even though he was a good six inches taller.

I turned around to the translator, bewildered.

'The referee is a sergeant. And our player is an officer,' he explained.

Our winger was tearing a strip off him.

'How dare you give a throw in to them! Reverse the decision. That is an ORDER!'

The referee's decision is final? Not here.

I gave our volatile winger such a dressing down at half time, in front of the whole team.

'Respect the referee. His decision is the law, whatever rank he is. You don't talk to him like that. You cannot challenge his decisions.'

'Yes, I *can*. I outrank him. I give the orders.'

'Not on the pitch you don't. There, he's in charge.'

He hated this criticism and I thought he was going to attack *me*. It was touch and go but I held my ground and eventually calmed him down. Come back Gerry Gow, all is forgiven.

Al-Raayan SC had bitter local rivals, Al Sadd SC. Fortunately, we beat them, home and away. I fulfilled my orders to win the league and get promotion. After one season, I felt my work was done. Mohammed was disappointed, as he expected me to stay and build on the success. But, as much as I enjoyed the experience (and I did get used to the heat, eventually), it was time to go. His parting shot to me was an accusation that I trained the players too hard, like 'donkeys'. And he made me wait for my final salary payment, though not as long as in Greece.

The following season they won the league title again. The great French World Cup-winning defender and manager Laurent Blanc was, up until February 2022, the Al-Rayyan SC boss, showing once again what money can buy.

31

JIMMY CALLS

I'd been back in Bristol from Qatar for a couple of weeks, enjoying the cool of an English summer, when Jimmy called. We hadn't spoken for a while. He'd returned to Fulham as chairman, having been brought in to save a club in crisis. They had nearly gone out of business, a result of a doomed merger plan with QPR. It was only the intervention of Jimmy that allowed the club to stay in business as he re-structured to become Fulham FC 1987 Ltd. They were mid-table in the Third Division, twenty-three years since they were in the First Division. Craven Cottage was one of the most pleasant grounds, sat by the River Thames, but it's handsome façade concealed tension and discord.

It had been a decade since I left Bristol City in 1980. The Fulham role was not an obvious golden opportunity to return to English League management. Jimmy confessed there was very little money for new players and the team had just narrowly avoided relegation. Pre-season confidence was low. And there was a manager already in place in Ray Lewington, who had not even been told about my appointment. Thanks, Jimmy.

If the roles had been reversed, I would have been really pissed off. It turned out Ray was much more than that. The way he saw it was effectively a demotion from gaffer to gofer. And he would make his anger plain from day one.

To try and nip any bad blood in the bud, we had a sit-down chat in my/his office. I explained I hadn't planned on taking his job, that Jimmy had put the deal together, and that I was joining to bring my experience of gaining promotion and to hopefully help the team get closer to that ambition of Second Division football. It made no difference. He had been demoted because of me. Now he was not in charge of *his* team and it was *my* fault. Not Jimmy's smartest move.

So, I couldn't trust him. But I didn't blame him. He was still around the players that a couple of days earlier he had managed. Now, he was the ex-manager, but still part of the management team. Who would they support? A group that were already low in confidence, fell even lower. My challenge was to gain their trust and respect. Leroy Rosenior – a goal-every-other-game striker, Simon Morgan (who played 350 times for Fulham), Gary Brazil (management at Nottingham Forest since 2014) and Gordon Davies (record Fulham goalscorer) were all part of the squad. We had some good, experienced players.

In the first home game that August, those players were well beaten by Cambridge United, setting the tone. Results were poor up to Christmas, never managing to escape the relegation zone. If home games were a struggle, away was torture – not winning a single point until November.

In January, I finally had enough money available to buy a much-needed striker – Phil Stant from Notts County for £60,000. He had been in the SAS and fought in the Falklands

War, so he didn't turn pro until he was twenty-four. An interesting character, he reminded me of some of the ex-soldiers I played with post-WWII, who had a different kind of world view, informed by what they'd seen in battle and perhaps still trying to forget. Losing at home to a much-improved Bury would be disappointing for players with this war background, but it's not going to ruin their evening. It's not that they lacked commitment or motivation, just a different perspective to the traditional pro.

After he signed, Phil decided he wanted to stay living in Northampton and commute every day to London for training. Request denied. But he became our top scorer that season – a natural goalscorer who gave us hope. But, by the end of the season, money was so tight the club decided they couldn't afford to pay his wages over the summer, so I would have to sell him. At Mansfield Town he was a prolific striker, then repeated it at Cardiff City. Stant was a guaranteed goal scorer I should have fought harder to keep, as the new season proved.

A brief respite from the many challenges came with an invitation to play in a pro-celebrity golf tournament, filled with minor TV faces and semi-pro golfers. It was one of those days where it wasn't quite happening, until the tenth hole. Pulling the seven-iron from my bag, I looked down the perfect fairway to the pin, 160 yards away. A sweet strike sent the ball on its way up towards the clouds, landing a couple of yards from the hole. It then continued to roll towards 'the cup' and rolled in. A hole in one! Wow. The tournament announced before we began that there would be a prize in the event of anyone achieving the feat. A set of silver cutlery? A cut-glass sherry decanter? No.

A brand new Jaguar XJ6 3.4. It was a bit of a step-up from my Ford. Sadly, it was only for professional players. Unfortunately, it even got a mention in the *Daily Telegraph*.

'Shame Dicks can't get Fulham to play as well as he plays golf.'

We finished twenty-first, just avoiding relegation. Mission accomplished.

But *only* because the FA had had to restructure the league system. The introduction of the Premier League meant that three teams, not four, were relegated, rescuing us from the Fourth Division.

The 1991-92 season brought a loan signing from Arsenal – nineteen-year-old Andy Cole. Released by manager George Graham to give him more game time, he'd only played once for the first team as a sub, so a drop of two divisions to a team in need of some skill and energy made sense for all parties.

Having been solely in charge of all my teams since Coventry City, it was a challenge having no discipline. I could have done with some Qatar army-type control. But it was my fault. I should have insisted from Jimmy on day one that if I came, Lewington went. But he was always there, undermining my position. On the training ground, in the dressing room, on the coach. I left him to run some training sessions, which was another mistake. He had the ear of the players, probably didn't miss any opportunity to cast doubt. Would I have done the same? Yes.

The one bright spot was Andy Cole. He was so hard to get close to on the pitch, with an incredible turn of pace. Teams just couldn't handle him. He was so quick that often the only way he could be stopped was by being scythed down, which gave us free kicks in attacking positions.

We lost our first three games but improved in September with a 3-0 win over Swansea City, two created by Cole, both effortlessly wrong-footing the opposition in their area. He was the difference between the sides to such a degree that their manager, Lou Macari, was quoted saying it was unfair players that good were allowed to be in the Third Division. Next up was Leyton Orient, similarly mid-table. It was a better, more urgent performance, that gave us another two points.

By the end of October, after winning three in a row, we were in the top ten and by early November, had lost just two in thirteen. Top performances at Bolton from Cole and Gary Brazil meant a 3-0 win. This was not relegation form – we were seventh. I hadn't exactly won over the dressing room (and Ray), but things were definitely less hostile. And the supporters seemed to be finally warming to me.

Cole was a completely natural and instinctive footballer. And even harder to get close to off the pitch, with a difficult attitude that made the manager/player bond virtually impossible. He kept missing training. I asked the physio what the issue was. He said that Cole insisted he was injured, but he couldn't find anything wrong.

So, after a two week absence, I challenged him.

'You've got to come out and train.'

'But I'm injured.'

'The physio says you're not. He can't find anything wrong.'

'Well, I know when I'm injured.'

'So, you know better than the physio?'

He shrugged his shoulders

'If you don't want to train, go back to Arsenal.'

'Oh… boss… er… I don't think..'

'If you won't train, you're no good to me. I'll call George and tell him you're coming back.'

He went quiet. Well, even more quiet. He sat on his own, distant from me and his teammates. On the coach, it was a seat for one. A loner. But on the pitch…

Then one day, with no warning, he left. We didn't see him again. George rang me. I told him what a mixed blessing Cole was. That he seemed to have a problem with authority and an attitude that made him difficult to work with. He agreed. Cole returned to Highbury but shortly after was off to a new club: Bristol City. Next was Newcastle United, where he was a revelation, a goal a game, and then it was on to Manchester United, where Fergie got the best out of him, becoming one of the top strikers in Europe, as United won the treble in 1999. He had eleven clubs by the end of his playing career. Maybe his character just wouldn't allow him to settle, so he kept moving on. Truly great players aren't always straightforward. For every Gary Lineker, there is an Andy Cole.

With no funds and no new signings, I focused on the youth, which led to one of my greatest ever player discoveries. The secretary of the London Sunday League Teams rang and asked for a match against our reserve team. They came to play on a Sunday morning at Craven Cottage. The performance of one of their players was so good, I put him straight into our reserve team to play Arsenal a couple of days later. George Graham was very keen to chat after that game.

'Blimey, Alan, your number two is useful.'

'Browne? Yes, we've just signed him,' I lied.

He was visibly disappointed.

So, I did sign him.

Corey Browne made his debut against Charlton in the League Cup, where he not only ran the game for ninety minutes from midfield but scored a brilliant equaliser. At eighteen. Everyone who saw him knew they were watching a rarity, someone so naturally gifted, comfortable all over the pitch and with either foot. An incredible prospect, the best I'd seen in thirty years. And so modest, just pleased to be there. He came from a tough south London council estate and, as man of the match, won a brand-new TV. The next day, his mum rang me in tears of joy, saying this was the first set they'd ever owned.

Four days later we went to Torquay United. Browne was brilliant, just as before, the best on the pitch and the inspiration for a great away win. Could he be the player to change our season? His maturity and speed of thought, changed the whole dynamic of our play. He was that good. Then, in the dying minutes, a reckless challenge floored him. I heard the scream. Browne's cruciate ligament was torn. Career. Ending. Incident. Again, if it had happened today, he would have probably recovered. He was the best young player I'd ever seen, his career over at eighteen. Another reminder of the fine line between fame and tragedy. It took just seven weeks from seeing him, signing him, playing him, to his life in football being over.

We had two tough away games and narrowly lost them both, followed by the second round of the FA Cup against Hayes, which was a west London derby. It was a chance to put a cup run together, to lift the team and fans after a blip in what had otherwise been a good season. Even though Hayes were six divisions below us, there was still the 'magic of the cup' to contend with.

As always, I fielded the strongest side. The night was more suited to kiting, such was the wind swirling around Craven Cottage. We faced a fired-up collection of plumbers, electricians and a chartered accountant. From the kick- off, it was obvious what they lacked in skill they more than made up for in commitment. Our chances in the first half couldn't be converted and it was goalless at the break. In the second half it was more of the same, though the longer the match went on, the more dangerous they looked – a realisation that maybe there was some history to be made here.

Just after the hour, they won a free kick thirty-five yards out. There was no apparent danger, unless Diego Maradona was a carpenter from west London. It turned out they had their own version. He hit it sweetly, stroking it up and over our wall, the ball spinning tantalisingly till it sailed past a despairing Jim Stannard and into the top corner. Who needs Diego when you have Colin Day, a builder from Hounslow? We pounded their goal, threw everything at it, with Morgan and Brazil coming close with desperate attempts to save the game – and face – but we just couldn't break through, with goal line clearances and keeper heroics until our misery was confirmed in an eighty-sixth minute counter-attack that resulted in their second. The final whistle signalled a pitch invasion by their fans.

My youngest daughter Melanie was there, with her future husband, Paul. He loved football and thought it would be the perfect way to see a match and meet his future father-in-law. So post-match we met, serenaded by fans who had stayed behind to share their feelings.

'Dicks out! Dicks out!'

Welcome to the family, Paul.

Two weeks later, I was fired.

Jimmy's first request when I arrived had been to reduce staff numbers, so I could have fired Ray Lewington then. But I didn't. I was older, perhaps a bit softer, and had lost that ruthless touch. It was ten years, after all. The foreign adventures had mellowed me. The hard-lined principles I held had wilted in the desert heat.

Losing that brilliant young talent Corey Browne, was a significant blow. You can only control certain elements of the job. It's all about one thing – the players. You can spend over £100m on an Enzo Fernandez, but will he transform the team?

Sometimes, players reach a point where they stagnate. For some often indefinable reason, they can't improve or perform in that environment and need to move on. This defines the manager – how you handle the players and the staff. Those that don't fit in, should go. If not, it will ultimately affect the whole team.

Me? I went to America.

32

SOCCER

I was living with Pam, wife number three, managing Carolina Dynamo in Greensboro, North Carolina, in the third tier of US soccer. It was a town the size of Portsmouth, with great sports facilities and a rich political history at the heart of the civil rights movement. I inherited a solid team - a multinational squad, that grew stronger through the season, made the A-League National Final and finished second in the league. We had striker Robert Rosario, ex- Norwich, Coventry and Nottingham Forest, who continued to score goals, before eventually going on to manage the side. I was voted USL Coach of the Year.

Leaving on a high, I moved 600 miles south to coach fourth-tier Cocoa Expos, based near Orlando, a challenge that lasted just one season as I was offered the manager's job at Charleston Battery in South Carolina. My replacement was Ricky Hill, the ex-Luton Town and England midfielder. Ricky has subsequently had a long and successful career in America, including managing Tampa Bay Rowdies. In his first spell with Cocoas Expos, as player-coach, he led them to two national championships and made Coach of the Year 1992. So, I was leaving the side in very safe hands.

The path from UK professional football to America was well trodden. From George Best signing in 1976 for the LA Aztecs, to numerous less high-profile players who fancied an adventure in warmer parts of the world on pitches that still had grass at Christmas. From Bristol City, players like Gary Collier and Len Bond moved. Along with the likes of Ashley Cole and Wayne Rooney, it's been a football land of opportunity since the 1970s.

On a trip back to England in 2000, I saw Maura for the first time in twenty years, in a reunion brilliantly contrived by my three daughters. We fell back in love. Amazingly, she forgave me for the past, and we made plans. Soon, she joined me in Charleston. We got married. I was a very lucky man to have a second chance. It was the Lyceum Ballroom moment all over again. My love had made it into extra-time.

My son Patrick lived down the coast in Orlando doing a great job at ESPN Wide World of Sports, so Maura and I got to spend plenty of time with him.

Tony Bakker was an Englishman, a Southampton supporter, who'd made money in the emerging world of computing. He had formed Charleston Battery in 1993. By now they were a second-tier club with a shiny new stadium just outside the beautiful, historic town of Charleston in South Carolina, unusual in America as it actually has buildings more than thirty years old. The squad came from the West Indies, Croatia, England, Ireland along with some experienced Americans like Paul Conway. The ground was modelled on an English club ground (5,000 capacity) including a pub, the Three Lions.

The American way is to find investors. Like David Beckham with Inter Miami, buy your way into a league system that's based on a 'no relegation policy'. It's the model for Major League Soccer and the National Basketball Association, nearly replicated closer to home in the cynical European Super League. The loaded word is 'franchise'. Perfectly acceptable in US sports circles, but something that strikes fear in the hearts of self-respecting European football fans. A system where the same wealthy teams play each other repeatedly, with no relegation or promotion.

As I'd managed in many countries before and was used to different ways of playing and interpreting the game, it was not too much of a culture shock to find out that we couldn't get relegated, because the fundamental truth of the game – it's all about winning – still applied. It just meant the forfeit for losing wasn't so devastating.

You adapt to the demands and structures of the culture you are in. Watch out for match-fixing in Greece; don't worry about relegation from the MLS. But are there more tense and exciting games than the English Football League play-off finals? Or an end of season relegation six-pointer?

In the first match, we played Colorado Rapids, a 3,400-mile round trip. I knew America was big but to have to recover from jet lag when travelling to a league game was a challenge. No surprise, we lost. For our first home match, a full house relaxed pre-match on the funfair and bouncy castle (a smart, family orientated experience) and enjoyed seeing us win.

The Battery are one of the oldest professional soccer clubs in America and won the USISL Pro League in 1996. The following year they became one of the original clubs of the A-League and were the first non-Major League Soccer club to build their own stadium.

We had some English boys. Nicky Spooner played for Bolton and was looking good when a crunching tackle meant he'd never play top-level football again. So, he went west, ended up at Charleston and played over fifty times for me before returning to the UK. Paul Conway was originally from Portland, having spent five seasons in the lower English leagues before returning home to play for us. In nearly 200 games he got over 100 goals and remains the club's highest scorer.

American soccer was still young, beginning in earnest in the 1970s. I remember England losing 1-0 to the USA in the 1950 World Cup in Uruguay, one of the biggest shocks in international football. The Americans were a hastily gathered collection of part timers, expected to provide nothing more than cannon fodder to one of the favourites to lift the trophy. A team that included my brilliant Chelsea teammate Roy Bentley, with Alf Ramsey and Billy Wright. Today's equivalent would be England losing to India. When Pelé signed for New York Cosmos in 1975, it was to kick-start the sport. But it had to compete with decades of baseball, football (American) and basketball.

The life suited us. I was in my mid-sixties managing without the pressure that comes with relegation and promotion. That fear of failure was not so acute. There was still pressure on getting results, but nothing like the English league. We were Atlantic Division champions that first season and reached the US Open semi-finals. On that cup run, we had a historic night at Blackbaud Stadium when we beat the top MLS side, DC United. It was equivalent to the Bristol City FA Cup win at

Leeds United, a giant-killing result and was the first time the club had reached that far in the competition.

I had one more moderately successful season but by the time that finished in 2001, we felt the final whistle had blown.

33

BACK HOME

We went home.

To Bristol.

Maura and I were second-time newlyweds, back with our beloved five children, eight grandchildren and six great-grandchildren.

Even after Maura sadly passed away in 2015, my family and sense of family remain my greatest inspiration and comfort.

THE END

DICKSY'S CLUBS

1952-1958	Chelsea	Appearances 33
1958-1962	Southend United	Appearances 85
1962-1967	Coventry City 248 games	Assistant Manager 120 won 70 drawn 58 lost
1967- 1980	Bristol City 611 games	Manager 202 won 174 drawn 235 lost
1982- 1983	Ethnikos Piraeus	Manager
1984- 1985	Apollon Limassol	Manager
1989-1990	Fulham 75 games	Manager 17 won 23 drawn 35 lost
1996 –1997	Carolina Dynamo	Manager
1999 – 2001	Charleston Battery	Manager

TRAINING DRILLS FROM 1970

<u>TECHNIQUES</u>

Coach:-

  (1)   To improve the accuracy of passing.

  (2)   The technique and skill of passing with the outside of the foot.

  (3)   The correct weighting of passes.

  (4)   The use of wall passes.

  (5)   The technique of lofted passing.

  (6)   The value of disguise in passing.

  (7)   Chest control for attackers.

  (8)   Ball control for defenders.

  (9)   Taking the pace off the ball.

 (10)   Receiving and turning with the ball.

 (11)   Controlling balls received at varying heights and speeds.

 (12)   Controlling to set up shooting chances.

 (13)   To improve dribbling skill to individual players.

 (14)   To understand when and where to dribble.

 (15)   The technique of screening.

 (16)   The technique of shooting on the volley.

 (17)   The technique of shooting on the turn.

 (18)   The technique of power shooting.

 (19)   Set up a realistic shooting practice with the emphasis on swerve.

 (20)   Set up a realistic shooting practice with the emphasis on chipping.

 (21)   Set up a realistic shooting practice with the emphasis on driving the ball.

 (22)   Forwards to finish low crosses.

 (23)   Instant shooting.

 (24)   The goalkeeper to improve his handling.

 (25)   The goalkeeper in shot stopping.

 (26)   The goalkeeper dealing with crosses.

 (27)   The goalkeeper on ground shots.

 (28)   The goalkeeper on distribution.

 (29)   Heading in attack.

 (30)   Heading in defence.

 (31)   Volleying in defence.

 (32)   Crosses to the far post.

 (33)   Crosses to the near post.

.../Contd....

UNDERSTANDING

Attacking:-

(1)   Coach one team to keep possession in a small-sided game.

(2)   Coach the correct supporting positions for the man in possession.

(3)   Coach one team in spreading out side to side to create space.

(4)   Coach closely marked players to make space as individuals.

(5)   Coach players to encourage penetrative passing.

(6)   Coach players when to take risks in passing.

(7)   Coach quick passing in order to make space.

(8)   Coach to improve the quality of passing in a small-sided game.

(9)   Coach to improve the timing and weighting of passes in a small-sided game.

(10)   Condition a small-sided game to emphasize dribbling techniques.

(11)   Condition a small-sided game to emphasize the use of quick passing.

(12)   Coach one side to achieve penetration in a small-sided game.

Defending:-

(13)   Coach players how to defend with their opponent receiving the ball facing his own goal.

(14)   Coach players how to defend against an opponent facing them in possession of the ball.

(15)   Coach defenders to cover each other.

(16)   Coach players for better understanding of when to mark players and when to mark space.

(17)   Coach defenders how to mark opponents in a small-sided game.

(18)   Coach one side in their defensive duties in a small-sided game.